Praise for
Seeing the
the Tr

"Dennis Sherwood has the ability to tame the most difficult and complex intellectual ideas, and to apply them to real situations in a language which is both down to earth and stimulating."
Peter Brown, Vice President Human Resources, Astra Zeneca

"If you are struggling with information overload, the paralysis of analysis; trying to tame the complexity of the busyness of business; or simply keen on finding ways to make better decisions, this is the book for you. Dennis Sherwood does a masterful job in providing a dynamic guidebook filled with how-tos, practical tools, and insightful techniques to enrich your future strategy, teamwork, and growth initiatives."
Patrick J. McKenna, Partner, Edge International, and co-author of First Among Equals, Beyond Knowing, *and* Herding Cats

"Dennis Sherwood offers a pragmatic view of a complex subject, rich in practical examples you can relate to. Essential reading for all managers."
Tim Cooper-Jones OBE, European NPI Project Director, Unilever

"This is a valuable guide for those who are currently trapped in a linear thinking mode. Dennis Sherwood demonstrates how systems thinking helps to break down complexity, and how individual actions affect others in a causal fashion. This book is full of real-life examples of how to use systems thinking in our day-to-day lives."
Andrew Yue, Director, Credit Suisse First Boston

"I managed technology for more than twenty years and thought I knew every-thing about building effective business systems, until Dennis Sherwood intro-duced me to systems thinking—it was like finding the missing pieces of all my jigsaws stacked neatly in a pile. Systems thinking is a no-brainer decision for the 21st century. Without it your business will never really fulfil its poten-tial. Worse, you may even lose what you have now—without ever knowing what went wrong. The question is not so much 'Why should we use systems thinking now?' It is more like 'Why the hell didn't we apply it sooner?'"
Colin Beveridge, IT director, author and visionary

"IT systems analysis and design is all about breaking problems down into smaller and smaller pieces until you are able to tackle them with simple programming instructions. But all IT professionals will recognise a common problem: when you build all the pieces back up into a system, it doesn't do what you wanted. This book gives a set of useful techniques on how to look at the problem as a whole and hopefully to avoid some of the unpleasant surprises. It doesn't replace the traditional analysis techniques—but introduces a new (and fun) one to the armoury."
Ruth Crook, Egg Bank

"For me, Dennis's enthusiasm and clarity of writing brings systems thinking to life. He makes this important business concept both simple to understand and exciting to learn."
Paul Smith, Group Managing Director, Accord plc

"One of the most precious skills that a communicator can have is the ability to convey complex ideas in a clear and readable way. Dennis Sherwood has this rare talent in abundance. To understand complex problems, we need to make them simple. The danger, however, is that we will over-simplify them and miss out crucial details. This book is about systems dynamics thinking … With clear explanations throughout, Dennis Sherwood demonstrates the value of this powerful thinking tool."
Rob Eastaway, creativity guru, author of What's a Googly? *and co-author of* Why Do Buses Come in Threes? *and* How Long Is a Piece of String?

"Good organisations only flourish when their people give their best. It is Dennis Sherwood's gift and achievement to show how effective systems thinking can help realise this happy state. He has a clarity of thinking and ease of communication which will enable managers and leaders to make sense of the complexities of their organisations and see the way ahead. In short, he really does help you see the wood/forest for the trees. This is an excellent book."
Tony Little, Headmaster Oakham School (1996–2002), Eton College (2002–)

"Dennis Sherwood develops the seminal insights of Jay Forrester and Ludwig von Bertalanffy into powerful practical tools for analysing and influencing the complex systems around us. The usefulness of his approach goes well beyond the world of business into that of government management and public policy making more generally."
Mark Allen, Deputy Director, Policy Development and Review Department, International Monetary Fund

"Dennis captures the very essence of why systems thinking is so relevant to management today. No one else I know has Dennis's unique ability to bring simplicity and clarity to what were, at first sight, impossibly complex situations.This book is essential reading to anyone wishing to understand the underlying drivers and dynamics of business models."
Henry Kenyon, Partner, PricewaterhouseCoopers

"This highly readable, practical guide to systems thinking makes it possible for the layman and the manager to make better sense of the world around them, to find leverage points where a small amount of effort can make a big impact, and to gain insights into why putting something right often has unforeseen knock-on effects, both good and bad."
Mark Batten, Managing Director, makingbreakthroughs

To Anny

Seeing the Forest for the Trees

A Manager's Guide to Applying Systems Thinking

Dennis Sherwood

NICHOLAS BREALEY
PUBLISHING

LONDON

First published by
Nicholas Brealey Publishing in 2002

3–5 Spafield Street
Clerkenwell, London
EC1R 4QB, UK
Tel: +44 (0)20 7239 0360
Fax: +44 (0)20 7239 0370

PO Box 700
Yarmouth
Maine 04096, USA
Tel: (888) BREALEY
Fax: (207) 846 5181

http://www.nbrealey-books.com

ISBN 1-85788-311-X

British Library Cataloguing in Publication Data
A catalogue record for this book is available from the
British Library.

Printed in Finland by WS Bookwell.

Contents

Acknowledgments   xv
Foreword   xvii

Prologue: What is systems thinking?   1
Systems thinking is a big idea   1
So what is systems thinking all about?   2
Connectedness   3
Why systems must be studied as a whole   5
The systems thinking toolkit   6
The benefits of systems thinking   7
How the book works   8

PART I: TAMING COMPLEXITY   11

1 The systems perspective   12
Systems   12
Emergence and self-organization   14
Feedback   16
Systems thinking   18
On with our journey…   24

2 Carrying the back office rock   25
The story   25
The context   26
The issue   27
A diagrammatic representation   27
Enriching the diagram   30
What happens as a consequence of error?   31
A nasty vicious circle   31
What else drives the ability to cope?   32
But what about cost?   34
There's still one thing missing…   35
Back to wisdom   38

3 Quality, creativity, and cutting costs   40
The story   40
The context   41
The picture   41
Another nasty vicious circle   42
What should we do?   43
Who's right?   44
Deciding policy   45

PART II: TOOLS AND TECHNIQUES   49

4 Feedback loops   50
The central role of feedback loops   50
Reinforcing loops   54
Balancing loops   55
Dangles, boundaries, and real systems   57
There are only two types of link—the S and the O   59
Distinguishing between reinforcing loops and balancing loops 59
The two fundamental building blocks   62
The importance of language   63
Are all links always either an S or an O?   64
Fuzzy variables   65
Ss and Os that work in one direction only   66
A final thought   68

5 The engines of growth—and decline   72
Vicious and virtuous circles   72
Vicious and virtuous circles really do have the same structure 73
The engine of growth   74
Patterns of growth   77
Exponential growth becomes very fast   83
Explicit and implicit dangles   85
Boom and bust   87
Reinforcing loops can be linked   94

6 Setting targets, seeking goals   103
More on balancing loops   103

Balancing loops in business   108
Balancing loops are often linked   114
Balancing loops and time delays   117
What is the definition of variance?   121
Time to reflect   125

7 How to draw causal loop diagrams   127
Rule 1: Know your boundaries   127
Rule 2: Start somewhere interesting   128
Rule 3: Ask "What does this drive?" and "What is this driven by?"   129
Rule 4: Don't get cluttered   129
Rule 5: Use nouns, not verbs   131
Rule 6: Don't use terms such as "increase in" or "decrease in"   132
Rule 7: Don't be afraid of unusual items   133
Rule 8: Do the Ss and the Os as you go along   134
Rule 9: Keep going   134
Rule 10: A good diagram must be recognized as real   135
Rule 11: Don't fall in love with your diagrams   136
Rule 12: No diagram is ever "finished"   136

PART III: APPLICATIONS   138

8 Stimulating growth   139
In real life, exponential growth does not go on for ever   139
Breaking through the constraints   146
The growth of urban populations   150
    The context   150
    The dynamics of population growth   150
    Driving economic prosperity   154
    Urban growth doesn't go on for ever   155
    The final causal loop diagram   160
    The moral of this story   161
Don't pedal harder, take the brakes off   162

9 Decisions, teamwork, and leadership   164
The talent problem   164
    The senior executive's perspective   166

The star's perspective   169
The perspective of the more junior staff   173
What is the best policy?   174
But that's all so obvious, isn't it?   178
Mental models   180
Teamwork   184
Outsourcing, partnering, and cross-boundary conflict   188
How the world looks to the buyer   189
How the world looks to the contractor   195
Is there a better way?   197
The systems perspective   201

10 Levers, outcomes, and strategy   **202**
Levers   202
Outcomes   204
How are the levers and the outcomes connected?   205
Levers, outcomes, and systems thinking   209
Levers, outcomes, and loops   209
Connecting the loops   213
The last link   217
What about the other levers?   221
A general business model   223
The big picture   226
Encouraging ambition, vision, and imagination   232
How to be creative   235
Back to levers and outcomes   238

11 Public Policy   **240**
Systems thinking also applies to matters of public policy   240
Back to population   241
What are the consequences of economic activity?   243
What is the structure of this system and how does it behave?   244
Gaia   247
Global warming   251
Linking the loops together   256
The impact of storms   260
The four horsemen ride again   263

This goes way beyond global warming   263
What should we do?   266

PART IV: HOW TO BUILD A "LABORATORY OF THE FUTURE" 271

12 Turbo-charging your systems thinking   272
   System dynamics   273
   System dynamics and spreadsheets   274
   Stocks and flows   278
   Stocks and flows in business   281
   Two more unifying concepts   286
   Causal loop diagrams and plumbing diagrams   287
   Modeling in ithink   292

13 Modeling business growth   302
   A business example   302
   Fuzzy variables   310
   Models for answers, models for learning   312
   Managing the marketing mix   316
   What policies would you invoke to optimize the business?   326
   Is the 80:20 split the best deal?   328

Epilogue: Complexity tamed   332

   Bibliography   333
   Websites   338
   Software   339
   Index   340

Acknowledgments

I thank many people for their help over the years. Let me mention specifically Alan Budd, Andrew Barton, Bruce Barnard, David Blood, Doug Smit, Harpal Lalli, Harsha Mistry, John Lawrence, John Morecroft, John Rountree, John Taylor, Judith Hackett, Kerry Turner, Michael Ballé, Nick Hester, Paul Deighton, Tessa Lanstein, Tim Beswick, Tony Vernon, and Warren Gemberling. Nicholas Brealey has been extremely helpful in sharpening the focus of this book and in clarifying both my thinking and the text; Chris Soderquist gave me some most apposite advice; Ben Russell was especially generous in advising me on the history of feedback; Sally Lansdell has been a most efficient and attentive editor; and special thanks to all those who most generously have written the endorsements. In addition — of course — I also thank my family, Anny, Torben and Torsten.

May I also thank those who have given permission for me to use or refer to their materials:

The Institute for the History and Philosophy of Science and Technology at the University of Toronto for the plate from *The Steam Engine Familiarly Explained and Illustrated* by Dionysius Lardner reproduced on page 19.

Bloomberg L.P. for the charts on page 92 and 93. Copyright 2001 Bloomberg L.P. Reprinted with permission. All rights reserved. Visit www.Bloomberg.com.

The Financial Forecast Centre™ for the data on which the chart on page 121 is based.

The United Nations Population Division, Department of Economic and Social Affairs, for the chart on page 245.

The Goddard Institute of Space Studies for the chart on page 266.

Dennis Sherwood
Church Barn, Brabourne, Kent
May 2002

Foreword

John Speed, Director, The European Court of Auditors

An alternative subtitle to this book might be "The application of rigorous common sense to strategic and policy-focused thinking for organizations." Because what Dennis Sherwood shows in a convincing and entertaining way is that by supporting common sense with the rigorous and structured techniques of causal loop diagrams and systems thinking, it is possible to address complex strategic issues in a manageable and understandable way.

Right at the beginning of the book Dennis points out the fundamental importance of taking a holistic view when addressing business and organizational problems. This rings true for managers in both business and public-sector organizations. As a manager in an institution of the European Union, I recognized immediately the validity of the approach to my own organization, which has a relatively decentralized structure and somewhat diffuse overall goals, and where the various sectors of the organization have their own vision of what is important and what are their priorities. In these circumstances there is a structural tendency to ignore the whole view. As we now, faced with enlargement, try to focus on the key goals for the whole institution, it is obvious—it's common sense again!—that we must take a holistic approach. Systems thinking and causal loop diagrams can be powerful tools for focusing on what is really important: seeing the forest for the trees.

I think that one of the most important messages in the book is indeed that systems thinking is about what, with hindsight, seems obvious. The paradox is that as one works through the causal loop diagrams, it takes time to determine what afterwards seems obvious! As Dennis points out, thinking through the links, the dangles, how to express the elements to include in the diagram, whether the causality effect is the "same" or "opposite" can make the brain hurt and the wastepaper basket fill up with diagrams that don't quite describe the situation. This is where the rigor has to be combined with the common sense; and, indeed, with a profound knowledge of the system being described. So a further valuable by-product of the approach is that one has to spend time making sure that one really does understand the business correctly.

Dennis has set out to show that the ideas in the book do not just apply to business organizations and business decisions. In Chapter 10 he does this by applying the techniques to a major issue of public policy, that of global warming. Global warming is a high-level public policy issue and it makes a most interesting and readable example. But for the purpose of showing the applicability Dennis could equally have chosen a more mundane strategic question facing a non-commercial organization, whether in the public sector or non-governmental. Wherever an organization has targets, and constraints, and complex interrelationships between the various elements that affect its performance, it is possible to apply systems thinking and draw causal loop diagrams. They may be more difficult—there are perhaps more "fuzzy variables" and fewer easily quantified ones such as profits or returns to investors—but they can still be used to great benefit.

Chapter 9, "Decisions, teamwork, and leadership," stressing the importance of understanding the different mental models that exist in an organization in order for effective teamworking to occur, is particularly relevant in public-sector organizations. In the admittedly specific environment of the European Union institutions this is especially important in light of the different backgrounds and cultures of the organizations' staff members. Even in a specialist institution such as ours (the Court of Auditors) where we are all supposed to be auditors, the traditions of audit across the Member States are very different, and combining them into one organization with a single culture so that the "telephone directory test" can work is a long task.

This is a useful and thought-provoking book, in that it makes managers want to get out their pens and paper and start trying to draw causal loop diagrams to analyze strategic issues for their own organizations. The way to do this is, of course, to get round a table and put brains together with a flipchart. Even better, invite Dennis to come round to help stimulate the process!

Prologue:
What is systems thinking?

Systems thinking is a big idea

This book is about **systems thinking**. Systems thinking is a big idea—the idea that you really can understand and tame the complexity of the real world. This complexity cannot be wished away, but if you look at the world in the right way, and have the confidence to embrace complexity rather than being cowed by it, it can indeed be tamed.

The essence of systems thinking is that the complexity of the real world can best be tamed by seeing things in the round, as a whole. Only by taking a broad view can we avoid the twin dangers of a silo mentality—in which a fix "here" simply shifts the problem to "there"—and organizational myopia—in which a fix "now" gives rise to a much bigger problem to fix "later." Taking a broad view, however, is not at the expense of missing the detail; much of business is of course about paying attention to those all-important details. Nor is it a question of broad brush versus detail; rather, it is one of taking a broad view in the context of the *right* detail, of truly—as the title of this book suggests—seeing the forest for the trees.

The prize you get from doing this is better, more robust, and wiser decisions. Decisions that are better because they have been taken by considering the problem in the round, in all its complexity; decisions that are more robust because they have been taken in the full understanding of their consequences, so that you will not be surprised by unforeseen circumstances; decisions that are wiser, because they stand the toughest test there is, the test of time. And whether you are in a commercial organization or a not-for-profit one, better decisions must mean better business, in the widest sense of the term.

To win the prize, you have to do two things:

➤ Be willing to tackle complexity head on.
➤ Be confident in using the systems thinking toolkit, enabling you to understand, describe, examine, and explore the complexity of the real world.

Here is how this book can help:

➤ It will convince you that complexity can be tamed, and will build your confidence in taming it.
➤ It will take you on an in-depth journey into systems thinking, so that you will be equipped to apply the tools and techniques yourself.

So what is systems thinking all about?

Systems thinking may well be familiar to you, especially if you have read Peter Senge's bestseller *The Fifth Discipline* or Arie de Geus's *The Living Company*, or indeed if you have had the benefit of attending one of their conferences or of participating in a systems thinking course at business school. In this case, I trust that this book will enhance your knowledge and that you will enjoy the many practical examples based on my experience in using systems thinking over the last 15 years in contexts as diverse as managing a busy back office, negotiating an outsourcing deal, and formulating business strategy.

For those of you to whom systems thinking is new, I hope that you will also enjoy the examples. In addition, you will find in this book everything you need to equip you with a good understanding of the tools and techniques.

Let me first explain the term "systems thinking," which at first sight can be rather offputting: The word "systems" appears to imply things to do with IT, and the use of "thinking" suggests something very cerebral and intellectual.

In this book I'm using the word "system" to mean "**a community of connected entities**," a definition that emphasizes the **connectedness** between the entities that comprise the system of interest. In this context, the opposite of a system might be called a "heap," for a heap is also composed of a number of entities, but in a heap the entities are just dumped together and are not interconnected. So a collection of people who happen to be in the same place at the same time—such as, for example, those who find themselves traveling on a bus together—constitute, in these terms, a heap (or, somewhat more politely, a random group), because they have no mutual interconnections; in contrast, the community of people working closely together on, say, a competitive bid have every opportunity to become a very special sort of system called a high-performing team, but only if they get their interconnectedness right.

The study of systems is therefore the study of the connectedness between those systems' component parts and, when a system is composed of component parts that are human beings, departments, or indeed businesses or organizations as a whole, the study of systems has immense relevance to our role as managers. Furthermore, as we will shortly see in more detail:

> If you wish to understand a system, and so be in a position to predict its behavior, it is necessary to study the system as a whole. Cutting it up into bits for study is likely to destroy the system's connectedness, and hence the system itself.
> If you wish to influence or control the behavior of a system, you must act on the system as a whole. Tweaking it in one place in the hope that nothing will happen in another is doomed to failure—that's what connectedness is all about.

Far from being an academic, ivory-tower activity, systems thinking is profoundly practical and pragmatic, and can apply to all aspects of business and organizational life. This book is full of real examples showing how systems thinking can beneficially be applied to problems such as:

> How to determine the right number of staff in a busy back office.
> How best to manage "stars."
> How to grow a business smoothly and continuously, avoiding boom and bust.
> How best to manage competition for scarce resources.
> How to build high-performing teams.
> How to negotiate partnering agreements across organizational boundaries.
> How to develop robust business strategies.
> How to design policies to tackle really big problems such as global warming.

Connectedness

As I have just pointed out, the connectedness between the entities constituting a system is a very important and fundamental concept in systems thinking, so let me take a moment to explain it in more detail.

I want you to imagine you are holding a small coin. What will happen if you drop it? Easy: It will fall to the ground.

In contrast, imagine what will happen if you drop not a small coin, but the price of one of your products by, say, 5 percent. Not so easy: If you decrease your price this single action could spark any number of different outcomes, from causing an increase in sales volume (as implied by basic economics), to triggering a competitive price war; from delighting those customers who rejoice in paying less, to alienating those customers who feel that a price reduction has destroyed their perception of exclusivity; from achieving your promotion as a reward for having met this quarter's targets, to the bankruptcy, three years later, of the company (your success gave you a lot of visibility, so that, soon after your promotion, you were headhunted by your major competitor, and you brought your immediate team with you, so stripping your former company of its major marketing talent).

All of these are possible consequences of that single event, the reduction in the price of your product; and there are a host of other possible consequences too. A Martian observing our world might on one occasion observe that a price reduction is followed by an increase in sales volume; on another by a decrease in sales volume; on a third by no change; with all sorts of other things happening too as time evolves. What would the Martian conclude? Perhaps that changes in sales volume are not in any way associated with changes in price; perhaps that, statistically, there is a one in four chance that people responsible for deciding to reduce prices subsequently get promoted; perhaps that the strange blue and green place is entirely capricious, behaving in a totally arbitrary, unpredictable—and therefore uncontrollable—way, and that he would be better off passing it by and seeing what Venus is like.

Is our world capricious, arbitrary, unpredictable, uncontrollable, mad?

No. It isn't so much a mad world as a complex one. The difference between dropping a small coin and dropping your price is the fact that the context in which a coin is dropped is very simple, whereas the context in which your prices are dropped is highly complex—a complexity driven by connectedness.

When you drop a coin, the only entities involved are yourself, the coin, and the ground. No one else, nothing else, is directly involved, and the events take place in a very bounded context. But when you drop your price, the situation is very different. Many entities are involved, and they are all connected together in one form or another. Your customers are connected with the price by virtue of their buying habits; your competitors are connected with the price by virtue of the behavior of markets; your colleagues are connected with the price by virtue of the impact that price changes have on the business itself, and on your political prestige within it; the government is connected with the price by virtue of its role in regulating commerce... and so it goes on. The event of dropping the price is not bounded, but has ripple effects extending over space and time almost indefinitely.

This ripple effect is a direct consequence of the connectedness between the various entities involved. If the connectedness were not present, the chain of cause-and-effect events would be bounded and stop quickly. However, because of the connectedness, the chain of cause-and-effect events is essentially unbounded, with one thing leading to the next again and again and again. Since there are so many entities involved, each of which can behave in so many different ways, giving rise to any number of possible consequences, it very quickly becomes quite impossible to predict with any confidence whatsoever what "the" outcome of the single action of dropping your price might be. We also begin to realize that the chain of causality goes backwards too. Why was it that we considered dropping the price in the first place? Was it driven by the launch of a competing product by a new entrant? Where does the chain of causality start, and where does it end?

No wonder that it is far, far harder to predict the outcome of dropping our price than that of dropping a small coin. It is all a question of connectedness. Events that are easily predicted are those that concern only a very few entities and are bounded in space and time; those that are much less easily predicted involve many highly connected entities, in which the cause-and-effect relationships extend widely over both space and time.

Why systems must be studied as a whole

I trust you are now convinced that it is the connectedness between the entities in a system that makes—or indeed allows—a system to behave as a system, to make, as the familiar idiom states, the whole greater than the sum of its parts. So if we want to understand systems, to discover what is going on to make the whole greater than the sum of its parts, then we must preserve that connectedness and study the system as a whole, in its entirety.

To many of us, however, such an approach is quite counter-intuitive. When confronted by complexity, our natural instinct is to seek to simplify matters by cutting the system of interest up into bits, then to study the bits, and finally to use our knowledge of the bits as a basis for understanding the system as a whole. This approach of cutting things up to examine the bits might give some insight into the behavior of the bits, but very often fails utterly to give insight into the behavior of a system as a whole, for two reasons:

➤ Cutting a system up into bits often destroys the system you are trying to understand. This, of course, is a matter of connectedness: As we have already seen, if you break the connectedness of a system, you break the system itself.

➤ Rather more subtly, many systems show characteristics that are not properties of any of their constituent parts. It therefore follows that no study, however exhaustive, of any individual constituent part will ever identify the existence of these system-level characteristics, let alone how they behave. Teamwork, for example, is a characteristic of the system we call a team, acting as a team, and—as every team manager, sports fan, and indeed business manager knows—knowledge of the individual players does not enable you to predict the behavior of the team.

Systems thinking avoids both of these traps, for the starting point of systems thinking is the recognition, and the acceptance, that complex systems *must* be studied intact, in the round, as a whole. This preserves that all-important connectedness and allows system-level characteristics to be observed.

The systems thinking toolkit

How, then, can you study complex systems as a whole, methodically and insightfully, without being overwhelmed by the system's inherent complexity?

That is where the systems thinking toolkit comes in. As well as being about an approach to tackling problems in the round, systems thinking also provides you with a set of tools and techniques to help you actually do it. The host of practical examples in this book will show you how, primarily using two main tools:

➤ **Causal loop diagrams,** which enable complex systems to be described in terms of cause-and-effect relationships.
➤ **System dynamics computer models,** which enable the time-dependent behavior of complex systems to be explored under a range of different assumptions.

Much of this book is about how you can use causal loop diagrams to describe a complex system, truly capturing its essence clearly and succinctly, so providing a platform for discussion, communication, and policy formulation. The book is therefore full of causal loop diagrams, each describing the causality underlying the complex situations in my list of "how tos" on page 3 and many more besides. I trust that you will find them clear and informative, and that they will truly help you "see the forest for the trees."

However, these diagrams have one shortcoming. As representations of the structure of a system on paper, causal loop diagrams are necessarily static and cannot describe how the properties of a system evolve over time. But computer simulation models can, and when you harness the logic of a causal loop diagram to the simulation capability of a computer—which is what **system dynamics modeling** is all about—then you can really "turbo-charge" your thinking.

The benefits of systems thinking

Together, causal loop diagrams and system dynamics computer modeling can be used to tame the complexity of the most complex systems, so delivering a package of very valuable benefits:

> ➤ Systems thinking can help you tame the complexity of real-world problems by providing a structured way of balancing a broad, complete view with the selection of the right level of detail.
> ➤ Causal loop diagrams—a visual method of capturing this now-tamed complexity—are a powerful means of communication, and their use can ensure that as wide a community as you wish has a genuinely, and deeply, shared view. This is enormously valuable in building high-performing teams.
> ➤ Causal loop diagrams can also help you identify the wisest way of influencing the system of interest. As a result, you can avoid taking poor decisions, for example decisions that look like quick fixes but are likely to backfire.
> ➤ System dynamics modeling is a computer modeling technique that allows you to simulate how a complex system, as expressed as a causal loop diagram, is likely to evolve over time. This provides you with a "laboratory of the future," so that you can test the likely consequences of actions, decisions, or policies before you are obliged to commit.
> ➤ Overall, systems thinking can help you take decisions that pass the most stringent test there is—the test of time.

How the book works

Structurally this book comprises thirteen chapters, in four parts, with this Prologue and a very brief Epilogue.

Part I, Taming Complexity, examines why complex systems must be studied as a whole, using two case studies as concrete examples. *Chapter 1, The systems perspective*, develops some of the concepts introduced in the Prologue. This leads to the first case study, *Chapter 2, Carrying the back office rock*, which concerns the problems of managing a busy back office as it strives to deliver a high-quality service under the relentless bombardment of an increasing number of transactions. In many macho back office cultures, the key performance measure of the back office manager is the size of the rock that can be carried without getting crushed. This may, from a Darwinian standpoint, ensure the survival of the fittest, but from an organizational standpoint is it wise?

Chapter 3, Quality, creativity, and cutting costs, is also set in what many people consider to be a glamorous context, this time the TV industry. The problem of interest, however, is by no means restricted to the media: how best to manage the dilemma posed when there is pressure on to cut costs, but quality and creativity are paramount. Together, these two case studies show how systems thinking in general, and the use of causal loop diagrams in particular, can tame the complexity of the real world, throwing a perceptive spotlight on to the key issues, so helping the management team take the best possible decisions.

Part II, Tools and techniques, presents the key fundamentals of systems thinking. *Chapter 4, Feedback loops*, introduces the feedback loop, the central concept of systems thinking, and shows that it comes in two varieties, the reinforcing loop and the balancing loop.

The first of these, the reinforcing loop, forms the subject of *Chapter 5, The engines of growth—and decline*. Reinforcing loops are the drivers of business growth, but they can, if things go awry, also exhibit catastrophic decline. This explains the boom and bust cycles we see so often. The other main building block, the balancing loop, is explored in *Chapter 6, Setting targets, seeking goals*, which will show how balancing loops are central to all systems that seek goals or targets. The business world is full of these systems, for every time you agree a budget or commit to a plan, you are in fact creating a balancing loop. The behavior of balancing loops therefore underpins the behavior of many businesses, and this chapter will explain just how this happens.

Part II concludes with *Chapter 7, How to draw causal loop diagrams*, which presents 12 golden rules to help you draw your own diagrams, so that you can use them to tame the complexity of whatever problems are directly relevant to you.

Part III, Applications, applies the tools and techniques to four very different real-world situations. The first, discussed in *Chapter 8, Stimulating growth*, is an examination of the fundamental goal of every business: how to grow a business smoothly and continuously even in the presence of constraints. It also explains why drinking tea gave a major boost to the industrial revolution!

Chapter 9, Decisions, teamwork, and leadership, throws the spotlight on decision making, and shows how systems thinking can assist in the formulation of wise policies. This chapter features two case studies. The first is a development of the television case we met in Chapter 3, and the second deals with an important issue that arises in all outsourcing and subcontracting situations: how to strike a balance between the dependency of the buyer on the contractor and the risk of cost escalation. A particular feature of this chapter is the role of systems thinking and the power of causal loop diagrams in helping build consensus, in the formation of high-performing teams, and in the exercise of leadership.

The most important decisions, of course, relate to strategy, and so *Chapter 10, Levers, outcomes, and strategy*, shows how systems thinking and causal loop diagrams can be used to help you formulate wise and innovative business strategies. This chapter features a generic systems thinking model for strategy, and a description of how this can be used as an integral aspect of the powerful process known as scenario planning.

The great majority of the practical examples in this book relate to business, but one of the strengths of systems thinking is that it can throw a very perceptive spotlight onto complex problems in domains well beyond business, such as health care and education. For those of you in the public or not-for-profit sectors—as well as for those of you in business who have an interest in the world beyond your company profit-and-loss account—*Chapter 11, Public policy*, presents a systems thinking case study of perhaps the most important long-term threat facing humanity today, global warming. From the causal loop diagram, you will be able to determine the wisest policies that we trust our politicians are taking, and you may also come to some conclusions for your own business. A further intriguing aspect of this chapter is that the structure of the causal loop diagram that we shall draw to represent global warming is strikingly similar to the one we drew in Chapter 10 to represent business strategy.

The tools and techniques discussed so far are "hand and mind tools," in that causal loop diagrams can easily be sketched by hand and their purpose is to stimulate the mind. *Part IV, How to build a "laboratory of the future,"* takes matters a step further by showing how these tools can be "turbo-charged" by harnessing the power of computer simulation. *Chapter 12, Turbo-charging your systems thinking,* introduces system dynamics, a computer-based simulation modeling technique that can take a causal loop diagram and use the power of the computer to explore how the appropriate system evolves over time.

Computer-based modeling is of course familiar to anyone who uses a spreadsheet. The power, range, and scope of system dynamics modeling, however, are vastly beyond those of the spreadsheet. System dynamics is truly turbo-charged and the range of "what-if" analyses that can be carried out can equip you with the most comprehensive laboratory of the future you can imagine — even to the extent of providing you with a control panel containing all the knobs, levers, and buttons you twist, pull, or press to run your business.

Having introduced the language of system dynamics modeling in Chapter 12, *Chapter 13, Modeling business growth,* builds on this foundation by drawing on the material in Chapter 8 to show how to build a generic system dynamics model of business growth.

That completes the book, and by then you will be in a strong position not only to use causal loop diagrams in your day job to help your decision making and enhance the performance of teams, but also to add real value by using causal loop diagrams as the basis for insightful computer models.

I trust you will enjoy the book — I have certainly enjoyed writing it! But I am well aware that it is not a light read. This is not one of those books that are piled high in every airport bookshop promising "five quick fixes for your business that you can learn in less than a minute without even thinking about it." Managing a business is complex and if there were some real quick fixes, everyone would know them and everyone would do them. Taming complexity is not a trivial task and so this book is not trivial. It requires your attention and concentration, but I trust that I have made it manageable by keeping the chapters short and building up the case studies step by step.

So let's start on our journey...

Part I
Taming complexity

In which we examine the fundamental principles of systems thinking and explore how one of the key techniques, causal loop diagrams, can be used to tame the complexity of two real-world situations: the determination of staff levels in a busy investment banking back office, and how best to cut costs in the quality-sensitive, highly creative context of a television company.

1
The systems perspective

Systems

A community of connected entities constitutes a system, and it is the study of systems as systems — with particular reference to the systems encountered in business — that is the theme of this book.

> **How can you predict the behaviour of a system?**
> A system is composed of a number of connected entities. If you wish to understand — and therefore be in a position to predict, influence, and ultimately control — the behavior of the system as a whole, can you achieve this solely on the basis of knowledge of the individual entities?

As we saw in the Prologue, there is an enormous temptation to answer this question with a "yes," for three reasons.

The first is very human: Sometimes we do not wish to see the complexity, because living in a simple world is much easier than living in a complex one. We want to deny the very existence of complexity, we want to believe that our actions will result in the effect we wish and only in that effect, however strong the evidence might be to the contrary.

The second is pragmatic: Surely it is an easier task to understand something smaller and simpler than to try to grasp the complexity of the whole.

And the third reason is attributable to the enormous success of the "understand the bits" approach in the development of science over the last four centuries. The essence of the scientific method is to observe the results of carefully crafted experiments, in which the experimental conditions have been deliberately designed to focus on the key items of interest, to the exclusion of everything else. In science, this process of dissecting out the specific aspects of a subject of interest for detailed study has worked well, and we are tempted to use the same approach whenever we have a problem to solve, even when the problem concerns the behavior of the apparently capricious, arbitrary, mad world around us.

However, there are some—indeed many—situations where this approach just does not work. Peter Senge makes this point very graphically in *The Fifth Discipline* by observing that "dividing an elephant in half does not produce two small elephants." If your objective is to understand how the system of an elephant works, and you decide to achieve this objective by cutting the elephant up in order to examine the properties of the bits, you are likely to be disappointed, for the act of cutting the elephant in half results in the transformation of a system that used to work very well indeed into two subsystems that don't work at all.

The reason for this, of course, is that the back half of an elephant is intimately connected to the front half. When you cut the elephant in half, this connectedness is destroyed. Since the essence of the system is its connectedness, it is no wonder that destroying the connectedness destroys the system.

As a consequence, if you want to understand a system, and so put yourself in a position to be able to influence its behavior or even control it, you *must* seek to understand the system as a whole. This may or may not require a detailed knowledge of the behavior of the component parts; what is certain is that knowledge of the parts alone is of only limited use in understanding the behavior of the whole—and in some cases, such knowledge can be counterproductive.

This, of course, is a central problem in management. The department you manage is part of a highly complex connected system, some aspects of which are within your own organization, many of which extend beyond your organization's boundaries. You understand your department well, and you feel confident taking decisions locally. Nevertheless, a decision that is totally rational within your own department might be suboptimal for the organization as a whole, and so your local action on your own part of the system might be counterproductive overall.

Suppose, for example, that in order to keep some key members of staff you give them an interim pay rise. This might be OK, but it might trigger jealousy elsewhere, so that a team working on a major bid no longer functions as well as it used to and the major bid is lost. That is just one very simple example of that familiar organizational problem in which a quick fix "here" or "now" results in a bigger problem "there" or "later."

Emergence and self-organization

Another reason why the "understand the bits" approach does not work when applied to systems is that systems display characteristics that are properties of the system as a whole, and are not characteristics of any of the individual component parts. Since these special properties exist only at the level of the system, no amount of study of the component parts will even identify their existence. So let's take a look at two of these special, system-level properties: **emergence** and **self-organization**.

Every organization I know has "teamwork" as one of its values and not being a "team player" is a cardinal sin. As I noted in the Prologue, true teamwork is a characteristic of a well-functioning, highly connected system—the system we call a team, a system composed of individual component parts, the team members. As we all know, the performance of a team, as a team, cannot be predicted from knowledge of the performance of the individual team members. High-performing teamwork is a characteristic that emerges when the conditions are just right, when the team really is behaving as a team. This is merely one example of *emergence*, whereby the whole does indeed become greater than the sum of its parts.

Sometimes, complex systems show a particular emergent property that is associated with the structure of the system itself. Consider, for example, a flock of birds. Small flocks often fly in the familiar V-shaped formation, with a "leader" bird at the apex of the V and the others in a neat echelon behind. Larger flocks form more globular shapes, but somehow the overall shape tends to stay coherent as the birds soar and wheel in the sky.

How are the shapes of these complex bird systems maintained? Are the "follower" birds told what to do by the "leader" bird? Is there a continuing flow of instructions, keeping the birds in order? Or do these patterns form naturally? Birds can communicate with one another and so some form of telling might be a possibility. Such an explanation, however, is quite impossible for other systems, such as hurricanes, that show large-scale structural coherence, even though they are composed of separate entities. Hurricanes are formed from water molecules, evaporated from the ocean, mixed in the air. Water molecules have no means of deliberate communication, yet hurricanes form huge vortices, in which the individual sub-microscopic molecules somehow act together to form coherent—and extremely powerful—macroscopic structures.

An important feature of all these systems is that they are not static; rather, they are vigorously dynamic. And dynamic systems can show some very surprising properties. Take, for example, the system of a bicycle and a rider. A bicycle cannot balance by itself, nor can the system of a bicycle and its rider when stationary. But when the system becomes dynamic, when the rider pumps energy into the system to make the bicycle move forwards, then suddenly the bicycle and the rider can stay upright, without wobbling. Dynamic systems can therefore exhibit stable structures without explicit external intervention. It happens quite naturally, as the system itself finds a stable dynamic state: the motion of a bicycle, the vortex of a hurricane, the wheeling of a flock of birds.

The emergence of a stable dynamic structure is known as *self-organization*, another important property of many complex systems.

To an external observer, one of the most obvious properties of a self-organizing system is a very high degree of order. A flock of birds is a well-ordered whole rather than a random crowd; the vortex formed by a hurricane has a specific, rather than arbitrary, structure; a moving bicycle, with its rider, remains upright rather than sprawled randomly on the ground. Often these highly ordered structures are maintained for long periods of time. Your heartbeat, for example, is another highly ordered, self-organizing system, which continues beating its regular pattern-in-time for the duration of your life.

Self-organizing systems maintain these highly ordered states because they all have another, rather subtle, characteristic in common. They all have a flow of energy passing through them, a flow of energy that connects any given system with its appropriate environment. When you ride a bicycle you pump energy into the system with your legs, energy ultimately derived from breathing oxygen from the air; a hurricane maintains its structure by means of flows of heat between itself and its surroundings; birds in a flock respond to the air currents created by the motions of their neighbors. Once again, it is the connectedness of the component parts of the system with each other, and of the system as a whole with its environment, that is the central reason for order being maintained, and indeed created. Self-organizing systems all exchange energy with their environments and so fall into a class referred to as "open" systems.

A corollary of this is the recognition that, if you want to create a system that maintains some degree of order and so does not disintegrate, the system must be an open one. This in turn requires that energy is continuously pumped into, and through, the system to maintain that order, with the consequence that when that energy flow ceases, the system will degrade. That is why a bicycle tips over when you stop pumping the pedals. When you go home tired after a hard day at the office, the energy you have been expending was exactly what was required to create the energy flow through your department and keep it well organized. The continuous pumping of energy into an organization is the very heart of leadership.

Feedback

Emergence and self-organization are properties of systems, as systems, that are visible to an observer. How do they arise? This is a question of much active current research, one particularly significant result of which is the recognition of the fundamental importance of **feedback**.

Let's return to our example of a high-performing sports team, say a soccer team. Such a team, at top level, is comprised of 11 superbly fit, independently willful, ego-rich, individual stars, each of whom is more than capable of "doing his own thing." But if each star does indeed do his own thing, hogging the ball, never passing, trying to keep the limelight to himself and denying the limelight to everyone else, the team will fail disastrously. For the team to show the emergent behavior of high performance, *the behavior of the individual must be constrained*, so that of all the possible choices an individual player can make at any instant ("Should I try to run through the defense or should I pass the ball?"), the choice actually made is the one that works best from the team's overall point of view ("I'll pass").

For this to happen, each player must continuously be receiving, and processing, a flow of information: information concerning the disposition of the opposing team's players and those of his own team. If a player were blindfolded so that he could not see which players were where, he would be unable to function. It is the continuous processing of this kind of information, coupled with the personal willingness of every player to constrain individual action, that allows the team, as a team, to display those wonderful moments when the emergent behavior of high performance shines through.

The flow of information within a system is known as *feedback*, which is a much broader use of the term as compared to feedback in connection with personal counseling, for example. The action of feedback, however, is not exclusively to control, to limit, or to constrain; sometimes, feedback operates to exaggerate or to amplify, an example being the way in which crowds—and indeed stock markets—can, under certain circumstances, become increasingly frenzied or panicked.

Feedback is also integral to another emergent property of many self-organizing systems, *self-correction*. As we have seen, the open, self-organized system of the bicycle-plus-rider shows the emergent property of maintaining dynamic stability, with the bicycle-plus-rider upright. One aspect of this emergent property is that the system is vertical, not at 27° or any arbitrary angle, and not violently wobbling: The system naturally stabilizes vertically. Only when cornering does the bicycle (or, more visibly, a motorcycle) lean over, and even then the angle of lean is very specific.

If the bicycle-plus-rider system goes over a small bump, the system will wobble. But it quickly stabilizes again, for the system is self-correcting, seeking to maintain its well-ordered, self-organized state despite the external disturbance. This is achieved through feedback: The rider senses the wobble, and very subtly adjusts his or her weight to compensate. This self-correcting mechanism works for small bumps, but if the bump is very large, the rider, and the bicycle, will tumble. In the language of systems, the original, self-organized system, in its state of well-ordered dynamic equilibrium, suffers an external shock with which its internal mechanisms of self-correction cannot cope. The system then becomes chaotic (the bicycle and the rider fall), until it reaches another stable equilibrium state, but a static rather than dynamic one (spread-eagled on the ground).

Many biological systems are self-correcting; biologists and physiologists call this "homoeostasis." You and I, for example, have a number of mechanisms that maintain our body temperatures stable at about 36.9°C. If it gets too cold we start to shiver, so causing the body to generate heat; if it gets too hot we sweat, so causing the body to lose heat. But these natural mechanisms have their natural limits: If we are too cold for too long, hypothermia sets in; if we are too hot, we might suffer heat stroke. These mechanisms are all driven by feedback, in which information concerning the external environment is fed back to our internal physiological processes; they all serve to maintain the self-organization of ourselves as systems.

As we shall see throughout this book, the concept of feedback is also fundamental to the understanding of management systems. In Chapters 9, 10, and 11 in particular we shall see how feedback, emergence, and self-organization combine to give guidance on how to build high-performing teams, how to deal with the complex issues that arise when trying to build relationships across organizational boundaries, how to create powerful business strategies, and how to gain a deeper insight into the major public policy problems of pollution and global warming.

Systems thinking

Systems must be studied as systems, intact and as a whole. Unfortunately, most of us are ill equipped to take such a "helicopter" view. Most of the problem-solving tools we learn in the educational system and in our professional careers endorse and encourage us to cut problems up; furthermore, our departmental, silo-like organizational structures make it almost impossible to take other than local, parochial actions.

If we are to understand systems as systems, we must use a new set of tools; if we are to take wise decisions, in the light of a deep understanding of the systemic implications of any action, we must act in harmony with our colleagues. Systems thinking is the combination of an approach to problem solving and a set of tools, techniques, and methods that equip us with just what we are looking for: an appropriate toolkit for understanding complex systems and their associated properties, as well as a framework for a more meaningful interaction with our colleagues.

The problem-solving approach of systems thinking is the recognition that complex systems are complex because of the connectedness between their individual component parts, and that to understand the system it must be examined as a whole. The tools, techniques, and methods are all designed to help this examination, to understand and document how the component parts are connected together, and to interpret and explore their collective dynamic behavior.

The foundations of systems thinking can be traced back to the ancient Greeks. Aristotle's *Metaphysica*, for example, comments: "Now anything that has a plurality of parts but is not just the sum of these, like a heap, but exists as a whole beyond its parts, invariably has a cause"—a 2,300-year-old version of our more modern idiom "the whole is greater than the sum of its parts." Many eastern philosophies also strongly advocate the holistic view, especially as regards the role of humankind as merely one component part of the universe; a theme that also forms an important feature of many religious and cultural traditions.

Some of the principles of systems thinking have been known for a very long time, particularly the use of feedback to control machines. Suppose that you want to control the speed of an engine so that it stays constant regardless of the load, for example to maintain the speed of a car as it is going uphill. One way of doing this is to monitor the speed of the engine and use this information to control the rate at which fuel is let into the engine. The slower the engine speed, the more the fuel is allowed in; the faster the engine speed, the more the supply of fuel is restricted. As long as the flow of information and the adjustments to the fuel supply are not too slow, the engine will run at a constant speed. This is exactly the way in which the cruise control on modern cars works; it is also exactly the way in which James Watt controlled the speed of the steam engines that he and Matthew Boulton built in the 1780s and 1790s by means of a device originally called a "whirling regulator" and now known as a "centrifugal governor" or "fly-ball governor" — a technology that continued to be used to control engine speeds until the relatively recent development of electronic methods.

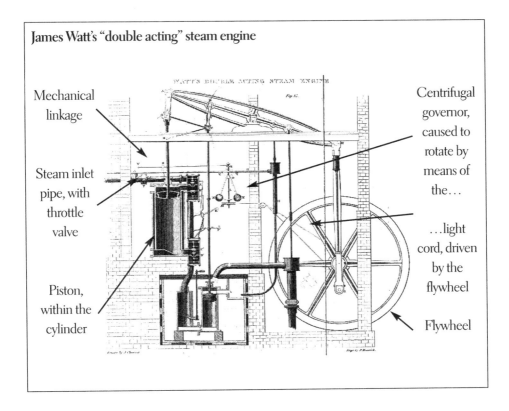

James Watt's "double acting" steam engine

Mechanical linkage

Steam inlet pipe, with throttle valve

Piston, within the cylinder

Centrifugal governor, caused to rotate by means of the…

…light cord, driven by the flywheel

Flywheel

The diagram on page 19 is a line drawing of one of James Watt's steam engines, the purpose of which is to make the large flywheel rotate. Steam from a boiler (not shown, but to the left of this diagram) passes through the steam inlet pipe via a "throttle valve" and enters the cylinder, so driving the piston. The way in which the steam is introduced into the cylinder powers the piston in both directions, hence the term "double-acting." The up-and-down motion of the piston rocks the horizontal beam (at the top of the diagram), so causing the flywheel to rotate. As it does so, a light cord causes the centrifugal governor — the dumb-bell-like structure in the center — to rotate, and the faster the rotation of the flywheel, the faster the rotation of the governor. As the governor rotates progressively faster the dumb-bells naturally move outward and upward, so activating a mechanical linkage that constricts the throttle valve on the steam inlet pipe. This reduces the flow of steam into the cylinder, so slowing the engine down, causing the flywheel to rotate more slowly. This in turn slows the rotation of the governor, causing the dumb-bells to drop, so releasing the throttle valve. This increases the flow of steam… with the overall result that the engine operates at a constant speed.

James Watt first used the centrifugal governor in 1788, but he did not invent it. That honor goes to one Thomas Mead, who in 1787 patented a similar device for use in windmills to control the distance between the millstones, so as to ensure the smooth milling of grain in different wind speeds.

What is happening here is that information on the output result of the engine (its speed) is being fed back to control the inputs to the engine (the flow of fuel or the flow of steam) and, as a result of this feedback, the engine constrains its behavior and self-organizes to run at a constant speed. James Watt understood the engineering perfectly, of course, but would not have recognized words such as "feedback" and "self-organizes"; nor indeed would the ancient Greek Ctesibius, who devised the earliest known example of mechanical feedback, a floating valve controlling the smooth operation of a water clock that he designed around 250 BC. The float valve, by the way, is another example of a remarkably durable technology: It was used by the Romans to control the level of water in their aqueducts, and it is a feature of our domestic plumbing systems to this day!

Throughout the industrial revolution and beyond, engineers continued to use feedback to control machines of increasing complexity and sophistication, but it wasn't until the 1930s and 1940s that systems were the subject of study in their own right. A major milestone in the development of systems thinking came in 1948, when Norbert Wiener, a professor at the Massachusetts Institute of Technology (MIT), published *Cybernetics*, which examines the bases of control with special reference to the pivotal role of the flow of information—this flow being what we now call communication—in getting control systems to work efficiently and effectively. This seminal work set many of the theoretical foundations for control theory, as used in many current aspects of computing, telecommunications, engineering, and robotics.

Also working at MIT in the late 1940s was Jay Forrester, an electrical engineer who was very much involved with the early development of computers. In the 1950s, Forrester became progressively interested in applying the concepts of control theory and feedback to wider issues of commerce and society, resulting in the publication of three major works. *Industrial Dynamics* (1961) examines many commercial and managerial systems such as inventory control, logistics, and decision making; *Urban Dynamics* (1969) studies the problems of urban society such as overcrowding and inner-city decay; and *World Dynamics* (second edition 1973) looks at problems such as population growth and pollution on a global scale. All of these books make extensive use of computer-based simulations to explore how the key properties of complex systems evolve over time, a technique pioneered by Forrester that he termed *system dynamics*.

Another major figure in the development of systems thinking, working not in the field of engineering but in biology, was the Austrian Ludwig von Bertalanffy. While at the University of Vienna between the two world wars, von Bertalanffy was particularly interested in how living organisms behave and develop. He recognized the importance of living organisms as open systems—systems, as we have seen, that do not operate by themselves, in isolation, but are intimately connected to their environments and maintain a high degree of order as a result of a flow of energy. Following his emigration to Canada in 1949, von Bertalanffy continued his work on biological systems, leading to his development of General System Theory, which articulates many of the principles describing the behavior of complex systems in general.

From these origins, the systems approach has, over the last 40 years, given rise to a host of disciplines, sub-disciplines, approaches, tools, techniques, methodologies, and indeed academic rivalries. Here is a checklist of the major themes:

➤ *Systems engineering* was pioneered in the US at the thinktank the RAND Corporation, and is primarily concerned with the design of complex systems so that they perform optimally: systems such as those required for the control of industrial plant and equipment, and military systems of command and control. Systems engineering draws on many of the methods of operational research and is also the basis of *systems analysis*, as applied to the design of computer systems.

➤ *Soft systems methodology (SSM)*, developed by Peter Checkland, recently retired from the UK's University of Lancaster, explicitly recognizes that in almost every real situation, people are intrinsically part of the system of interest. Since people often have multiple, different, competing, or simply unclear objectives, SSM asserts that the most beneficial approach is one of enriching all the participants' knowledge and understanding of the situation, rather than a "scientific" search for the "best" answer.

➤ *Complexity theory* and *chaos theory* are two closely related areas of active current academic study, for example at the interdisciplinary Santa Fe Institute in New Mexico. These are especially concerned with the study of *complex adaptive systems* (open systems that naturally change their structures and behaviors in harmony with changes in their environments) and the search for the rules, and ideally the mathematical explanations, underlying self-organization and emergence.

➤ *Management cybernetics* was developed in the UK by Stafford Beer. It features the Viable Systems Model, a framework for determining the characteristics of systems that are sustainable, with the goal of designing a self-organizing organization.

System dynamics itself has continued to flourish since its early days in the 1950s, and MIT's System Dynamics Group, founded by Jay Forrester in 1956 at the Sloan School of Management, is still regarded by many as the world center of excellence not only in computer simulation, but in systems thinking in general. It was, for example, a team from MIT that did the research for the Club of Rome that culminated in the publication, in 1972, of *Limits to Growth*, which, building on Forrester's *World Dynamics*, stimulated much—often vigorous and contentious—public debate on the fundamentally important issues of the progressive depletion of the earth's resources and the problems of pollution.

Systems thinking is a very broad field and it would be impossible to cover all the tools, techniques, methods, and approaches in a single book. My choice is therefore to explore in detail those that I have found most useful. They are drawn primarily from the MIT heritage and comprise two main tools: the use of *causal loop diagrams* to describe the complexity of real systems, highlighting the connectedness of the component parts; and *system dynamics* computer simulation modeling, which enables you to explore how the behavior of any given complex system evolves over time.

For those of you who would like to find out more about the various other approaches, I trust that the following list of sources is helpful.

Some systems thinking sources

There are many books on systems thinking and its applications, as detailed in the Bibliography. Here are thumbnail sketches of some of those I have found particularly valuable.

Two of the foundation stones of systems thinking are *Cybernetics, or Control and Communication in the Animal and the Machine*, by Norbert Wiener, first published in 1948 with a second edition in 1961, and *General System Theory* by Ludwig von Bertalanffy, first published in 1968 and revised in 1976.

Industrial Dynamics, by Jay Forrester, was first published in 1961 and shows how a holistic, systems thinking approach can throw great light on a host of problems such as sustaining a business, managing complex supply chains, the dynamic behavior of markets, and effective management policy making and decision making.

The Limits to Growth, published in 1972, presents the findings of the Project on the Predicament of Mankind, a study initiated by the thinktank the Club of Rome, and carried out by an international team of multidisciplinary experts led by Dennis Meadows of MIT. Their conclusions, at the time highly controversial, sounded a crystal-clear warning bell about the dangers of depleting natural resources. Together with Rachel Carson's *Silent Spring*, published 10 years earlier, *The Limits to Growth* made a major contribution to the environmental movement.

The Fifth Discipline, by Peter Senge, first published in 1990, became a business bestseller and is probably the best-known book on systems thinking. A particular feature of this book is the emphasis on systems thinking as a management process, rather than as an analytical or mathematically based technique.

Business Dynamics, by John Sterman, was published in 2000 and is a natural complement to *The Fifth Discipline*. It is an extremely well-written, complete, and rigorous description of systems thinking and system dynamics modeling, as befits the credentials of the author, who is the current Director of the System Dynamics Group at MIT.

Systems Thinking, Systems Practice by Peter Checkland, as well as being the primary source for soft systems methodology, contains a very informative review of the development of systems thinking and its position in the overall development of ideas. First

published in 1981, the 1999 edition contains a 30-year retrospective of how systems thinking in general, and soft systems methodology in particular, have developed.

The Heart of the Enterprise by Stafford Beer, published in 1978, is the main source on his
Viable Systems Model; some practical insights based on this model are described in *The
Viable Systems Model: Interpretations and Applications of Stafford Beer's VSM*, edited by
Raul Espejo and Roger Harnden, published in 1989.

Systems Thinking: Managing Chaos and Complexity, by Jamshid Gharajedaghi, published in 1999, gives a highly thought-provoking analysis of the current state of the art in systems thinking and related fields, and provides much insight as to future developments.

The second edition of *Complexity*, by Roger Lewin, published in 2001, is an up-to-date,
non-mathematical account of complexity theory, drawing on examples from fields as
diverse as physics, chemistry, biology, economics, linguistics, and anthropology. It also
includes a chapter on the applications of complexity theory to business.

On with our journey...

Let's continue our journey into systems thinking by seeing how complex systems can be described, and therefore understood, by using a particular type of
pictorial representation known as a causal loop diagram. The next two chapters demonstrate the practical use of causal loop diagrams in the context of
two case studies drawn from my consulting work. The first examines the problem of how to determine the right number of back office staff in an investment bank; the second looks at the consequences of a cost-reduction program
in a media company.

2
Carrying the back office rock

The story

Many organizations have a "back office," an administrative function that processes all the transactions resulting from the customer-facing "front office." This story, based on my personal experience, is about a central dilemma that faces all back office support functions: How many staff should be employed and how do we best minimize costs?

To be specific, my stage is an investment bank, where the primary role of the back office is to process the transactions executed by the front office market traders and stockbrokers who buy and sell securities, commodities, and currencies. This is a high-profile, high-profit, high-tension environment, portrayed vividly in Michael Lewis's book *Liar's Poker* and in *Wall Street*, the film starring Michael Douglas. Although my story is set in these particularly dramatic surroundings, it applies to back office support functions everywhere.

The characters in my story represent five communities. First, we have the back office managers, those responsible for the delivery of the service and also for controlling costs in each of the various back office departments. In investment banks these people are experienced, tough cookies who work all hours to keep things going. A day's transactions must be processed in a day to avoid backlogs, and in times when the markets are booming the number of transactions to be processed can be huge.

Secondly, we have the back office staff, those whose job it is to ensure that each transaction is processed correctly, and whose time is spent entering data, correcting errors, dealing with exceptions, handling queries, chasing up problems, and all the rest. These people are often young and inexperienced, willing to accept the demands of a tough environment for generous salaries and the prospect of rapid promotion.

Thirdly, we have the IT department. Securities trading is totally reliant on IT systems, from the "rocket science" that the traders use in connection with their decisions to buy or sell, to the transaction processing systems that record the trades and settle the cash. Clever IT systems are a real source of competitive advantage in such a fast-moving industry and the imperative for the IT function is to get systems in as fast as they possibly can.

Fourthly, the HR function. Many investment banks have a very macho culture and under these conditions the HR function is primarily involved in personnel administration (that's politically correct code for hiring, and especially firing) rather than management and organizational development.

And finally the directors. Directors in investment banks are usually young, vigorous, decisive, tough, enormously successful, and even more enormously wealthy. They have the gift of patronage and promotion, as well as the sanction of causing rapid and undignified departure. So everyone wants to keep the directors happy.

The context

In most investment banks, power and status lie with the front office: the people who make the trades or do the deals, the people who bring in the revenue. Those in the back office are often regarded very much as "second-class citizens" and the back office as a whole is always in a defensive political position internally, since it doesn't contribute directly to revenue but very visibly contributes to cost. Given the volatility of securities markets, investment banks seek to minimize costs in general, and especially those costs that are not directly associated with generating revenue. Back offices are continually under pressure to hold costs down or reduce them, and that usually translates into restrictions and ceilings on headcount.

"How many staff are on your establishment?" a visitor might ask a back office manager.

"Twenty-three."

"Oh. But you must have far more than twenty-three people out there."

"Oh, yes. In fact, we have about sixty people in the department right now."

"Sixty? I thought you said your establishment was twenty-three?"

"I did. And it is. The others are all temps."

"Temps?"

"Yes, temps. When the transaction volumes surge we need more people, and since the headcount is capped the only way we can handle things is to get in temps. And of course when the market volumes drop, we can get rid of all the temps at short notice…"

"I see. So about how long have you had so many temps?"

"Well, the markets have been active for quite a while. Let me think… I guess we've had forty or so temps—give or take a few—for about three years now."

The issue

This story is not an exaggeration; I expect you have come across similar examples. Sometimes the translation of cost control into headcount restrictions can lead to strange places. Not only can the cost of employment of temps, contractors, or consultants be more expensive than the cost of the equivalent number of full-time employees, but there are also considerations of loyalty, and the capture—or loss—of organizational knowledge.

An important question is therefore: "How can we determine what the staff establishment should be?" To me this is not the central issue, however. The central issue is more fundamental, and one that the more macho investment banks do not recognize, let alone talk about. It is what I call the back office's "ability to cope."

The concept of the "ability to cope" captures what to me is the essence of the back office role. To do its job properly, the back office must be able to cope with all the demands made on it: the processing of transactions, the handling of queries, the provision of useful management information, the generation of ideas to improve processes. And the greater the ability to cope, the better the service to the front office in particular, and the business as a whole in general. Conversely, if the ability to cope is eroded, all sorts of things can go wrong: Backlogs mount up and queries multiply, people get stressed and work increasingly long hours, maybe the sickness rate increases. And, most importantly, people make more mistakes.

A diagrammatic representation

The last paragraph is one way of describing the situation, but it is somewhat wordy. A much more succinct representation is as a diagram, Figure 2.1 overleaf.

This diagram shows the central concept, ABILITY TO COPE, linked to two other concepts, SERVICE QUALITY and INCIDENCE OF ERROR. The direction of

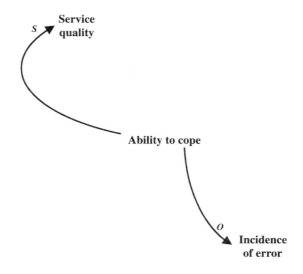

Figure 2.1

the arrows is important, for each arrow indicates a cause-and-effect relationship: ABILITY TO COPE drives both the SERVICE QUALITY and also the INCI-
DENCE OF ERROR. You will also notice two small symbols, S and O. These are
also important, because they indicate the way in which the cause-and-effect
relationships work.

   Let's imagine that our ABILITY TO COPE is (for whatever reason) becoming
stronger. As our ABILITY TO COPE increases, what effect will this have on the
SERVICE QUALITY and the INCIDENCE OF ERROR? I believe that the SERVICE
QUALITY will, in general, improve, and that the INCIDENCE OF ERROR will,
simultaneously, decrease. According to how I see the world, as the ABILITY TO
COPE increases, so does the SERVICE QUALITY. To indicate that the nature of
this cause-and-effect relationship is such that these two variables move in the
same direction, the diagram shows the S by the head of the arrow. The cause-
and-effect relationship linking the ABILITY TO COPE and the INCIDENCE OF
ERROR works the other way: As the ABILITY TO COPE increases, the INCIDENCE
OF ERROR decreases—they move in *opposite* directions, hence the O.

   What happens if, for whatever reason, our ABILITY TO COPE begins to
decrease? Let's determine this from the diagram and then check our deduc-
tions against common sense. The S linking ABILITY TO COPE and SERVICE
QUALITY indicates that these move in the same direction, so if our ABILITY TO
COPE goes down, the diagram tells us that the SERVICE QUALITY will go down
too. That makes sense. And as the ABILITY TO COPE goes down, the O by INCI-

DENCE OF ERROR indicates that this will move in the opposite direction, implying that this will increase. That makes sense too: As our ABILITY TO COPE decreases, we get more stressed and we make more errors.

The diagram works whether or not our ABILITY TO COPE increases or decreases, and so one diagram can cater for both eventualities.

Causal loop diagrams

Diagrams like this are called **causal loop diagrams** or **influence diagrams**, and this book is full of them. Confidence in drawing these diagrams, and in reading them, is the heart of what this book is all about, and so I'll be taking things steadily to help build your confidence. Now is a good time to pause for a moment and check that you're happy with the arrows, their directions, the Ss and the Os, and the feature of the diagram that it works both when the ABILITY TO COPE is increasing as well as when it is decreasing. Some people, by the way, prefer to use the symbols + instead of S and – instead of O. In practice, provided you are consistent the choice of symbols is immaterial — what is important is that the directionality of each cause-and-effect link is clearly understood and explicitly identified.

One particular aspect you might like to think about for a moment or two is the direction of the arrow from ABILITY TO COPE to SERVICE QUALITY, capturing the idea that the SERVICE QUALITY at any time is determined by the ABILITY TO COPE at that time. You might be thinking: "Aha! The arrow is the wrong way round! Surely, if I decide what SERVICE QUALITY I want, then I can use this to determine what my ABILITY TO COPE should be. If this is the case, shouldn't the arrow should go from SERVICE QUALITY to ABILITY TO COPE, but still with an S?"

That's a good question. In fact, the arrow is the right way round — let me explain why. In drawing causal loop diagrams, the terminology needs to be succinct but it also needs to be absolutely clear. In the diagram, the term SERVICE QUALITY means the service quality as delivered in practice. This is a different concept from the target I might set, or aspiration I might have, for what I might wish the service quality to be. I agree that the target I might set for service quality does influence how I might plan my ability to cope, but that is an issue not addressed in the diagram (not yet, anyway). The diagram as drawn focuses on actualities, not aspirations: My actual ABILITY TO COPE drives the SERVICE QUALITY I actually deliver, and so the arrow is in the direction shown.

Targets, budgets, and goals are very important in business and we will spend quite a lot of time seeing how these may be represented in causal loop diagrams, particularly in Chapters 6 and 8. For the moment, let's keep to the actuals.

Enriching the diagram

We can now enrich the diagram by examining the key driver of the ABILITY TO COPE. This is the WORKLOAD on the department, which itself is driven by the VOLUME AND VARIETY OF TRANSACTIONS that the department has to process. The direction of causality is such that, as the VOLUME AND VARIETY OF TRANSACTIONS increases, so does the WORKLOAD (implying an S); and as the WORKLOAD increases, our ABILITY TO COPE goes down (an O). These two new features can be represented as in Figure 2.2.

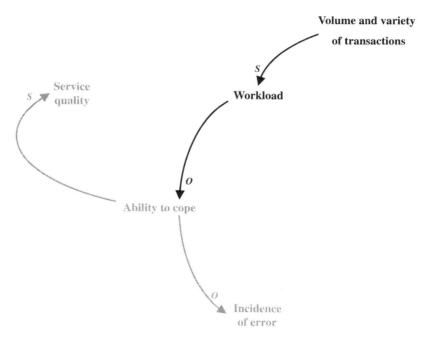

Figure 2.2

In this diagram the items that appeared in the previous diagram are shown in a lighter tone and newly introduced items are in black. I will use this convention throughout the book, so that, as causal loop diagrams are built up, you can very easily see the progression of successive features.

What happens as a consequence of error?

Generally, when errors occur there are increasing demands on all staff—especially supervisors and managers—to sort things out. Quite often, for example, supervisors and departmental managers will get sucked into the problem, since the more junior people may lack the knowledge of how to solve it or may no longer be trusted since they made the mistake in the first place. The more senior people end up doing not only the job they should be doing but the jobs of their subordinates too, and this puts a STRAIN ON MANAGEMENT, which itself increases the WORKLOAD (Figure 2.3).

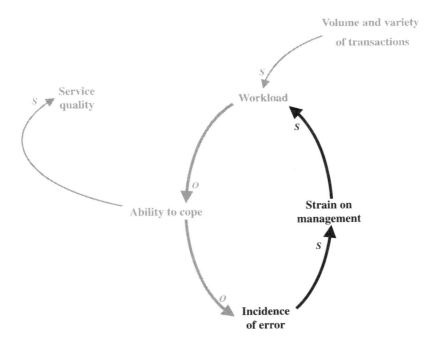

Figure 2.3

A nasty vicious circle

The central part of the diagram, which I have now emphasized with heavier arrows, shows a very special feature: a singularly nasty vicious circle. As the WORKLOAD increases our ABILITY TO COPE diminishes, so increasing the likelihood of INCIDENCE OF ERROR. This in turn puts a STRAIN ON MANAGEMENT, further increasing the WORKLOAD and pushing the INCIDENCE OF ERROR even higher…

Those of you who have worked in or seen a busy back office might recognize this as the world in which the back office manager lives. That is why they have to be tough, because they are always having to carry ever heavier rocks.

What else drives the ability to cope?

I would argue that the main contributor to the back office's ABILITY TO COPE is the availability of the right number of effective staff, where the concept of EFFECTIVE STAFF CAPACITY represents a combination of HEADCOUNT and TRAINING. HEADCOUNT alone is not enough, since if the staff are untrained they could well be of very little help (Figure 2.4).

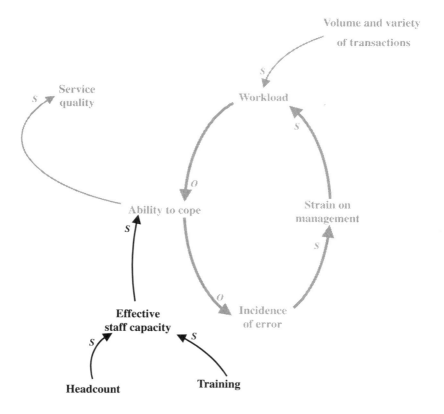

Figure 2.4

"But what about the availability of good IT systems?" I hear you say. "Doesn't that help the ability to cope?"

Yes it does. But does it do that directly? In my view, good IT systems certainly improve the ABILITY TO COPE, but primarily by reducing the WORKLOAD. The greater the use of high-quality, EFFECTIVE IT SYSTEMS, the lower the WORKLOAD, since good systems enable large volumes of transactions to be processed without manual intervention (Figure 2.5).

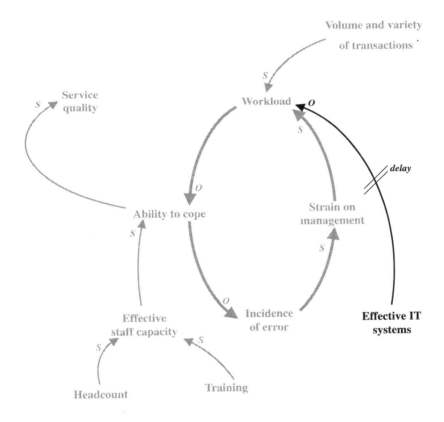

Figure 2.5

This diagram introduces another new feature: the *time delay* that is often associated with the development and delivery of good systems.

Time delays

Most cause-and-effect relationships are associated with time delays, in that it is very rare for an action to give rise to its result instantaneously. You are probably thinking, correctly, that it takes time for people to be trained (implying a delay between TRAINING and EFFECTIVE STAFF CAPACITY), and perhaps even more time for good people to be recruited (hence another delay between HEADCOUNT and EFFECTIVE STAFF CAPACITY). So why have I introduced a delay explicitly between EFFECTIVE IT SYSTEMS and WORKLOAD, but not elsewhere? The answer is one of emphasis: There are time delays everywhere, but this one is especially important.

But what about cost?

The diagram is not yet complete, for there is an important element still missing: COST. The HEADCOUNT, good TRAINING, and EFFECTIVE IT SYSTEMS all cost money, so we can introduce COST as shown in Figure 2.6.

This diagram now shows the management dilemma. The tendency of that vicious circle in the middle is to spin away, making life progressively more difficult for the back office with each successive turn. This can be mitigated in two different ways: by introducing more EFFECTIVE IT SYSTEMS (albeit with a time delay), or by increasing the EFFECTIVE STAFF CAPACITY through having a well-trained, appropriate staff establishment. The problem, however, is that people, training, and systems all cost money. The "good" of optimizing our ABILITY TO COPE is therefore in direct conflict with the "good" of minimizing COST.

How can this dilemma be resolved? In many instances, by power. And in an investment bank, those who hold the power are the directors, whose main motivation is to minimize costs. So they will impose headcount restrictions, minimize training, and divert systems development resources to front office support—which generates income—rather than to back office developments, which just increase cost. So the end game is an ordeal in which the back office managers are tested to see just how big a rock they can carry before they are crushed. When that happens, that manager is fired and a new one appointed to continue carrying the rock.

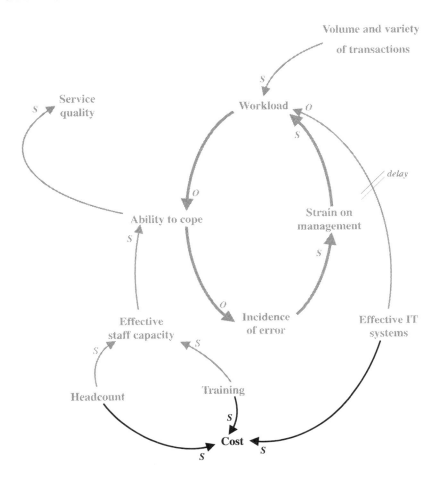

Figure 2.6

There's still one thing missing...

The diagram is not yet complete. There is one important aspect missing, one
that is often overlooked.

What is missing from the diagram? The answer is in Figure 2.7 overleaf.

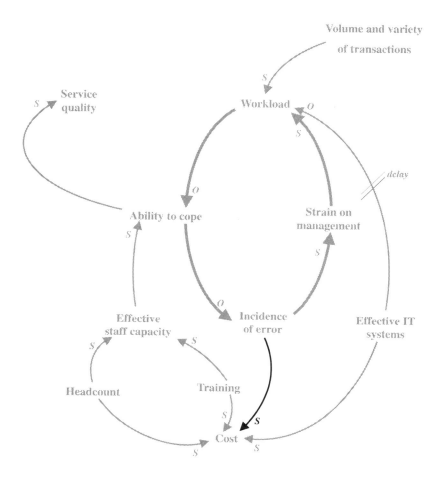

Figure 2.7

The missing item is an arrow: an arrow linking INCIDENCE OF ERROR to COST; an arrow with an S on it. Errors are not free, for they incur costs of two types. The first is the cost of correcting the error, this being absorbed in the extra workload and hassle. But the second is the intrinsic cost of the error itself, as expressed, perhaps, in terms of compensation to a client, or—more likely in the securities industry—the cost of having to go into the market to buy some securities (when the price has inevitably gone up) or to sell some securities (when the price has plummeted down). And sometimes, that can cost real money.

The recognition of this last link has a significant impact. In its absence, the only items driving cost are the headcount, training, and IT, all of which act to increase cost. So in times of active cost cutting, or more benign times of cost control, it is the headcount, training, and IT budgets that get scrutinized, challenged, and cut. And the burden is thrown back on to the ever-suffering back office manager to carry a bigger rock.

However, as soon as that link from INCIDENCE OF ERROR to COST is recognized, another cost driver is explicitly on the table: the cost of errors. It is this that resolves the dilemma between the "good" of being able to cope, and the conflicting "good" of controlling cost. If the ABILITY TO COPE diminishes, the INCIDENCE OF ERROR goes up, but so does the COST. Starving the back office of well-trained people and quality IT systems therefore might be *adding* to cost, rather than diminishing it. There must be some point at which the investment in people, training, and systems is such as to hold the error rate at a low level, so that the cost of error is acceptable. And since the cost of error is measurable—particularly in an investment bank—it must be possible to determine what level of expenditure is sensible to invest in people, training, and IT, with an eye on the expected fluctuations in transaction volumes, so that the back office can deliver a high level of service without being crushed by the rock.

This story is real. And when I drew this last diagram at a workshop, attended by some directors, back office managers, back office staff, HR managers, and IT managers, an important lightbulb went on. At one level, people thought, "That's obvious—of course things are like that. The diagram looks pretty, but it doesn't tell us anything new." The fact that the diagram is "obvious" is important, for the diagram must represent reality and so must be recognized as such. And since the diagram is "obvious," it cannot contain any surprises. Nevertheless, that's not necessarily the same thing as saying nothing new.

What this diagram actually achieved in my workshop was a realization that no one—no one at all—was actively managing the whole system, as a whole. The back office people were stuck on their treadmill and prevented by the culture from even acknowledging the concept of the ability to cope; the IT people were always arguing for better systems, but usually having their resources primarily devoted to the front office rather than the back office; the HR people were always on the phones to the temp agencies and had very little power in policy making; the directors were usually very narrowly focused on cost control. And the only people who knew about the incidence of error were the internal auditors, who swept up the mess afterwards!

Even in a very sophisticated organization, no one was looking at the whole picture. Each manager was being very conscientious in managing their "bit," but the successful management of all the bits was suboptimizing the management of the whole. This, of course, is a natural consequence of most organizational structures and the power of local performance measures. All managers, quite legitimately, strive to manage their own local bits, to exceed their own personal performance measures. The problem is that the only point at which the whole system comes together in its entirety is on the desk of the chairman—and he's too busy to get into the detail!

So the lightbulb that went on was all about the importance of managing the whole as well as the parts, of seeing the interconnectedness of decisions, and of taking a collective, non-parochial view. As a result of that workshop, the organization adopted a new series of procedures and policies, so that departmental managers could still manage their departments to the best of their abilities but, in addition, they collectively agreed to implement a process whereby cross-boundary issues could be discussed and resolved with wisdom.

Back to wisdom

Take another look at Figure 2.7 on page 36, which contains several significant features. At its center is that vicious circle: the treadmill from WORKLOAD, through ABILITY TO COPE, INCIDENCE OF ERROR, STRAIN ON MANAGEMENT, and back to WORKLOAD. The back office manager strives to stop this from running out of control, but if there is a surge in business (so causing a leap in VOLUME AND VARIETY OF TRANSACTIONS), or if the "rocket scientists" invent some fancy (and probably complex) new financial product for which no system has yet been built (so causing another leap in VOLUME AND VARIETY OF TRANSACTIONS), or if there is a systems failure (so causing a sudden increase in WORKLOAD), or if a key person resigns or is sick (so diminishing the ABILITY TO COPE), that rock gets heavier.

Obviously this diagram can be taken to extremes, because you can envisage a situation in which the HEADCOUNT has risen so high that the ABILITY TO COPE is far in excess of any likely WORKLOAD. The SERVICE QUALITY has long since reached a plateau, the INCIDENCE OF ERROR is as close to zero as you could reasonably expect, and the COST has gone through the roof. This profligacy is not commercially sensible; but nor is the opposing tendency, the situation in which the pressure to control costs has been exerted so strongly that there are real issues around the ABILITY TO COPE and the INCIDENCE OF ERROR. What we are seeking is that region of sensible commercial balance, where the EFFECTIVE STAFF CAPACITY, and its interaction with EFFECTIVE IT SYSTEMS, in the context of the VOLUME AND VARIETY OF TRANSACTIONS, has been determined so as to ensure that the back office's ABILITY TO COPE is never unduly jeopardized, where the INCIDENCE OF ERROR is low and controllable, and where the COST of the entire system has been optimized. That's what wisdom is all about.

Another feature of the diagram is the fact that *everything is connected to everything else*, implying that if you take an action over here, sooner or later something pops up over there. So if (yet another) round of cost cuts is being implemented, sooner or later the benefit of reducing cost will result in the undoubted disbenefit of an error—and in the securities industry, the cost of even a single error could well wipe out six months of cost cutting.

This interconnectedness, associated with inevitable time delays, is what makes managing organizations so complex and difficult. Try as we might to fix something locally, sooner or later there are repercussions somewhere else. Some may take the view that as long as their department is fine, they don't care what happens elsewhere, so the factory manager, incentivized on production efficiency, fills the warehouse with finished goods, which then become "marketing's problem." Some may take the view that the time delays are sufficiently long that they will have been promoted by then, so who cares what chaos they bequeath to their successors?

Such cynical views are not held by wise managers. Wise managers want to understand and think through the likely consequences of their possible actions; they want to understand the complex interconnectedness of real business problems; they do not simply wish to pass the buck of responsibility down the line or to their successors; they appreciate how organizational boundaries can lead to counterproductive short-sightedness and parochialism; they want to understand issues completely and holistically; they want to anticipate the impact of the time delays. If they can do this, they are in a much stronger position to take decisions that will stand the test of time, decisions that are truly wise.

3
Quality, creativity, and cutting costs

The story

"You know what will happen, don't you?" asked Jonathan aggressively.

"Lot of things will happen, I'd imagine. What do you have in mind?" replied Tony, trying to keep his voice calm.

"The key issue is quality," continued Jonathan. "Everything we do as producers is about quality, and that's why viewers watch our programs. If you persist in enforcing those cost cuts, our quality will drop, our viewers will start watching the other channels, our ratings will go down, and that will be the end of us."

"I agree with Jonathan on that one," chipped in Clare. "Once we lose the ratings war, we'll never be able to recover."

"And when the ratings start dropping, the advertisers will start kicking up..." added Anne.

"Hitting our revenue line..."

"And causing us to cut even more costs. What a mess!"

"I think it's worse than that," said Paul, the HR director. "What I'm worried about is the damaging effect all this cost cutting will have on our key staff. Some of our producers are very hot properties, you know, let alone our star presenters. If they get fed up, their motivation will suffer, and eventually they'll walk. And if they walk, we'll be even worse off!"

"And what about our creative talent? Our creatives are the very heart of our business. Are we going to start rationing their pencils?"

"I hear all that. And I understand it all too," said Tony, trying to bring the meeting back under control. "The fact remains, we have to cut costs somehow. How can we best do this without suffering all the problems we've identified?"

The context

That conversation is a pretty accurate (but highly abbreviated) reflection of one in which I participated at a TV production company. The box in which they find themselves is by no means unfamiliar whatever industry you're in: how to cut costs without damaging the business.

The immediate reaction of Jonathan, a producer, is that the impact of a cost cut is to reduce quality ("Yes, we can continue to make costume dramas, but we'll have to shoot everything from the front, since we won't be able to afford costumes for the actors' backs!"). Paul, consistent with his HR role, highlights the likely effect that cost cutting will have on morale; and Clare and Ann articulate the ultimate threat: that the viewers will go away, and that the advertisers will no longer buy time in their programs. As Jonathan (possibly triumphantly) puts it, what a mess. This, however, doesn't solve the problem, so Tony, the MD, tries to bring the meeting back to the realities of life.

Drawing a causal loop diagram

If you have a paper and pencil to hand, draw a causal loop diagram that you feel captures the essence of the conversation.

What are the key items in the diagram? How are they sequenced and linked? What are the directions of the arrows? Are there any additional items, not explicitly mentioned in the story, that you think are important to add? Where are the Ss and the Os? How does the whole thing fit together?

If you don't have these materials easily available, stop for a moment to compose a diagram in your head.

The picture

Here, as they say on TV cookery shows, is one I prepared earlier (Figure 3.1 overleaf).

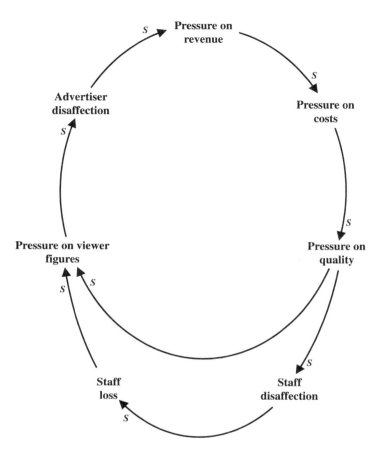

Figure 3.1

Another nasty vicious circle

Here's an explanation of my causal loop diagram.

The starting point is what I call the PRESSURE ON COSTS, which, as Jonathan stated, puts PRESSURE ON QUALITY (hence the S). This, in its turn, has two consequences: First, there is a direct impact on those who watch the programs that might be of reduced quality, causing PRESSURE ON VIEWER FIGURES (another S); secondly, and at the same time, picking up the point made by Paul, the continued PRESSURE ON QUALITY increases STAFF DISAFFECTION (an S again), which drives STAFF LOSS (with an S), and when the stars depart, this too can contribute to the PRESSURE ON VIEWER FIGURES (S once more).

As the PRESSURE ON VIEWER FIGURES mounts, this increases ADVERTISER DISAFFECTION (S), putting PRESSURE ON REVENUE (S), so aggravating the already existing PRESSURE ON COSTS (S once again).

This is another nasty vicious circle (or rather a pair of vicious circles), and one that is probably rather familiar.

How does this diagram compare to the one you compiled or had in your head? Don't worry if they're different—compiling these diagrams requires quite a bit of practice, and I'll be giving some guidelines on how to do it in Chapter 7. For the present, the most important thing is that you feel comfortable with my diagram, especially the sequence of items and all the Ss. Also, are you convinced that the diagram captures the essential features of the story? You will have noticed, I'm sure, that the diagram is not an exact transcript of the story; no one, for example, explicitly used the terms PRESSURE ON COSTS or ADVERTISER DISAFFECTION, and different parts of the diagram were discussed at different times and not necessarily in the "right" sequence.

This, of course, is very realistic. When people are discussing a problem, they describe it in terms that reflect what they perceive and what they think is important, as well as emphasizing the issues that that they wish to argue about or defend. One of the major benefits of compiling a causal loop diagram is to portray the whole story, independent of parochial, narrow, or short-sighted interests.

What would you do?

Imagine that you're Tony, the MD. What actions would you take to stop the vicious circle going out of control?

What actions do you think would be advocated by the other people: Jonathan, Clare, Anne, Paul?

What actions do you think they will agree on?

What should we do?

Let's eavesdrop on their conversation.

"I had a rather tricky session with one of our presenters just yesterday," said Paul. "She's received a very attractive offer from elsewhere, and she was asking—quite directly—for a salary increase. She wasn't exactly blackmailing us, but it was pretty close. I really think, as a matter of some urgency, we should budget for some substantial rises. I realize that doesn't save money, but it certainly will stop the viewers from going away."

"I disagree," said Jonathan. "Not only is that very short-sighted, as well as quite unwise, it is simply a license for everyone else to blackmail us too. Once you start down that road, it will never stop. To me, the issue is all about quality. I think we should agree the quality standards we wish to achieve, and commit never—just never—to compromise. Once we draw this line in the sand, that will be that."

Clare and Anne exchanged glances and then Clare spoke. "I'm afraid I disagree with both of you. I think we're looking in the wrong place altogether: We should be cutting overhead, not the costs in our core activities of making programs. Can't we save money in IT or accounting or something? Isn't everyone these days talking about outsourcing?"

"That's amazing!" exclaimed Anne. "Clare, you've used exactly the same words as I was going to, at least to start with. But you ended up in a wildly different place. I was going to say, just like you, that I disagree with everyone; I was also going to say that we're all looking in the wrong place. And now I've heard what you said, Clare, I think the same is true of you too. This is exactly the wrong argument. We shouldn't be talking about cutting costs at all. We should be talking about how we can generate new sources of revenue. Shouldn't we be exploiting our most successful programs as brands and make money through merchandising? And what about investing in a website, or a series of websites linked to our shows? All this talk about cutting costs makes me gloomy. What business ever achieved success by cutting costs all the time?"

Tony shook his head. "Well, folks, thanks for all that. So far I've heard four totally different and contradictory things: buy our staff off, define quality standards, get rid of all our accountants, and start selling T-shirts. Why can't we ever agree on anything? Why don't we see the world the same way? And what are we actually going to do?"

Who's right?

So if you were Tony, what would you do? Who is right? Which is the wise decision?

In my view they're all right. All of these suggestions are quite plausible ways of tackling the problem, so it is not a question of "right" or "wrong," it is a question of "different." What is going on here is a genuine disagreement on policy, a sincere articulation of the different choices that different people would make. And these different choices have different impacts and consequences. Upping the salaries could lead to generalized "blackmail," but it does have the benefit of being an action that can be implemented very quickly; generating revenue from other sources does take the pressure off costs — eventually — but in the short term costs are likely to increase as funds are spent on creating a merchandising operation. All the suggestions have some merit; all have consequences; all also have different political agendas. We're back to the issues of choice and wisdom.

These four suggestions aren't the only possibilities. Take a look at the next diagram (Figure 3.2 overleaf).

This is an enhancement of the previous diagram, in which I have added, around the perimeter of the central two vicious circles, a number of possible actions, each of which acts primarily on one of the items in the central loops. You will also see that each of these new items is linked into the loops by an O. For example, the greater the exploitation of NEW REVENUE SOURCES, the lower the PRESSURE ON REVENUE from program production; likewise, the stronger the OVERHEAD COST CONTROL, the lower the PRESSURE ON COSTS in the mainstream activities.

Each of these items therefore acts as a brake on the vicious circle, arresting its relentless spinning, bringing the business back under control. The diagram also shows some suggestions not mentioned in the story: STAFF DISAFFECTION might be alleviated by INVOLVEMENT, this being an encapsulation of all the best features of change management ("We're all in this together, folks, so let's sort it out"); PROGRAM INNOVATION represents the possibility of producing new types of TV show, which have either a different cost structure or are less dependent on "stars," but which still hold the viewers; maybe there is scope for negotiating NEW DEALS with the advertisers, so mitigating ADVERTISER DISAFFECTION.

Deciding policy

I often do this example as an exercise in my workshops. After drawing the vicious circles, I ask the participants to think about what actions they would take and then, without consulting each other, to write them down and rank them in order of impact. I go round the group and ask each person to state the single action that they would take, the single action that they believe

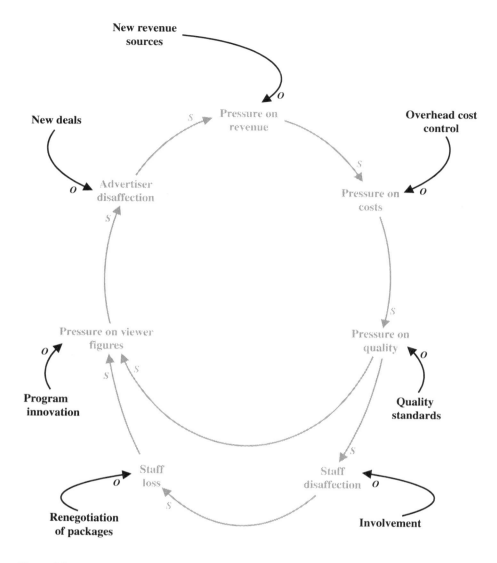

Figure 3.2

would have the most beneficial effect. By the time I have gone round the group, I have usually written at least half a dozen different actions on a flipchart.

I then ask: "So what do we collectively decide to do?"

This always leads to a lively debate. Those who believe that "quality is king" argue vigorously for drawing a line in the sand; the HR community advocates involvement; the entrepreneurs come up with any number of ideas for merchandising; everyone agrees that the overhead should be cut.

None of these policies is intrinsically "wrong," none is "right"—they're just different. Different as regards the specific actions to be taken, different as regards the time required for them to come into effect, different in terms of the costs of implementation, different in terms of their consequences; indeed, the last causal loop diagram is by no means complete, for all the policies feed back elsewhere, especially to PRESSURE ON COSTS. Despite the complexity of all this, people can and do make personal assessments of all these factors—and more—in their own minds and decide which policy they believe to be the most effective. And different people will come to different conclusions.

What is happening in this debate is the articulation of sincerely held views about what individuals genuinely believe to be for the best. Sometimes these beliefs are well founded, sometimes they are driven by short-sightedness and parochialism, but they are all passionately held. And if someone really believes that the best thing to do in this situation is to define quality standards, they will argue that case passionately against all-comers.

How, then, are such strongly held, individual beliefs reconciled? How can we collectively decide on a shared, committed policy? How can we be wise?

Is it a question of power, in which the most senior person, or the one who shouts the loudest, "wins"? Or is it an "armed truce," in which we all agree to do a little of everything? Or is it a more thoughtful process?

To me the determination of wise policy is the heart of business decision making and, once again, it is not a question of choosing between "right" and "wrong"—it is a question of deciding between sincerely held, passionately argued beliefs.

One of my sincerely held, passionately argued beliefs is that diagrams like the ones we have been using in this chapter can be enormously helpful in assisting this debate. Using causal loop diagrams helps the group think through the range of potential policies and the likely consequences of the various alternatives. Not only does this open people's minds ("Program innovation, I hadn't really thought of that"), but it also prevents the dangers of tunnel vision ("The only way to sort this one is by…"), since there is never an "only way." Wisdom is all about identifying all the possible ways and determining the best.

In my view, one of the most powerful ways of encouraging that wisdom is to look at complex problems holistically, teasing out how all the parts are mutually interconnected, and representing that complexity in a succinct, meaningful way in a well-constructed causal loop diagram. So in the next chapter we will examine in more detail the fundamental building block from which all causal loop diagrams are formed: the feedback loop.

These things have all happened

All of the policies discussed in the television example have been put into practice over the last several years. For example:

> Many television companies have cut costs and overhead.
> In the UK, the BBC had a major "culture change" program for several years, seeking to involve all its staff in the cost-cutting exercise.
> The newspapers carry frequent stories about television celebrities who are either negotiating greatly increased packages, or moving from channel to channel or from company to company.
> Many television companies are heavily involved in generating additional revenues from activities such as merchandising videos and DVDs, pop music, books and magazines, and the linking of programs to websites.
> There are a multitude of examples of program innovation, notably "fly-on-the-wall" documentaries in which real-life scenes are broadcast (such as the activities in busy airports or hotels), as well as "reality" shows with members of the public in various situations, such as *Big Brother* where a group of people live in a house together for a number of weeks and progressively vote each other out until there is one winner of a large cash sum. Most of these are cheaper to make than studio programs and, very importantly, they do not carry "big star" names, thus avoiding costs and also preventing dependence on the star. What was that about quality standards?

Part II
Tools and Techniques

In which we examine in detail one of the main techniques in the systems thinking toolkit, the causal loop diagram.

Chapter 4 explores the generic structure of feedback loops and shows that these come in two, and only two, basic types: the reinforcing loop and the balancing loop.

Reinforcing loops act as virtuous circles and can be used to represent the growth engine driving every business. However, as we shall see in Chapter 5, the same structure can also act as a vicious circle, so business boom can quickly become business bust. We shall also see how competition for shared resources can be represented by two reinforcing loops acting together—a systems thinking structure that underlies much conflict and can also be used to determine how that conflict can be best managed.

Balancing loops cause a system to converge toward a target and Chapter 6 will show how these systems thinking structures underpin all those aspects of management concerned with budgets, goals, targets, and plans.

Finally, Chapter 7 sets out 12 golden rules that will help you draw your own causal loop diagrams.

4
Feedback loops

The central role of feedback loops

The examples discussed in the previous two chapters—managing a busy back office, and the problem of managing quality in a TV company—demonstrate the value of taking a broad perspective when confronted by difficult choices, choices made difficult by the complexity of the problem. Faced by such complexity, it is so easy to be tempted to take a narrow, parochial view and jump to quick decisions. This temptation is driven by our organizational structures, our performance measures, and our natural desire not only to avoid complexity, but also to be seen to be "decisive"; isn't one of the attributes of a wise manager the ability to take quick decisions?

Certainly decisiveness is an important attribute, for no business could survive if top managers agonized endlessly, in pangs of self-doubt like Shakespeare's Hamlet. However, decisiveness does not imply rashness or recklessness; to be seen to be decisive does not require you to take decisions so quickly that sensible alternatives have not been examined and the corresponding consequences explored. Wisdom, surely, is about taking decisions that are well founded and well considered.

One way of contributing to this is to ensure that the context of the decision is explored on a broad prospective: broad in terms of both scope (so a decision on staffing levels in the back office recognizes the costs of error as well as the costs of employment) and also time (over time, an unwise decision on headcount will cause the employment of lots of temporary staff, and much organizational learning and knowledge will be lost).

As outlined in Part I, systems thinking provides a suitably broad perspective and causal loop diagrams are a very powerful way of capturing the essence of complex systems. As we have already seen from the diagrams shown so far, causal loop diagrams portray cause-and-effect relationships, but they do so in a way that emphasizes the complete, highly interconnected nature of the problem of interest; they capture the way everything is connected to every-thing else.

They also capture that intrinsic, highly important feature of complex sys-tems that we met in Chapter 1, the feature known as *feedback* (see pages 16–18). Feedback manifests itself in causal loop diagrams by the presence of one or more continuous, closed loops: loops representing chains of causality that link back on themselves, loops with no beginning and no end, loops in which everything is ultimately connected to everything else, loops known as **feedback loops**.

Take, for example, the causal loop diagram of the back office shown on page 36, where the central feature is the treadmill loop represented in Figure 4.1.

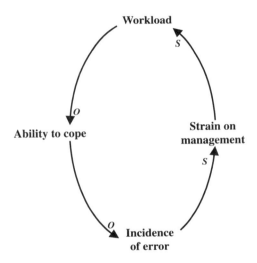

Figure 4.1

This loop has no beginning and no end, since all the parts of the loop are connected to all the other parts. These connections are not necessarily direct from one part to another, because there may be intermediate steps; further-more, there may be time delays between various elements. Ultimately, how-ever, all the elements are interconnected. This is therefore our first example of the central feature of all causal loop diagrams, the feedback loop.

As a moment's thought will show, a feedback loop has the property that any break in the loop, however small and wherever it may be, has the effect of destroying the loop itself. This is similar to the story of the elephant (see page

13), where cutting it in half destroyed the system of interest. It is indeed elegant that our study of the behavior of systems, which are themselves formed by the interconnections between individual component parts, is facilitated by diagrams whose central features are closed, continuous loops in which each element is connected to every other element.

A similar closed structure is the feedback loop forming the central feature of the TV company example (Figure 4.2).

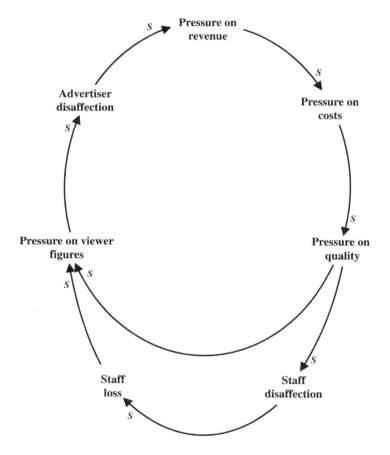

Figure 4.2

This, in fact, shows two interlinked feedback loops acting together, each reinforcing the other. Once again, everything is linked to everything else and the loop has no beginning and no end.

Feedback loops are everywhere

Feedback loops are, literally, everywhere. Take, for example, the trivial-seeming task of pouring a cup of coffee or tea, something we do without consciously thinking about it umpteen times a day. What does this simple task have to do with feedback loops?

In fact, this simple task would be impossible to accomplish in the absence of a feedback loop, as you can quickly discover if you try to pour a cup wearing a blindfold. The key feature of the feedback loop in this case is the information you monitor by watching the level of the liquid in the cup as you pour. As you see the level rise, this feedback, through your eyes and your brain, causes you to stop pouring just as the cup becomes full.

The system comprising the position of your hand, the rate at which you pour, the level of coffee in the cup, your observation of this level with your eyes, and the signal back from your brain to your hand forms a feedback loop. If you break the loop—as, for example, by wearing a blindfold to stop your eyes from observing how the level of the coffee in the cup is rising—you continue to pour until the cup overflows and the system fails.

The fundamental tenet of systems thinking is that real, complex problems are best described in terms of networks of interconnected feedback loops. The examples we have met so far are relatively simple, but, as we shall see during the course of this book, causal loop diagrams for real systems can soon become complex, consisting of networks of many interconnected individual feedback loops. The fact that these diagrams are complex is no surprise, for the problems they are describing are themselves complex. But however complex the final diagram, the underlying structure is the feedback loop, and the examination of complex diagrams to identify each of the individual feedback loops from which they are composed is one of the main ways in which the complexity of the real world can indeed be tamed.

Yes, everywhere

Here's another feedback loop.

It's been a long day, the trains were late, the traffic was horrible, and it's been pouring with rain. I finally arrive home, feeling grumpy and wanting my wife to fuss over me. My wife has also had a hard day and so she wants me fuss over her. I, however, am waiting for her to give me attention, and since she doesn't, that makes me grumpier still. Oh dear.

Overleaf is my loop:

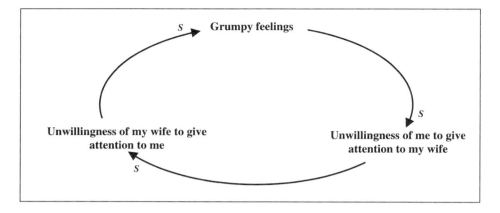

Feedback loops are a central feature of all causal loop diagrams, and their existence is a diagnosis of the completeness of any diagram: If ever you find you have drawn a diagram that does not contain any feedback loops at all, you know you have not yet described the corresponding system fully. The test is not reliable the other way about. Even if you have at least one closed loop on your diagram, that does not indicate that the diagram is necessarily complete, because there may be additional, as yet undocumented, loops that are relevant to the system in question. Nevertheless, the completion of the first loop shows that you are heading in the right direction and, as your understanding of the real system becomes more perceptive, you will add more loops until you reach a point where you believe that your diagram captures the system, succinctly and completely, and the complexity of the real world is then tamed.

Much of this book is about giving you confidence in how to do this, so let me turn now to two important classes of feedback loop, known as the **reinforcing loop** and the **balancing loop**.

Reinforcing loops

Take another look at the main loop in the TV example (Figure 4.3). This loop acts as a vicious circle: The stronger the PRESSURE ON COSTS, the stronger the PRESSURE ON QUALITY, in turn pushing up the PRESSURE ON VIEWER FIGURES, so increasing ADVERTISER DISSATISFACTION, enhancing the PRESSURE ON REVENUE, and putting even more PRESSURE ON COSTS. With each successive turn of the circle, things get progressively worse.

This situation, in which an initial event—the PRESSURE ON COSTS—is progressively enhanced and reinforced with each spin of the loop, is known as

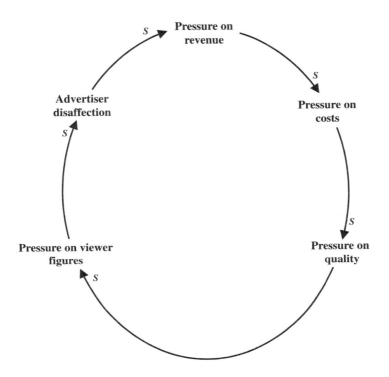

Figure 4.3

positive feedback, and the associated causal loop diagram is known as a *positive feedback loop* or *reinforcing loop.* As portrayed in the diagram, this loop acts as a vicious circle in which each relentless spin of the loop squeezes the pressure on costs ever more tightly. Reinforcing loops do indeed have this progressive effect, but, as we shall see in the next chapter, it does not have to be vicious—it can also be virtuous, since reinforcing loops acting as virtuous circles are the fundamental engines of business growth and success.

Reinforcing loops are a very important building block and we shall spend quite some time exploring their behavior in the next chapter. In the meantime, however, let's turn to another important building block, the balancing loop.

Balancing loops

Figure 4.4 overleaf is another causal loop diagram, which represents the pouring of a cup of coffee.

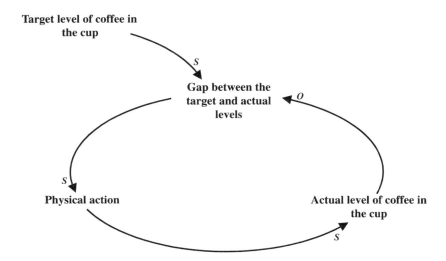

Figure 4.4

As we saw in the box on page 53, pouring a cup of coffee is an example of a real feedback loop and this diagram shows the loop in question. Let me explain.

What is happening when we pour a cup of coffee is that we have an objective in mind, the TARGET LEVEL OF COFFEE IN THE CUP. This target is usually "nearly full" but it doesn't have to be: It might be half a cup, or whatever. For the purposes of this example, let's assume that our target is half a cup.

As we pour the coffee into the cup, our eyes are watching the level of the coffee rise and, at any instant, we are assessing the GAP BETWEEN THE TARGET AND ACTUAL LEVELS. It is this assessment in our brain that causes us to control our PHYSICAL ACTION, which in this case is the positioning of our hand, which in turn determines the rate at which we are pouring coffee into the cup. At the start, when the gap between the target and actual levels is relatively large (when the cup has only a little coffee in it), our physical action is a relatively rapid rate of pouring, hence the S.

Our physical action, of course, affects the ACTUAL LEVEL OF COFFEE IN THE CUP, such that the greater our PHYSICAL ACTION the greater the ACTUAL LEVEL OF COFFEE IN THE CUP, so there is an S here too. However, as the cup fills and the ACTUAL LEVEL OF THE COFFEE IN THE CUP *in*creases, the gap between the target and actual levels *de*creases, so this link is an O. As the gap between the target and actual levels gets progressively smaller, our PHYSICAL ACTION becomes progressively gentler and the ACTUAL LEVEL OF COFFEE IN THE CUP rises progressively more slowly, until a time is reached when the GAP BETWEEN THE TARGET AND ACTUAL LEVELS becomes zero. At that point, our PHYSICAL ACTION stops and the cup is, as intended by the target, half full.

The overall action of the loop is therefore to control the ACTUAL LEVEL OF COFFEE IN THE CUP and guide it toward the TARGET LEVEL OF COFFEE IN THE CUP, such that when the target is reached, the PHYSICAL ACTION stops. And that last S, the one linking the TARGET LEVEL OF COFFEE IN THE CUP to the GAP BETWEEN THE TARGET AND ACTUAL LEVELS, indicates that, for any given ACTUAL LEVEL OF COFFEE IN THE CUP, the greater the TARGET LEVEL, the greater the GAP BETWEEN THE TARGET AND ACTUAL LEVELS, as indeed makes intuitive sense.

This form of feedback, in which a system seeks a particular goal, is known as *negative feedback*, and the corresponding causal loops are called *negative feedback loops* or *balancing loops*. Balancing loops are in fact very common. Filling a cup of coffee, controlling your domestic heating to a steady temperature using a thermostat, and taking action to bring your business actuals into line with your budgets are all examples of balancing loops in action.

You probably didn't think that pouring a cup of coffee was so complicated! But as we all know, it's simple to get distracted when pouring a cup of coffee—the phone rings, a child asks a question, or whatever—and this can easily break the feedback loop as our attention turns away from the gap between the target and actual levels while our physical action stays the same. A few moments later, we have a mess. Yes, the feedback loop is real.

Dangles, boundaries, and real systems

Although all feedback loops represent closed, continuous loops with no beginning and no end, some causal loop diagrams also include items outside the closed loops but linked to them: for example, the TARGET LEVEL OF COFFEE IN THE CUP in the balancing loop. These are known as *dangles*.

Dangles fall into two categories:

➤ *Input dangles*, representing targets, goals, or objectives to be achieved; or external drivers of the system; or specific parameters that determine particular external values.

➤ *Output dangles*, representing the overall results of the operation of the system.

The TARGET LEVEL OF COFFEE IN THE CUP in the balancing loop is an example of the first of these, because it represents our goal of filling the cup half full. We have also seen examples of some of the others. If you refer back to the causal loop diagram for the back office (see page 36) you will see three dangles: SERVICE QUALITY and COST, both of which are output dangles representing the overall results of the back office system, and the VOLUME AND VARIETY OF TRANSACTIONS, which is an input driver.

Dangles define the boundaries of the system of interest. The concept of a system boundary might appear to be in conflict with the holistic emphasis of systems thinking: Surely, if we wish to take a holistic view, there can be no boundaries.

In fact, the objective of taking a holistic view is not in conflict with the existence of boundaries. The issue is to draw the boundaries in the right place, so that they encompass the system of interest as a whole but without including unnecessary or extraneous material.

In the balancing loop, for example, our system of interest is the pouring of a cup of coffee, and a dangle is the TARGET LEVEL OF COFFEE IN THE CUP. In terms of wishing to understand how the balancing loop operates so that this target can be achieved, the existence of the target is all that concerns us. We could, if we wish, ask "Why is the target half a cup?" and so introduce into the diagram concepts such as "desire to quench thirst" and "dependence on caffeine" or whatever, and these items might well be relevant under certain circumstances. In the context of understanding the convergence of the system on the target, however, these are extraneous and so the TARGET LEVEL OF COFFEE IN THE CUP is safely left as a dangle.

The choice of when to leave dangles and when to trace their causality is a matter of judgment, exercised in the context of a wish to understand the behavior of a particular system of interest. What we are seeking, of course, is a balance between unnecessary complexity and the mistake of falling into the "half elephant trap." In practice this can always be done, although you might find that you have filled several wastepaper baskets with torn-up diagrams before you have identified the precise point of balance in any particular instance.

Very occasionally, you will see causal loop diagrams that contain no dangles at all, with all the items being part of one complete loop or another. This situation is rare. Much more commonly, especially for causal loop diagrams of business systems, you will find a number of interconnected feedback loops, driven by a (usually small) number of input dangles representing policies and objectives, and resulting in a (once again usually small) number of output dangles representing the results of the system's activities. This general structure is borne out by the diagrams you have already seen, as well as all the diagrams to come.

There are only two types of link—the *S* and the *O*

All the causal loop diagrams we have seen so far have been of the form

Cause   Effect

in which the CAUSE is at the tail of the linking arrow and the EFFECT at the head. Furthermore, each link has been assigned with an *S* if an *increase* in the cause drives an *increase* in the effect (for example, as our ABILITY TO COPE increases so does our SERVICE QUALITY); or an *O* if an *increase* in the cause drives a *decrease* in the effect (for example, as our ABILITY TO COPE increases the INCIDENCE OF ERROR decreases). Are *S* and *O* the only possible designations for a link, or are there any other possibilities?

In fact, a moment's thought will show that *S* and *O* are mutually exclusive conditions and that there are indeed no other possibilities. The situation in which an increase in the CAUSE neither increases nor decreases the EFFECT is not a third case; rather, it's an indication that there is no cause-and-effect relationship to start with!

Any individual link in a causal loop diagram must therefore be either an *S* or an *O*—there are no other possibilities. The fact that *every* link must necessarily be either an *S* or an *O* is the first of a number of rather startling unifying concepts within the framework of systems thinking, and sets the scene for some further important principles, the next one being a way of using the number of *S*s and *O*s around any single loop as a diagnostic of whether the loop is a reinforcing loop or a balancing loop.

Distinguishing between reinforcing loops and balancing loops

The action of a balancing loop—convergence to a target—is very different from that of a reinforcing loop, which amplifies itself on every turn. Why is it that these loops behave differently? The answer lies in the structure of the two loops and, in particular, the patterns of the Ss and the Os around them. Indeed, if you look at the reinforcing loop shown on page 55 there are no Os in the loop at all, since every link is associated with an S.

The balancing loop on page 56, however, contains a single O, and it is this one O that makes all the difference. When the action of the loop reaches the link with an O, something that is getting *bigger* (in this case, the ACTUAL LEVEL OF COFFEE IN THE CUP) translates into something that becomes *smaller* (again in this case, the GAP BETWEEN THE TARGET AND ACTUAL LEVELS), and this serves to dampen things down. In the reinforcing loop there is no such dampening effect, and so the loop spirals away, reinforcing itself on each successive turn.

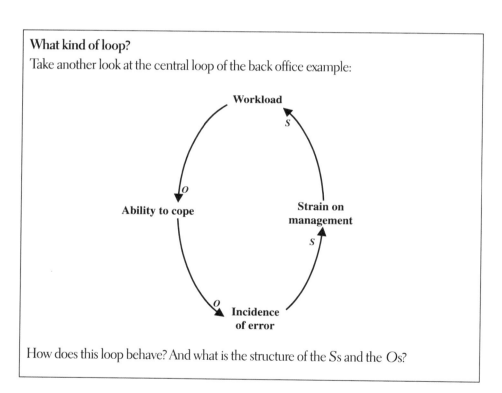

What kind of loop?
Take another look at the central loop of the back office example:

How does this loop behave? And what is the structure of the Ss and the Os?

Let's take the behavior first. As the WORKLOAD increases our ABILITY TO COPE diminishes (that's the O), and as our ABILITY TO COPE diminishes this increases the INCIDENCE OF ERROR (that's the second O). An increase in the INCIDENCE OF ERROR then increases the STRAIN ON MANAGEMENT (that's the first S), and this in turn increases the WORKLOAD (the second S).

In response to an initial increase in the workload, the action of a complete turn of the loop is to increase the workload yet more, demonstrating that the behavior of the loop is one of reinforcement. This is therefore a reinforcing loop but, as we have seen, it is not structured from a continuing series of Ss; rather, there are two Ss and two Os.

Is there a pattern emerging? We have now seen two reinforcing loops (the TV loop and this one) and one balancing loop (the coffee cup). Looking at the Os rather than the Ss, we see that whereas the balancing loop has a single O, the two reinforcing loops have either no Os at all or two Os. Mathematically, zero counts as an even number so, if there is an even number of Os, could it be that they "cancel out" in pairs, so making the loop a reinforcing loop as if they were all Ss?

This is just like in arithmetic. If we associate S with +1 and O with –1, then can we determine the nature of the loop by multiplying all the +1s and –1s round the loop? A loop comprising only Ss will multiply out to +1 and so is a reinforcing loop. But since $-1 \times -1 = +1$, a loop with two Os and any number of Ss will also multiply out to +1 and so will be a reinforcing loop, as will any loop with an even number of Os. Hence the term "positive feedback." A loop with an odd number of Os, on the other hand, will always multiply out to –1 and will always behave as a balancing loop, hence the term *negative feedback*.

Identifying reinforcing loops and balancing loops

For any closed, continuous loop, go round the complete loop and count the total number of Os.

➤ If the number is **even** (remembering that zero counts as an even number), then the loop will be a **reinforcing** loop, strengthening on each turn.
➤ If the number is **odd**, then the loop will be a **balancing** loop and will act to seek some goal or target.

In practice, when you do this ensure that:

➤ You go round the complete single loop, without missing any links out.
➤ You count only the Ss and Os within the loop itself.
➤ You are happy that all the Ss and Os have been correctly identified.
➤ You check out the logic too!

This applies to all closed loops, no matter how many items there are around the loop and no matter how complex the loop. It must always work, since, as we have seen, all links are either Ss or Os. Such a simple rule to help us distinguish between a reinforcing loop and a balancing one is the second of the fundamental, unifying principles identified by systems thinking that we will meet in this book.

The two fundamental building blocks

> All closed, continuous loops are either reinforcing loops or balancing loops.

This third unifying principle is an immediate consequence of the fact we have just established that reinforcing loops can be distinguished from balancing loops according to whether the number of Os around the loop is even or odd. If you count the number of Os around a loop the result must be either even or odd; there are no other possibilities. It therefore follows that...

> **There are only two fundamental building blocks**
>
> Since the number of Os in any closed, continuous loop can only be either even or odd, any single loop can only be either a reinforcing loop or a balancing loop. There are no other possibilities.

This is an enormously powerful unifying principle. It states that, no matter how complex a system might be, the fundamental building blocks from which it is composed can be of *only* two types: reinforcing loops or balancing loops. In practice, real systems are comprised of many loops all interacting together, with a number of dangles on the side, representing, as we have seen, targets, results, or external drivers. However, no matter how many loops we might have or how they are mutually interconnected, the fundamental structures are just two: Any single closed, continuous loop must be either a reinforcing loop or a balancing loop.

Given the importance of these two building blocks, the next two chapters will explore in depth how each of them behaves in isolation. This will then set the stage for us to examine what happens in more complex situations in which reinforcing loops and balancing loops are acting together. But before we look at reinforcing and balancing loops in more detail, there are three more points about Ss and Os that I need to make.

The importance of language

Take a look at the causal loop in Figure 4.5.

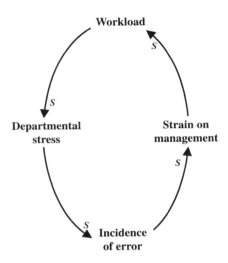

Figure 4.5

This is very similar to the back office causal loop we have seen before, but there are two differences. First, I have changed the concept ABILITY TO COPE to DEPARTMENTAL STRESS and, as a result of this, the two Os in the previous diagram have changed to Ss. There are now no Os at all and so this is a reinforcing loop: As the WORKLOAD goes up so does DEPARTMENTAL STRESS, increasing the INCIDENCE OF ERROR, adding to the STRAIN ON MANAGEMENT, and adding even further to the WORKLOAD in the now familiar way. This is of course describing the same situation as the previous diagram—I have merely chosen different words. As a result of choosing different words, the specifics of which items have an O and which have an S have also changed (that's the second difference), *but the situation being described, and the behavior of the loop, are still the same.*

This is also an important principle. The actual behavior of a system must be independent of the words we choose to describe it, for, as this example shows, different words can be chosen to describe the same thing. One of the marvels of systems thinking, however, is that the end result is still robust and still gives the correct description of the system's behavior, regardless of the specific words used.

This does not imply that we can be sloppy when drawing causal loops, using any words we like. The choice of words is very important, because we must use succinct, apposite phrases and we must ensure that anyone who might look at the diagram can quickly understand exactly what is meant. However, once we choose our language and we ensure that the Ss and Os are fit for purpose, the behavior of each loop will give an accurate portrayal of how the real system actually behaves.

Are all links always either an *S* or an *O?*

As I am sure you are now well aware, central to the drawing and use of causal loop diagrams is the clear and unambiguous identification of each link as either an S or an O. Furthermore, the fundamentally important distinction between a reinforcing loop—which amplifies itself on every turn, so acting as either a virtuous or a vicious circle—and a balancing loop—which shows the very different behavior of seeking a particular goal—depends not only on the S or O nature of each link, but also on the maintenance of this identity under all conditions. If a particular link were to behave sometimes as an S and at other times as an O, the same structure would sometimes behave as a reinforcing loop, sometimes as a balancing loop.

Can this happen? Are all links always either an S or an O, or is it possible for the same link to act sometimes as an S and sometimes as an O?

Behind this rather technical question is the more fundamental question: *Are there situations in the real world that sometimes show S-type behavior and sometimes O-type behavior?*

In fact there are. Consider, for example, the concept of GENEROSITY TO STAFF, as shown by a benevolent boss, and that of STAFF PRODUCTIVITY. In a benign world, these would be linked by an S:

Generosity to staff   Staff productivity

implying that as GENEROSITY TO STAFF increases, STAFF PRODUCTIVITY increases.

Not all worlds, however, are benign and you might well be thinking: "If you are so generous as to be over the top, wouldn't the staff start taking advantage and slack off?" The answer is probably yes. In this case, it appears as if the link is flipping from an S to an O. As our GENEROSITY TO STAFF increases, initially STAFF PRODUCTIVITY increases too, but as our GENEROSITY TO STAFF becomes excessive, STAFF PRODUCTIVITY begins to go down. We now have the problem that this link sometimes behaves as an S and sometimes as an O.

There are a number of ways of resolving this ambiguity, one of which is to state, in a note to a causal loop diagram, that it only applies to a specified set of circumstances. Rather better, in my view, is to enhance the diagram to cater for both eventualities (see Figure 4.6).

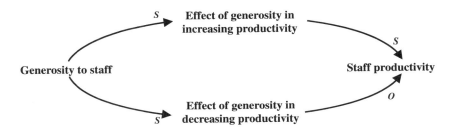

Figure 4.6

This diagram explicitly recognizes that acts of GENEROSITY TO STAFF might have two results, one of which is to increase STAFF PRODUCTIVITY, the other to decrease it. Each of these links is now unambiguous and stable, but they act perhaps at different times, or under different circumstances, which themselves can be included in the diagram if you wish. So if you are ever faced with a situation of this nature, in which one link appears to be able to act as either an S or an O depending on certain conditions, it is always possible to enhance the diagram to make all the possible behaviors explicit, unambiguous, and robust.

Fuzzy variables

In Figure 4.6 I introduced two additional concepts, which I have termed the EFFECT OF GENEROSITY IN INCREASING PRODUCTIVITY and the EFFECT OF GENEROSITY IN DECREASING PRODUCTIVITY, both of which are related to the GENEROSITY TO STAFF by an S, capturing the idea that the greater the

GENEROSITY TO STAFF, the greater the appropriate effect. These "effect" concepts do exist but are rarely talked about, and even more rarely measured. They represent a class of concepts known in systems thinking as **fuzzy variables**, concepts that are important but rather nebulous; concepts that we all understand and that can readily be described using terms such as "strong" or "weak" even if we don't usually ascribe numerical values to them.

Systems thinking actively encourages you to recognize variables of this nature, since they often underpin critical elements of our businesses. We have already seen several examples of fuzzy variables, such as the ABILITY TO COPE, which was central to the back office story, and the PRESSURE TO REDUCE COSTS, the prime driving force in the television story. Later chapters will discuss in some detail fuzzy variables such as the EFFECT OF HAVING GOOD STAFF ON ATTRACTING AND RETAINING CUSTOMERS and the EFFECT OF ADVERTISING ON SALES, and will show how they can be quantified. For the moment, let me flag up that fuzzy variables can often be very helpful in many situations, including resolving potential ambiguities regarding a link that sometimes appears to be an S and sometimes an O.

Ss and Os that work in one direction only

There is one more subtlety about Ss and Os that I would like to mention. However, it is something of a detail, so you may like to skip this section. The issue concerns Ss and Os that work in one direction only. To explain what is going on, let's consider once more the first two links we examined at the start of the back office story (Figure 4.7).

As we now know, the key diagnostic of whether a link is an S or an O, as applied in this case to the ABILITY TO COPE, is the question: *As the* ABILITY TO COPE *increases, does the* SERVICE QUALITY *(or the* INCIDENCE OF ERROR*) increase or decrease?* Since the SERVICE QUALITY increases and is moving in the same direction as the ABILITY TO COPE, we designate this link an S. Conversely, since the INCIDENCE OF ERROR decreases we designate this second link an O.

I then showed (see page 28) that these links also work the other way around. If the ABILITY TO COPE decreases, the SERVICE QUALITY decreases, preserving the "sameness" of the link; likewise, as the ABILITY TO COPE decreases, the INCIDENCE OF ERROR is likely to increase, so preserving the "oppositeness." The fact that the links can preserve their S or O nature in both directions in this way is one of the strengths of causal loop diagrams.

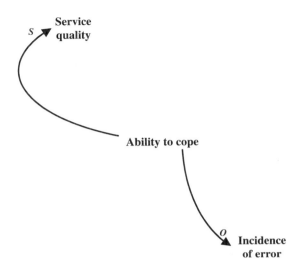

Figure 4.7

There is, however, a particular situation in which the S or the O works in one direction but is invalid in the other. We have already had one, somewhat disguised, example of this. Let's return to the coffee filling example, but instead of referring to PHYSICAL ACTION, let me use the more obvious term ACTION OF POURING COFFEE INTO THE CUP to describe more explicitly what the physical action is in this case. This is the link to the ACTUAL LEVEL OF COF-FEE IN THE CUP (Figure 4.8).

Figure 4.8

As I increase the ACTION OF POURING COFFEE INTO THE CUP, there is no doubt that the ACTUAL LEVEL OF COFFEE IN THE CUP increases, and so this link is indisputably an S. But what happens as I *decrease* the ACTION OF POURING COFFEE INTO THE CUP? In fact the ACTUAL LEVEL OF COFFEE IN THE CUP con-tinues to increase, but more slowly. So here we have a case in which a *decrease* in the ACTION OF POURING COFFEE INTO THE CUP is causing an *increase* in the ACTUAL LEVEL OF COFFEE IN THE CUP, suggesting that an S has suddenly become an O.

This apparent change in behavior is driven by a change in directionality: As the ACTION OF POURING COFFEE INTO THE CUP increases, the ACTUAL LEVEL OF COFFEE IN THE CUP increases too, and the S is abundantly clear. The problem arises when we investigate what happens when the ACTION OF POURING COFFEE INTO THE CUP decreases, since this does not drive a decrease in the ACTUAL LEVEL OF COFFEE IN THE CUP.

As a moment's thought will show, it can't—ever. It is in fact quite obvious that the act of pouring coffee *into* a cup can never, under any circumstances, *decrease* the level of coffee in a cup—the action of pouring coffee into something is intrinsically unidirectional. The fact that what is happening physically can act in one direction only is reflected by the apparently perverse behavior of the causal loop diagram; this causal loop diagram can work in one direction only as well.

Once again this is often a question of language, and that is why the diagrams I used before refer to PHYSICAL ACTION, rather than to the ACTION OF POURING COFFEE INTO THE CUP. As we shall see in Chapter 5, the term PHYSICAL ACTION can refer not only to pouring coffee *into* the cup, but also to pouring it *out*— and pouring coffee out of a cup surely does reduce the actual level of coffee in the cup!

So a word of caution. Some causal loop diagrams—or rather the words used in some causal loop diagrams—describe a reality that in practice can work in one direction only. And when we try to examine what happens in the other direction, some Ss seem to flip to Os or vice versa. These one-way links can arise from time to time—another example is described on page 152—and these anomalous links can sometimes cause confusion if you are using the "reversibility test" to help you determine whether a link is an S or an O in the first place.

As this discussion has demonstrated, the reversibility test is not fail-safe; there are a specific set of conditions, described in detail on page 290, when it doesn't work. This test should therefore not be used as a determinant of whether a link is an S or an O. It is far safer to keep to the question: *As the* ABILITY TO COPE *(or whatever) increases, does the* SERVICE QUALITY *(or whatever) increase or decrease?* If it increases the link is an S, and if it decreases the link is an O. This always works.

A final thought

Drawing and using causal loop diagrams is at the heart of systems thinking. A clear, concise diagram can be enormously beneficial in seeing the forest for

---

S or O? The ultimate test

Getting the Ss and Os right is important. The general rule of thumb "If an increase in a CAUSE drives an increase in an EFFECT then the link is an S, otherwise it's an O" is in fact a simplified version (but a very useful simplified version nonetheless) of the ultimate fail-safe test as given in John Sterman's book *Business Dynamics*. It's a bit of a brain buster, but here goes:

> ➢ If a CAUSE increases, such that the EFFECT increases above what it would have been otherwise; or if a CAUSE decreases, such that the EFFECT decreases below what it would have been otherwise, then the link is an S.
> ➢ If a CAUSE increases, such that the EFFECT decreases below what it would have been otherwise; or if a CAUSE decreases, such that the EFFECT increases above what it would have been otherwise, then the link is an O.

---

the trees, in clarifying explicitly how things work, and in capturing the essence of complex situations. As a consequence, these diagrams support enhanced teamwork, effective and clear communication, robust policy formulation, and wise decision making.

As we have seen, however, it isn't simply a matter of jotting down one or two idle scribbles. A good causal loop diagram requires insight to compile and demands considerable clarity and precision of thought. In my view, these are "good things" and I fully appreciate the effort that needs to be devoted accordingly. Perhaps the most challenging aspect is to sort out the Ss and the Os, and I trust that this chapter has helped build your confidence in doing this.

However, if you are still feeling a little shaky about this, please don't be concerned. I hope you will find the summary box overleaf useful and, as you read on, you will find many more examples of causal loop diagrams in practice, accompanied by what I trust you will find to be clear and helpful descriptions of the realities that the diagrams are seeking to capture, all of which will convincingly demonstrate how causal loop diagrams really can help you tame complexity.

In Chapter 7 I present 12 "golden rules" that will help you do just this. In the meantime, Chapter 5 takes a deeper look at the behavior of the first of the fundamental building blocks of systems thinking: the reinforcing loop, the engine of growth.

Systems thinking in one box

The way in which real systems evolve over time is often bewilderingly complex. Systems thinking enables us to tame that complexity, offering an explanation of why a system behaves as it does, and providing insights into the system's likely behavior in the future.

The key is to understand the *chains of causality*, the sequence and mutual interactions of the numerous individual *cause-and-effect relationships* that underlie the system of interest. These chains of causality are captured in a *causal loop diagram*, in which each cause-and- effect relationship is expressed by means of a link represented by a *curly arrow*:

Cause   Effect

Links are of only two types: S links and O links. If an *increase* in the CAUSE drives an *increase* in the EFFECT (for example, as the VOLUME AND VARIETY OF TRANSACTIONS I have to process increases, my WORKLOAD increases too), then the link is an S; if an *increase* in the CAUSE drives a *decrease* in the EFFECT (as my WORKLOAD increases, my ABILITY TO COPE is likely to decrease), then the link is an O.

	S		or		*O*
Cause	**Effect**			**Cause**	**Effect**
(increase)	**(increase)**			**(increase)**	**(decrease)**

Causal loop diagrams of real systems are composed primarily of closed, continuous chains known as *feedback loops*. There are only two fundamental types of feedback loop: the *reinforcing loop* and the *balancing loop*. Reinforcing loops are characterized by having an even number of Os around the loop (with zero counting as an even number); balancing loops have an odd number of Os.

The action of a reinforcing loop is, as its name implies, to amplify the original effect on each turn. Reinforcing loops therefore behave as a *virtuous* or *vicious circles*, depending on the circumstances. The action of a balancing loop is quite different: The system seeks to *achieve or maintain a target or a goal*. For example, the action of a thermostat in a heating system maintains the ambient temperature at a constant level; likewise, the objective of many budgeting systems is to steer the corporation toward a set of pre-determined goals.

All real systems are composed of interlinked networks of reinforcing loops and balancing loops, often in conjunction with a (usually small) number of *dangles*, which represent items that determine the boundary of the system of interest, such as the output results of the system or the targets or goals that drive it.

Compiling a good causal loop diagram for a real system requires deep knowledge of the system, as well as the insight to see the forest for the trees. It also encourages the explicit articulation of relationships that we all know are present but are rarely talked about (such as the relationship between the WORKLOAD and our ABILITY TO COPE), and the recognition of *fuzzy variables*, which are important but difficult to measure, such as the EFFECT OF HAVING GOOD STAFF ON ATTRACTING AND RETAINING CUSTOMERS.

Systems thinking and the use of causal loop diagrams offer many benefits:

➢ By encouraging a holistic view, both as regards scope and time, *systems thinking avoids parochialism and short-termism*.

➢ By capturing chains of cause-and-effect relationships in a causal loop diagram, *systems thinking makes explicit our mental models*, our fundamental beliefs about how the world works, the fundamental beliefs that underpin our decisions and our actions.

➢ This in turn enables our own mental models to be compared to the mental models of our colleagues, so *providing a better basis for high-performing teams*. Causal loop diagrams therefore offer a powerful means of communication.

➢ Causal loop diagrams can also be a means of exploring alternative policies and decisions so that their consequences can be anticipated in advance. *This enables you to avoid quick-fixes that are likely to backfire, or decisions that you might regret later*.

➢ Overall, *systems thinking puts you in the strongest possible position to take decisions that pass the most stringent test there is: the test of time*.

5
The engines of growth—and decline

Vicious and virtuous circles

Take another look at the central part of the back office diagram (Figure 5.1).

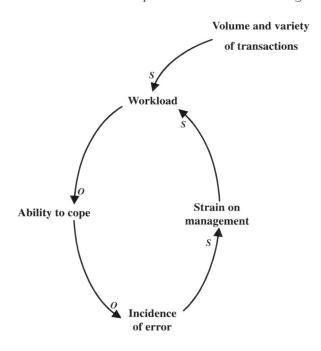

Figure 5.1

Suppose that something happens in the stock markets so that the activity on the exchanges goes down. This reduces the VOLUME AND VARIETY OF TRANS-ACTIONS and so reduces the WORKLOAD. As a consequence, the ABILITY TO COPE is enhanced and so the INCIDENCE OF ERROR goes down. This alleviates the STRAIN ON MANAGEMENT, so reducing the WORKLOAD even further, so enhancing the ABILITY TO COPE even more…

This is certainly the behavior of a reinforcing loop, since on each turn of the cycle the effect is progressively reinforced. But what is happening now is good news rather than bad: The system is behaving as a *virtuous circle* rather than as a *vicious* one. Nevertheless, the diagram—the descriptions as well as the structure of the Ss and the Os—is exactly the same as it was before. How can the same diagram behave as both a vicious and a virtual circle?

Vicious and virtuous circles have the same structure
Structurally, reinforcing loops are characterized by having an even number of Os. Behaviorally, these loops can act in either of two ways: as virtuous circles or as vicious ones. Whether a loop behaves as a virtuous circle or a vicious one in practice depends on how the loop is triggered.

This is another wonderful unifying insight provided by systems thinking: Virtuous circles are the *same* as vicious ones, it all depends on how they are triggered. In the case of the back office, if the WORKLOAD is reduced, perhaps by a reduction in the VOLUME AND VARIETY OF TRANSACTIONS or perhaps by the provision of some powerful, new EFFECTIVE IT SYSTEMS (see page 34), this triggers a virtuous circle in which our increasing ABILITY TO COPE provides steadily better SERVICE QUALITY. However, by the same token if the WORKLOAD suddenly increases, this triggers a vicious circle and the SERVICE QUALITY soon becomes eroded.

This is indeed a precarious situation, in which the *same system* behaves either benignly or malevolently depending on external stimuli. How can we stabilize this? How can we avoid the situation in which a system that starts as a virtuous circle suddenly becomes vicious? This is the all too familiar "boom and bust" cycle of many businesses, of which more shortly.

Vicious and virtuous circles really do have the same structure

Take another look at the TV example, but use different language to see how this apparently vicious circle is also a virtuous one. What happens, for example, if the company has a hit show and there is suddenly a significant increase in revenue (see Figure 5.2 overleaf)?

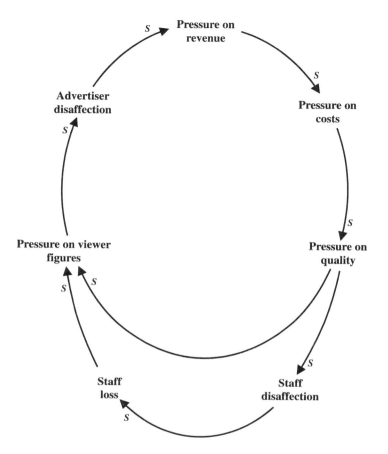

Figure 5.2

Suddenly the pressure on revenue is relaxed, and this takes the pressure off costs. The argument about quality goes away, and not only does this increase the quality of our programs, and so enhance our viewer figures, but staff are no longer disaffected and are pleased to stay. The advertisers are no longer upset and so the revenue stream continues to increase...

Now that's a virtuous circle I could live with!

The engine of growth

This description of the TV example, using the language of a virtuous circle rather than that of a vicious circle, represents a powerful driver of business growth. Indeed, central to every business is a growth engine of this type, which we can represent by a generic causal loop diagram such as that in Figure 5.3.

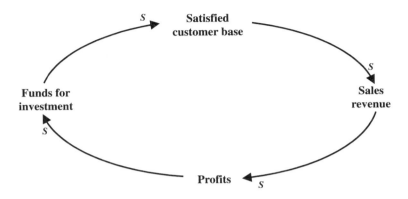

Figure 5.3

All real businesses are obviously far more complex than this diagram implies, and we shall explore much of that complexity throughout the rest of this book. Nevertheless, ultimately every business, from the largest multinational to the smallest corner shop, is trying to make this virtuous circle spin ever faster, growing the business with each turn.

The larger our SATISFIED CUSTOMER BASE, the higher our SALES REVENUE, from which (all being well) we make our PROFITS. These PROFITS provide the FUNDS FOR INVESTMENT, which we can use for product development, marketing, advertising, channel extension, or whatever, the ultimate objective of which is to increase our SATISFIED CUSTOMER BASE, either by making our existing customers even more satisfied or by attracting new customers. This further increases SALES REVENUE and PROFITS, providing an even bigger pot of FUNDS FOR INVESTMENT... And so this virtuous circle spins away and our business grows and grows. Once we have kick-started the loop with some initial investment funds, how can we keep it turning for ever?

Quiz time: How does your business grow?
With reference to Figure 5.3, showing a generic structure of business growth, and assuming (for the moment) that this diagram is a complete and accurate representation of reality, how does the sales revenue grow over time?

In particular, which of the following four graphs would you choose?

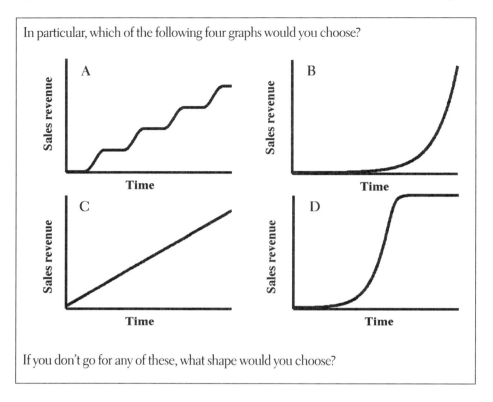

If you don't go for any of these, what shape would you choose?

In fact, for the causal loop shown in Figure 5.3, the sales revenue will evolve over time as in graph B. Let me explain why this is what happens and the others don't apply.

Let me first eliminate graphs A and D. Both of these show initial growth but then slow down. Graph D stops growing altogether, with the sales revenue stabilizing at a constant amount; graph A grows in fits and starts, with periods of growth interrupted by periods of stability. Although we have all seen examples of this type of business development in practice, such behavior is impossible for the causal loop as drawn: Given an initial trigger of investment, each turn of the loop adds increasingly more revenue, relentlessly. Since there is nothing shown in the diagram that stops the loop from spinning, it doesn't: It spins away, for ever, adding yet more and more revenue with every turn. The diagram has no indication of a limit of any sort, and so graphs A and D cannot represent the behavior of the loop as drawn.

"That's nuts," I hear you say. "No business can grow for ever, without any limit at all! What happens when the customer base exceeds the whole population of the world? It must stop growing sometime!"

Your point is correct: No business grows for ever, without any limits at all. But—sorry to be pompous about this—the question wasn't: "What is the real behavior of the business?" It was: "With reference to Figure 5.3, showing a generic structure of business growth, and assuming (for the moment) that this diagram is a complete and accurate representation of reality, how does the sales revenue grow over time?"

Since the loop, as drawn, keeps on spinning without limit, the behavior of the sales revenue must be growth without limit, as implied by graphs B and C. The fact that neither of these graphs can represent the actual behavior of a real business over a long time indicates that the causal loop, as drawn, is an incomplete representation of reality. To capture the fact that, eventually, all markets must saturate, we need to enhance the diagram and add some new features. We shall see how this can be done on pages 140–9. For the moment, let's get back to the behavior of the loop as drawn.

Patterns of growth

Because the loop, as drawn, contains nothing to constrain it from spinning away for ever, it must exhibit unlimited growth, as, for example, represented by either graph B or graph C. But which one? The difference between these two graphs lies in the nature, the pattern, of the growth. Graph C is a steady straight line. Graph B shows a quite different behavior: It starts rather more slowly, but after a while growth suddenly shoots off, becoming increasingly more rapid, far outstripping the linear growth.

We talk of growth when successive measures of an event—say sales revenue—become progressively bigger. In principle there are many different patterns of growth, all of which can be recognized by a series of numbers in which each is bigger than its predecessor, or by a graph in which the line goes steadily upward as you move toward the right.

Of all these possible patterns of growth, two are particularly special. Here is one:

Sales revenue, $'000, in each successive year									
1	2	3	4	5	6	7	8	9	10
500	850	1,200	1,550	1,900	2,250	2,600	2,950	3,300	3,650

The characteristic pattern here is that the year-on-year increase in revenue is constant. In this particular case, the revenue for any one year is $350,000 more than the previous year, consistently. This pattern is known as linear growth, because a graph of the sales revenue over time is a straight line, like that shown in graph C.

Here is another pattern:

Sales revenue, $'000, in each successive year									
1	2	3	4	5	6	7	8	9	10
500	630	794	1,000	1,260	1,587	2,000	2,520	3,175	4,000

The pattern here is not so obvious, but there are two clues. The first is found in years 1, 4, 7, and 10, for which the sales revenue figures are $500,000, $1,000,000, $2,000,000 and $4,000,000 respectively, showing that the revenue is doubling every three years. The second clue is more subtle and concerns the sales revenue growth over any year expressed as a ratio of the sales of the preceding year. For example, over year 4, the revenue grew by $1,000,000 − $794,000 = $206,000. The ratio of the growth over year 4 to the revenue during year 3 is $206,000/$794,000 = 0.26. And over year 6, the revenue grew by $1,587,000 − $1,260,000 = $327,000, and the corresponding ratio is the same: $327,000/$1,260,000 = 0.26! In fact, as a few moments with a calculator will show, this ratio is constant across all the data.

The constancy of this ratio means that, if you are given the ratio (in this instance 0.26) and a starting value ($500,000), it is then easy to calculate the sales in each year. Over year 2 the increase in sales is 0.26 × $500,000 = $130,000, so the total sales are $500,000 + $130,000 = $630,000. Over year 3 the increase in sales is 0.26 × $630,000 = $164,000, so the total sales are $630,000 + $164,000 = $794,000; and so on.

This process is recursive. Given an initial, base value for the sales revenue (in this case $500,000) and a growth rate that is constant throughout (in this case 0.26), the pattern of sales revenue growth can be calculated by following this method:

1 Take the starting value.
2 Multiply this by the growth rate to compute this period's growth in revenue.

3   Add this figure to the starting value to compute this period's total revenue.
4   Take this as the starting value for the next time period, and go back to step
    2.

This is rather clumsy. Far neater is the representation of this process as a feedback loop (Figure 5.4).

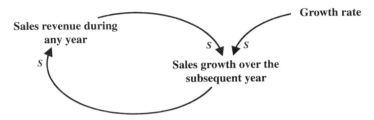

Figure 5.4

Aha—this is a reinforcing loop! And because it's a reinforcing loop, the SALES
REVENUE DURING ANY YEAR will grow with every turn. But since the SALES
GROWTH OVER THE SUBSEQUENT YEAR depends on the SALES REVENUE DURING
ANY YEAR and this itself is growing, then the SALES GROWTH OVER THE SUBSE-
QUENT YEAR will also grow. The sales growth each year is therefore not con-
stant, but grows year on year. As a result, a graph of this pattern will curve
progressively upward, like graph B (Figure 5.5).

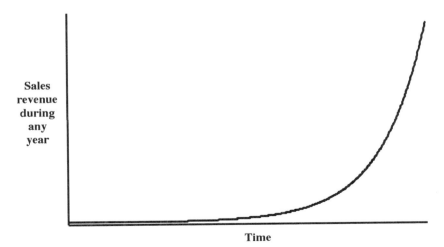

Figure 5.5

This pattern of growth has a special name: *exponential growth*. It is also the pattern exhibited by *all* reinforcing loops. The starting point, and the rate at which the growth takes place, will vary according to the specific circumstances, but the fundamental truth is that all reinforcing loops exhibit this very special pattern of growth.

This pattern, of course, is very familiar. Here, for example, is the identical pattern, as exhibited by compound interest (Figure 5.6).

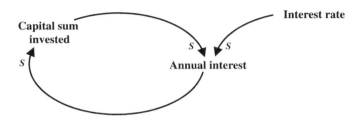

Figure 5.6

And in Figure 5.7 is the same pattern again, this time as exhibited by any living population.

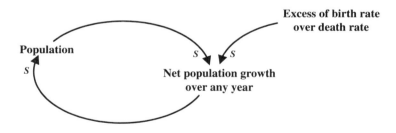

Figure 5.7

You will have noticed that all these loops contain a dangle, specifying an appropriate form of growth rate. This dangle acts as a driver of the system, determining how fast the reinforcing loop will spin. Dangles that play this role are known as *rate dangles*.

Rate dangles explain why reinforcing loops can show decline as well as growth: It depends on whether the growth rate is a positive or a negative number. With reference to the business example, see Figure 5.8. If the GROWTH RATE is a positive number, the SALES GROWTH OVER THE SUBSEQUENT YEAR is also positive, and so the SALES REVENUE DURING ANY YEAR increases with each

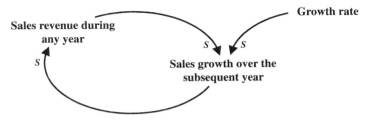

Figure 5.8

turn of the loop. However, if the GROWTH RATE is a negative number, the SALES GROWTH OVER THE SUBSEQUENT YEAR becomes a negative number and the SALES REVENUE DURING ANY YEAR is diminished, so creating a vicious circle of exponential decline (Figure 5.9).

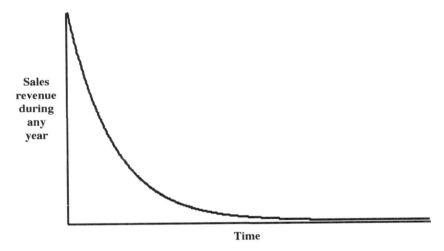

Figure 5.9

The behavior of all reinforcing loops
All reinforcing loops show either exponential growth or exponential decline, depending on how the loop is triggered.

This is yet another startling unifying principle: *All* reinforcing loops show either exponential growth or decline, depending on how they are triggered. It doesn't matter what the loop actually is or what the concepts are: They all show the same fundamental behavior. It doesn't matter whether the system is some invested capital growing by compound interest or being eroded in value by inflation, or the population of bacteria in a laboratory culture growing by cell division or being killed by a test drug: If the system is one that can be described by a reinforcing loop, exponential growth or decline is what you will observe. Amazing—some may grow or decline relatively rapidly, some relatively slowly, but the fundamental behavior is the same.

Just one word of caution concerning the identification of exponential growth from time series data and the corresponding graph. For example, take a look at the graph in Figure 5.10, which shows the rise in the population of a small community toward the end of the 1800s.

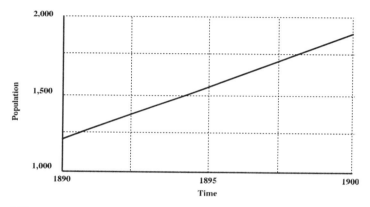

Figure 5.10

This looks linear, but in fact it isn't. As reference to the scales will show, it is a small portion of Figure 5.11.

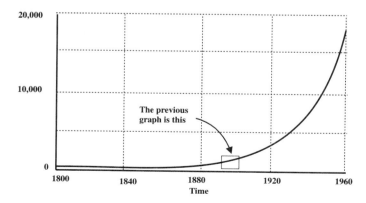

Figure 5.11

This is of course an exponential graph. However, if you take a small enough extract, the shape can appear to be linear. So take care when you interpret the underlying behavior of data from a small sample, particularly if the system under study operates over relatively long time scales: What you observe at first sight can sometimes be quite misleading. Also, exponential growth always starts very slowly, and it can be quite some time before the very rapid growth becomes apparent, as the next story demonstrates.

Exponential growth becomes very fast

> **Quiz-time: The story of the frogs**
> A colony of frogs is living happily on one side of a large pond. At the other side of the pond is a lily-pad. One day, a chemical pollutant flows into the pond, which has the effect of stimulating the growth of the lily-pad so that it doubles every 24 hours. This is a problem for the frogs, for if the lily-pad were to cover the pond entirely, the frog colony would be wiped out.
>
> ➤ How would you describe the growth of the lily-pad?
> ➤ If the lily-pad can cover the entire pond in 50 days, on what day is the pond half covered?
> ➤ The frogs have a method of stopping the growth of the lily-pad, but it takes them 10 days to put their method into effect. What proportion of the pond's surface is covered at the latest possible time the frogs can take action to save themselves?

The pattern of growth is one in which the size of the lily-pad doubles over equal periods of time, in this case every 24 hours. As we have seen, this is one of the characteristics of exponential growth. Indeed, all living populations will inevitably grow exponentially, the actual rate of growth at any time being the difference between the birth rate and the death rate, as shown by the causal loop diagram on page 80.

If it takes 50 days for the lily-pads to cover the pond, and if they double every day, then the pond will be half covered at the end of the 49th day—not at the end of the 25th. If the growth is linear, then half the pond will indeed be covered at the end of the 25th day, which is the answer usually given to the second question, largely because most people can envisage linear growth much more easily than exponential growth. But the growth is exponential, doubling every day, and so it takes just one day for the lily-pads to grow from half cover to full cover.

Once exponential growth gets going, it gets going really fast; by the same token, exponential growth starts really slowly. The third question throws a spotlight on exactly this point.

This question states that the frogs can stop the lily-pads, but the total time required to implement their plan is 10 days. So the latest time at which they can start their action is by the end of day 40 after the pollution incident; if they were to start at any later time, they would be racing against the lily-pads—and the lily-pads would win. There is absolutely nothing the frogs can do if the clock were to tick past the end of day 40 without their taking action. They would be doomed.

How much of the pond would be covered at that time? The easiest way to work this out is backward. We know that the pond was fully covered by the end of day 50; by the end of day 49 it was half covered; by the end of day 48 the pond was half of a half—that is, one quarter—covered; by the end of day 47, the fraction covered was $\frac{1}{2} \times \frac{1}{2} \times \frac{1}{2} = (\frac{1}{2})^3$; and so on. This implies that the fraction covered at the end of day 40, the latest time at which the frogs can take action, was $(\frac{1}{2})^{10}$.

Now $(\frac{1}{2})^{10}$ is quite a small number—0.00098 in fact, or rather less than one thousandth. So with 10 days to go to certain doom, less than one-tenth of one percent of the surface of the pond would be covered by the lily-pad!

From the point of view of the frogs at their end of the pond, they would have to notice, and take action on, a very small event, far, far away. If they failed to do anything until the danger really loomed—say, when they noticed that the pond was quarter or even half covered—it would be way, way too late.

Exponential growth—the natural behavior of all reinforcing loops—can be very misleading. It starts off so slowly that you hardly notice it. But all of a sudden it's overwhelming.

So next time you read a newspaper article or watch a television program about global warming, the depletion of fossil fuels, the hole in the ozone layer, or the decline in the number of species of birds or insects, you might like to think about the frogs too—a theme that we will explore in more detail in Chapter 11.

Caulerpa taxifolia

On 9 February 2001, the BBC screened a 50-minute program, *Horizon*. Below is part of the synopsis of the program in the TV listings magazine *Radio Times*.

Giant cloned alien monster loose in US waters

No, not a trailer for a terrible sci-fi movie, but the headline from a deadly serious on-line report about a serious, deadly offshore phenomenon: killer algae that are very hardy, have no natural predators, and are highly toxic to marine life and humans.

This week's *Horizon* tells how, in the 1980s, aquaria brightened up their tanks with hardy and beautiful green algae, *caulerpa taxifolia*. By 1984, the organism had escaped from the Oceanographic Museum in Monaco, and established a small colony in the Mediterranean under the museum's windows. Now, less than 20 years later, the algae have gone from an isolated aquatic curiosity to a global eco-disaster.

Caulerpa first spread a green carpet across much of the Mediterranean. British waters are too cold for it to gain a foothold, but last year it reached the Pacific, appearing off the coasts of California and Australia.

French ecologist Alexandre Meinesz first raised the algae alarm in 1989, but in his recent book *Killer Algae* he concludes that after years of denial, prevarication and inaction, "its eradication, envisaged at the beginning of the invasion, can now be classed only as a utopian dream."

Ever felt like a frog?

Explicit and implicit dangles

The causal loop diagram in Figure 5.12 is complete, in that it explicitly contains the dangle specifying the growth rate.

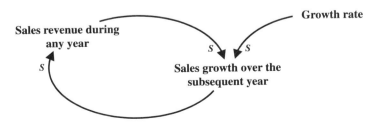

Figure 5.12

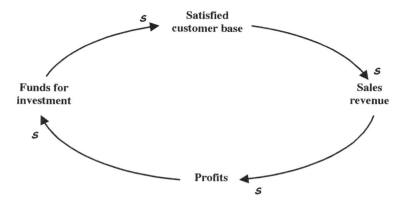

Figure 5.13

In contrast, the diagram in Figure 5.13 does not explicitly contain any dangles. Rather, the dangles associated with this loop are implicit—even without the dangles, we can still read this diagram as a reinforcing loop and recognize that it will show exponential growth or decline.

We can, of course, include the dangles if we wish to (Figure 5.14).

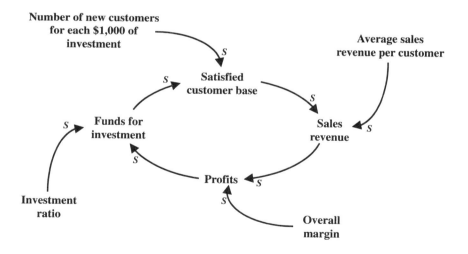

Figure 5.14

In this diagram, the AVERAGE SALES REVENUE PER CUSTOMER specifies the SALES REVENUE for any given SATISFIED CUSTOMER BASE; the OVERALL MARGIN determines the total PROFITS for any given SALES REVENUE; the INVESTMENT RATIO represents the company's policy on how much of the PROFITS is

ploughed back as FUNDS FOR INVESTMENT; and the NUMBER OF NEW CUS-
TOMERS FOR EACH $1,000 OF INVESTMENT captures the effectiveness of the
company's direct mail campaign (or whatever). The overall result of all these
determines, at any time, the overall growth rate of the business. In fact, if you
use 5,000 for the initial SATISFIED CUSTOMER BASE, $100 for the AVERAGE
SALES REVENUE PER CUSTOMER, 20 percent for the OVERALL MARGIN, 65 percent for the INVESTMENT RATIO, and 20 as the NUMBER OF NEW CUSTOMERS
FOR EACH $1,000 OF INVESTMENT, you can reproduce (subject to rounding)
the figures for the exponential growth shown in the table on page 78. Different numbers will give different rates of growth, but whatever the numeric values the overall structure of the feedback loop is unchanged—it is, and always
will be, a reinforcing loop. And if the parameters driving the loop remain constant, it will grow or decline exponentially, for ever.

Sometimes the explicit depiction of all the dangles adds clutter without
enhancing clarity. Causal loop diagrams therefore always show all the relevant
closed feedback loops—since it is these that determine the fundamental structure—but many deliberately omit the majority of the dangles and show only
those that actively contribute to the diagram's message. As we have seen, the
dangles that are included usually represent key external policies, targets, or
drivers; those that are omitted usually relate to ancillary parameters, such as
those shown on the last diagram, that can be inferred from the overall context.

Boom and bust

Back to business. At 12.25 pm on the afternoon of 17 October 2000, just outside a town called Hatfield in the UK, a train crashed en route from London
to Leeds while traveling at around 115 mph. Four passengers were killed and
thirty-three injured. The immediate cause was a broken rail, but the more
fundamental cause was the failure of Railtrack—the organization charged
with the maintenance and upkeep of the nation's tracks, stations, and signals—to carry out an effective program of track inspection, maintenance, and
repair. However, many people believed the underlying cause to be even
deeper, and attributed it to the fragmentation of the UK's rail industry following the privatization, between 1994 and 1997, of British Rail, the nationalized
industry that had hitherto run the entire system.

In the old days under British Rail, all the tracks, the signals, the stations,
and the trains were run in a unified way, and accountability for the system as

a whole rested with British Rail. At privatization, however, a host of different companies were awarded 25 separate franchises to run the trains, while the newly created company Railtrack plc—floated on the UK stock market on 20 May 1996 at an opening price of 390p per share—assumed responsibility for the tracks and signals. No one entity has responsibility for the entire, highly interconnected system, so, said many people, no wonder something terrible happened. And the disaster at Hatfield was the third since privatization: seven people were killed in an accident in Southall, West London, on 19 September 1997, and thirty-one were killed in an accident close to Paddington Station, also in West London, on 5 October 1999.

In the weeks and months following the Hatfield disaster, Railtrack implemented an extensive program of emergency work, but carrying this out required some lines to be closed; at the same time, many parts of the network that weren't closed were subject to speed restrictions. The disruption was immense. Journeys that were originally scheduled to take an hour might take four, if they ran at all; Railtrack was obliged to give many millions of pounds of compensation to the train operating companies who were no longer able to run their trains, and therefore lost customer revenue through no fault of their own; the passengers became very angry indeed; and the UK's internal airlines had a bonanza.

Quiz time: Where's the loop?

Here is an extract from one of the UK's leading newspapers, *The Times*, dated 24 November 2000:

…the one positive development since the old British Rail was abandoned was that the total number of passengers increased steadily. But the rail companies, some of whom are not far from bankruptcy, will shortly face an awful vicious circle. They will need to invest in order to attract customers back to the rails, yet will not have the resources to do this if their income is shrinking.

Do you see that this is a real systems thinking story, *par excellence*? What is the underlying causal loop? And how does it behave?

The causal loop diagram underpinning this story is in fact one we have already seen (Figure 5.15).

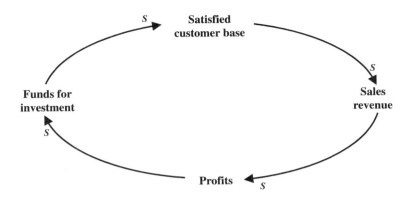

Figure 5.15

As the story from *The Times* describes, soon after privatization the SATISFIED CUSTOMER BASE went up as more people traveled on the trains, and so the SALES REVENUE and PROFITS of the operating companies increased. This provided more FUNDS FOR INVESTMENT, further enhancing the SATISFIED CUSTOMER BASE, with the result that the rail industry was creating a potentially powerful engine of exponential business growth.

Then came the series of crashes. The first, at Southall in 1997, did not have a major impact, because the public accepts that from time to time accidents do happen. The second crash, at Paddington in 1999, created much more public outrage, and the Hatfield crash just one year later proved to be very much the last straw. Not only was this a psychological shock to customers—rail passengers have very high expectations of safety—but, very suddenly, the reliability of the service plummeted and the SATISFIED CUSTOMER BASE plunged. Almost overnight, the SALES REVENUE fell, PROFITS disappeared, there was little prospect of there being any FUNDS FOR INVESTMENT without significant help from the government...

The article from *The Times* states explicitly that the rail companies "face an awful vicious circle." What had been a virtuous circle had, as a result of a single, sudden shock, flipped into the nastiest of vicious circles. Bust followed boom—exponential growth suddenly became exponential decline (Figure 5.16 overleaf).

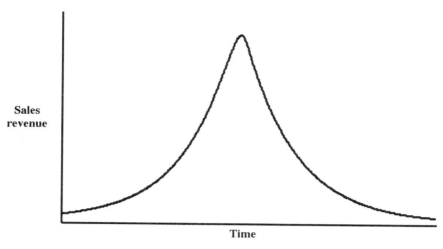

Figure 5.16

Boom and bust cycles are by no means uncommon in business and give rise to two questions:

> How come the bust happens so quickly and dramatically?
> Once the bust has started, how come it's so hard to stop?

Systems thinking, and the very simple causal loop diagram we have just been examining, shed perceptive light on both these questions.

The bust sets in so quickly because the *fundamental structure of the system has remained exactly the same*. What initiates the bust is usually the occurrence of an external event—maybe just a single one—which flips the reinforcing loop from exponential growth to exponential decline, from boom to bust. In the case of the UK railways, it was the Hatfield crash that suddenly made a hitherto satisfied customer base very unsatisfied indeed. There are many other examples from elsewhere in the business world.

Ratner's jewelry chain

During the 1980s one of the UK's business golden boys was Gerald Ratner, who built up a nationwide network of jewelry shops, selling gold chains, cheap watches, household gifts, and the like. Ratner was hailed and fêted as a wondrous businessman and his company boomed to success. And then, on 24 April 1991, Ratner was invited to address the UK's

Institute of Directors. In his speech, Ratner attributed his success to the fact that his jewelry shops sold "crap" (his word, not mine).

Not surprisingly, this speech was widely reported in the newspapers and on television and, also not surprisingly, his hitherto loyal customer base, which included many teenage girls who regularly bought a new piece of jewelry for the weekend, suddenly decided that they would make their purchases elsewhere.

This was a shock that the business could not sustain, and so bust followed very soon afterward.

The bust is hard to arrest for three reasons. First the surprise: The bust sets in so quickly that everyone is taken unawares. Secondly, because the structure of the system—the engine of business growth that has been so carefully nurtured—is unchanged, management just doesn't know what to do differently, especially since the cause of the shock is often outside the business system itself. In the rail example, the crash happened in Hatfield, a town just north of London, but the consequences were felt across the entire country. And thirdly, there is the unrelenting dynamic property of exponential decline itself—the enormous power of the exponential flywheel, once it gets going. Remember the frogs?

The end of the line

On the morning of Sunday, 7 October 2001, the UK's lead news item was the announcement by the UK government that it had decided to appoint an administrator to take over the affairs of Railtrack. In essence, the privatized Railtrack plc was being wound up and taken over by the government. Here is how the news was broken in the headline article in that day's *Sunday Times*:

Bankrupt Railtrack begs for state rescue

Railtrack, the company that owns Britain's rail network, is teetering on the brink of bankruptcy and is in rescue talks with the government. Ernst & Young, the accountancy firm, is expected to take over day-to-day running of the company tomorrow as Railtrack executives give up attempts to rescue the group from its critical financial position ... Railtrack is expected to announce tomorrow that the trading of its shares on the London Stock Exchange will be suspended pending an eventual delisting.

And this is a graph of Railtrack's share price over the five years to 7 October 2001:

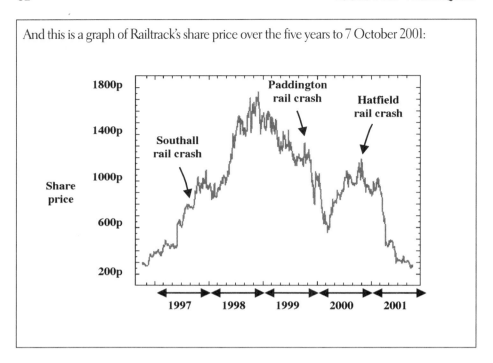

If a business is lucky and has enough resilience and inertia—and funds—to survive the downward plunge without going into liquidation or receivership, it might survive to grow again, as Railtrack appeared to be recovering after the Paddington crash, and as IBM actually did recover after its initial failure to recognize the importance of the PC market. However, Railtrack couldn't in fact recover from Hatfield, and within a year it folded.

Quiz time: The dot-coms
Opposite is a graph of the NASDAQ share price of Amazon.com, the most successful of the new breed of e-based businesses, over the five years from 1997–2001.

It shows boom and bust again. What do you consider to be the underlying causal loop?

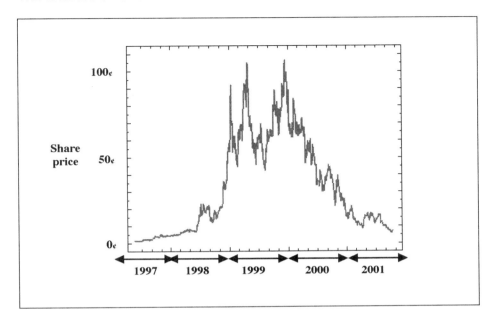

My vote goes for something like Figure 5.17.

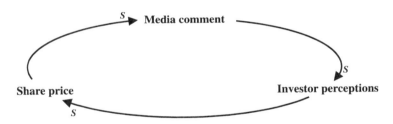

Figure 5.17

Favorable MEDIA COMMENT, as expressed in the newspapers and on radio and tele-vision, begins to influence INVESTOR PERCEPTIONS: The world is becoming wired, so why drive to the mall when I can get everything I need merely by clicking my mouse? As more and more investors perceive that it is a good idea to invest in the dot-coms the SHARE PRICE rises, and of course the media then emphasize how suc-cessful the dot-coms are becoming... Exponential growth kicks in once more.

Then something happens—maybe one or two influential journalists stick their necks out, maybe a bank starts calling in its loans to some dot-coms that are consuming cash as if it were a free good. And suddenly INVESTOR PERCEP-TIONS change—maybe these new-fangled dot-coms are a little too risky, per-haps I would be better off investing my savings in something a bit more tangible, with a verifiable track record. And so the SHARE PRICE falls and, if this happens quickly, it can initiate a seemingly unstoppable exponential decline.

This causal loop does not refer specifically or only to the technology of the dot-coms. The investment boom and bust cycle has been around for centuries—from tulip mania in the Netherlands in the mid 1630s, to the UK's "South Sea Bubble," which spectacularly burst on 10 September 1720, to the margin-stimulated boom and bust of the late 1920s. The underlying causal loop is the same; only the context is different.

As we have now seen many times, systems thinking provides some wonderful unifying insights into the true behavior of complex systems.

Reinforcing loops can be linked

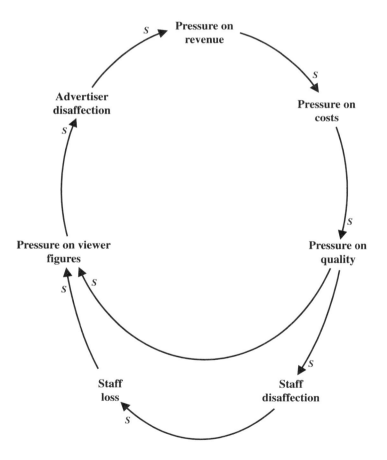

Figure 5.18

Figure 5.18 is the causal loop diagram of the TV example once more. As we have already seen, this is formed from two reinforcing loops that reinforce one another and, when the loops act as virtuous circles rather than vicious ones, this cooperative action can be a powerful engine of growth.

This is just one example of two linked reinforcing loops. Figure 5.19 is another, which is quite common in business and elsewhere.

Figure 5.19

I have a goal to reach, so my desire to achieve MY GOALS is strong. You too have your goals, so your desire to achieve YOUR GOALS is equally, and as validly, strong. But to reach our goals we both need to use resources—perhaps investment funds, perhaps people, perhaps equipment—and the greater MY NEED FOR RESOURCES, the greater MY CONSUMPTION OF RESOURCES, and the same is happening for you. However, these resources are shared and drawn from a common resource pool, which is finite and limited by the TOTAL RESOURCE CAPACITY. The greater MY CONSUMPTION OF RESOURCES, the fewer the RESOURCES LEFT AVAILABLE either for you now (because I've taken them all) or for us both in the future, hence the O. By the same token, the greater YOUR CONSUMPTION OF RESOURCES, the fewer RESOURCES LEFT AVAILABLE for me (another O).

The larger the TOTAL RESOURCE CAPACITY, the larger the RESOURCES LEFT AVAILABLE for any given total level of resource consumption, hence the S on that link, and when there is plenty of resource to go around and both our needs can be satisfied easily, there is no problem. But eventually, as the RESOURCES LEFT AVAILABLE become progressively scarcer, MY FEAR THAT YOU WILL NOT LEAVE ENOUGH RESOURCES FOR ME builds (that's another O) to a point at which

I begin to take rather different actions. Maybe I stockpile resources secretly so that you don't get your hands on them; maybe I overbid for resources to ensure I have some contingency. Either way, my NEED FOR RESOURCES gets even bigger. And simultaneously, the same thing is happening to you.

The structure here is formed from two interconnected reinforcing loops driven by two input policy dangles (see page 57)—our respective desires to reach our own goals—and a third input dangle specifying the TOTAL RESOURCE CAPACITY. The action of this system is to make the scarce resources even scarcer, as you and I compete on each relentless turn of our respective reinforcing loops.

How does this happen in business?
Does this situation ever arise in business? If so, in what contexts? What happens? And what about contexts outside of business?

In my experience, this diagram is at the very heart of many business situations. Maybe it's the argument over budgets, where we are all competing for bigger slices of a finite investment cake; maybe it's about the staffing of project teams, when I want Alison on my team and you want her on yours; maybe it's about access to the IT development team; maybe the "finite resource" is the market space, where we are both competing for clients even though we work for the same firm. These situations arise outside business too, from problems between neighbors about noise (the finite resource in this case being peace and quiet) to conflicts between neighboring states about, say, access to the water provided by a single river than runs through both territories.

There are a number of possible outcomes to this situation, of which the most common is shown in Figure 5.20.

We'll have a row or maybe we'll go to war. CONFLICT escalates, eventually resulting in a reduction in the NUMBERS COMPETING FOR RESOURCES, so that all the RESOURCES LEFT AVAILABLE become mine. That seems to solve the problem—but does it?

The presence of CONFLICT has introduced two further loops: As the level of CONFLICT increases, there is a progressive reduction in the NUMBERS COMPETING FOR RESOURCES (hence the O), and as the number of competitors decreases, the RESOURCES LEFT AVAILABLE for the winners increase (another O). So—if I'm the

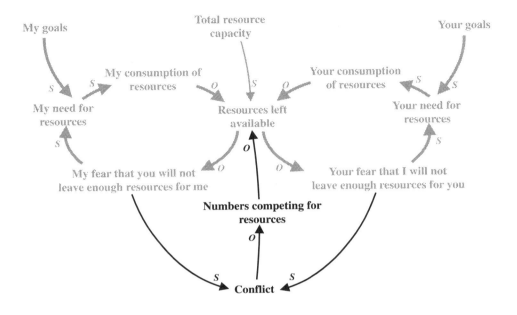

Figure 5.20

winner—this relieves MY FEAR THAT YOU WILL NOT LEAVE ENOUGH RESOURCES FOR ME, which reduces the likelihood of further CONFLICT, at least for a while.

Tracing that loop around shows that it contains three Os, so it is a balancing loop. The structure is therefore now two linked reinforcing loops interacting with two linked balancing loops, the overall effect of which is to introduce some stability eventually, even if this is at the expense of some of the original players. However, even when there is only one player left, if the resource in question is something truly finite like good agricultural land, water, or oil, there is always the possibility that the last remaining player will use all the resources up, even if there are no explicit competitors.

Putting the brakes on

This example is an instance of a very important general rule: The action of a balancing loop, when operating in conjunction with a reinforcing loop, is to slow down the rate of (positive or negative) growth that the reinforcing loop would have exhibited in the absence of the interconnected balancing loop.

To verify that this is the case, take another look at Figure 5.20 and consider the operation of the reinforcing loops alone. As MY NEED FOR RESOURCES increases, so does MY CONSUMPTION OF RESOURCES, depleting the RESOURCES LEFT AVAILABLE. This aggravates MY FEAR THAT YOU WILL NOT LEAVE ENOUGH RESOURCES FOR ME, so stimulating MY NEED FOR RESOURCES even more, with the result that the reinforcing loop increases in intensity with each spin.

Now add in the balancing loops. Once again, a depletion of the RESOURCES LEFT AVAILABLE for me aggravates MY FEAR THAT YOU WILL NOT LEAVE ENOUGH RESOURCES FOR ME, but now two actions are triggered. MY NEED FOR RESOURCES is increased as before, but simultaneously CONFLICT breaks out. And if this results in aggression, this in turn causes a reduction in the NUMBERS COMPETING FOR RESOURCES. The greater the reduction in the NUMBERS COMPETING FOR RESOURCES, the more the RESOURCES LEFT AVAILABLE.

As a result of the action of the balancing loop, the RESOURCES LEFT AVAILABLE are now subject to two influences: a continued depletion attributable to MY CONSUMPTION OF RESOURCES (and a symmetrical effect attributable to YOUR CONSUMPTION OF RESOURCES) and, simultaneously, mitigation (possibly with a time lag) attributable to the REDUCTION IN THE NUMBERS COMPETING FOR RESOURCES. The net effect is that the RESOURCES LEFT AVAILABLE are greater than they would have been in the absence of the balancing loop, implying that the runaway behavior of the reinforcing loop has been slowed down, if not absolutely stopped.

This explanation is totally generic and applies to any reinforcing loop interacting with any balancing loop: The action of the balancing loop is to put the brakes on. The severity with which this happens depends on the context, but the general rule that the action of the balancing loop is to limit the growth of the reinforcing loop is universally true. Accordingly, as we shall see on page 143, a combination of a reinforcing loop and an interconnected balancing loop is known as the "limits to growth" structure.

Fortunately, out-and-out conflict is not the only possible outcome of our two synchronous reinforcing loops. Before having a row or a war, perhaps the situation in Figure 5.21 happens first, in which an APPEAL TO HIGHER AUTHORITY limits CONSUMPTION OF RESOURCES for both of us.

As every parent knows, it is mum (or dad) who in the end decides which television channel squabbling children will watch—and the wise parent also remembers to check in from time to time to make sure that the dominant child has not switched back. The other solution—to buy a second television set and

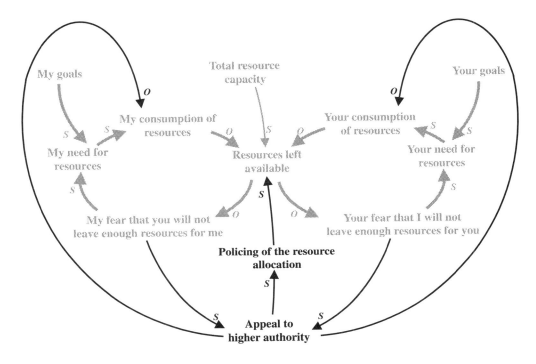

Figure 5.21

so increase the TOTAL RESOURCE CAPACITY—is not shown on the diagram!

As every middle manager knows, it is the boss who arbitrates on staff allocation disputes; as every director knows, it is the managing director who has the final say on investment decisions; as every MD knows, it is the government monopoly or antitrust regulator that stops one company dominating the industry; and as every citizen hopes, maybe the United Nations will bring those crazy warring politicians to their senses. But, as the history of the League of Nations relates all too tragically, an APPEAL TO HIGHER AUTHORITY has meaning only when coupled with effective POLICING OF THE RESOURCE ALLOCATION.

However, let's not become too gloomy, because there is also a third possibility (Figure 5.22 overleaf). This one is different, since it captures the idea that, instead of competing for the scarce resources, the players see the sense in cooperating and in seeking to agree how the resources can best be shared. The stronger my RECOGNITION OF THE NEED FOR COOPERATION, the greater MY WILLINGNESS TO PARTICIPATE IN A COOPERATIVE GOAL-SETTING PROCESS, the outcome of which is to influence MY GOALS to be more in line with the RESOURCES LEFT AVAILABLE to both of us. Rather than arguing about how to

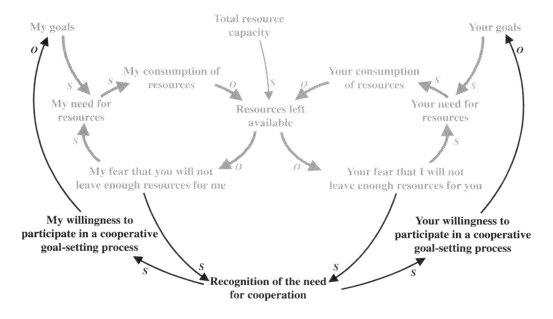

Figure 5.22

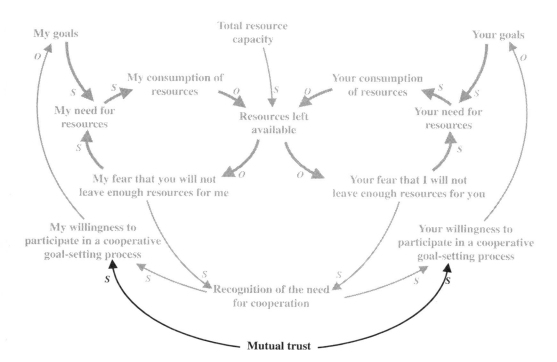

Figure 5.23

carve up the RESOURCES LEFT AVAILABLE, we'll agree our goals and limit our respective CONSUMPTION OF RESOURCES accordingly. This approach also introduces two balancing loops, but they interact with the reinforcing loops in a different way, as the diagrams show.

Which approach leads to a more robust long-term solution? It depends on your world-view. If you are a Darwinian, believing in the survival of the fittest, you will opt in the first instance for the policeman, and in the second for the army. If you have a different outlook, you will pray for wisdom. Nevertheless, wisdom itself depends on a very scarce commodity indeed (Figure 5.23).

If I don't trust you, I'll sit at the negotiating table and smile, but behind your back I'll be doing all sorts of other things, just in case. Maybe you have to prove your word by reducing your goals first; but then why should you trust me to do likewise? However, if we can trust each other, surely this approach is much more sustainable, especially if we agree that it would be a good idea to see if we could discover ways of increasing the TOTAL RESOURCE CAPACITY. So perhaps some of the resources I would otherwise consume might best be devoted to a SEARCH FOR NEW OR RENEWABLE RESOURCES, because not only do I see the need for a broader set of goals, but MY GOALS and YOUR GOALS have become aligned (Figure 5.24 overleaf).

This final causal loop diagram is a complex—but I trust fully intelligible—network of six interconnected feedback loops: the original two reinforcing loops, and four additional balancing loops. With one exception, every item on the diagram is a component of at least one loop, the sole exception being MUTUAL TRUST. That is the only dangle and its presence—or absence—drives the whole system. To me, that rings powerfully true.

That story was all about how two reinforcing loops, linked through the sharing of a common resource, can act together to cause conflict, and we explored three different ways in which the situation might be managed. Each of these introduced two additional balancing loops, acting in different ways according to the policies invoked. Two sought to reduce the conflict by changing the rules by which the scarce resource was allocated; one changed the rules by which the demand for the scarce resource was generated in the first place. All three approaches, however, act in the same generic way: The two balancing loops brake the otherwise runaway exponential growth of the two reinforcing loops.

We shall explore the interactions between reinforcing loops and balancing loops in much more depth in Chapter 8. In the meantime, Chapter 6 examines the behavior of the second fundamental building block of systems thinking, the balancing loop.

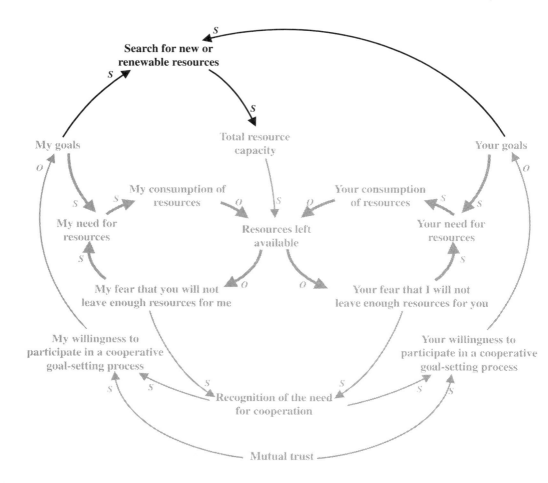

Figure 5.24

6
Setting targets, seeking goals

More on balancing loops

Figure 6.1 is a balancing loop that we examined earlier, the causal loop diagram describing how to pour a cup of coffee.

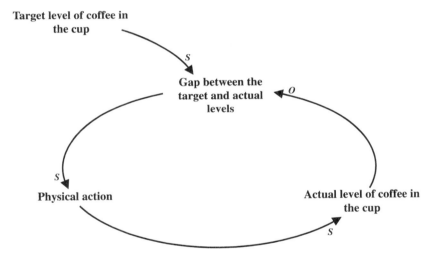

Figure 6.1

How does this loop behave?

Take a moment to refresh your memory about this loop and check that you understand it, especially the Ss and the O. Assuming that I am pouring the coffee carefully, draw a graph showing the behavior of the ACTUAL LEVEL OF COFFEE IN THE CUP over time.

This loop contains an odd number of Os and so is a balancing loop, in which the ACTUAL LEVEL OF COFFEE IN THE CUP converges on the TARGET LEVEL OF

COFFEE IN THE CUP. If I am pouring carefully, the behavior of the ACTUAL LEVEL OF COFFEE IN THE CUP over time is like Figure 6.2.

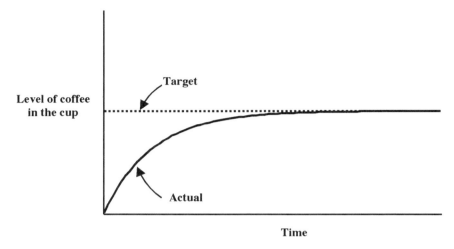

Figure 6.2

As can be seen, the ACTUAL LEVEL OF COFFEE IN THE CUP steadily approaches the TARGET LEVEL OF COFFEE IN THE CUP, and once the target has been reached the system stays unchanged indefinitely.

What happens if I am not particularly careful when I am pouring?

Imagine for a moment that I am distracted for a moment while I am pouring the coffee into the cup. What happens? What actions do I take? How does this relate to the causal loop diagram? And what does a graph of the behavior of the ACTUAL LEVEL OF COFFEE IN THE CUP over time look like?

That exercise—especially the third question concerning the causal loop diagram—is not trivial, so take a moment or two to think about it.

As you will recall, the target level of coffee in the cup was set as half a cup, so if I am distracted only for a moment, I will overfill the cup beyond the halfway point, but I am likely to notice this before the cup overflows and makes a mess. What happens then? I carefully tip the cup and pour some excess coffee out, but if once again I am not too careful, I might tip too much out and so I will have to put some more in again. Eventually, after some to-ing and fro-ing, I get it just right.

How does this relate to the causal loop diagram? Let me explain, and I'll do so slowly since it needs careful thought. I'll take it from the time at which I have noticed that I have overfilled the cup beyond the halfway mark, and I have just stopped pouring. At this instant, the ACTUAL LEVEL OF COFFEE IN THE CUP is *higher* than the TARGET LEVEL OF COFFEE IN THE CUP. If I define the GAP BETWEEN THE TARGET AND ACTUAL LEVELS as the target level minus the actual level, then, in this case, this computes to a *negative number*. Furthermore, the more I have overfilled the cup beyond the halfway mark, the more negative this number becomes.

Moving around the loop, the S linking the GAP BETWEEN THE TARGET AND ACTUAL LEVELS and PHYSICAL ACTION tells us that these two items move in the same direction. As the GAP BETWEEN THE TARGET AND ACTUAL LEVELS becomes progressively more negative, so does the PHYSICAL ACTION. But what on earth might a "negative physical action" mean? If a positive physical action is pouring coffee *into* the cup, then a negative physical action can mean only one thing: We have to pour coffee *out of* the cup. This, of course, is exactly what happens. What we have now discovered is that the causal loop anticipates this and tells us what to do—the negative value of the GAP BETWEEN THE TARGET AND ACTUAL LEVELS instructs us to pour the coffee out.

There is also an S linking PHYSICAL ACTION to the ACTUAL LEVEL OF COFFEE IN THE CUP, so if the PHYSICAL ACTION is negative, the effect on the ACTUAL LEVEL OF COFFEE IN THE CUP is negative too, implying that the actual level *reduces*—as, of course, is true as we pour the coffee out of the cup.

Health warning: Here comes the part that many people find mind-bending. The causal loop diagram shows an O against the link from the ACTUAL LEVEL OF COFFEE IN THE CUP to the GAP BETWEEN THE TARGET AND ACTUAL LEVELS. This implies that they move in opposite directions. So if the ACTUAL LEVEL OF COFFEE IN THE CUP is reducing, the GAP BETWEEN THE TARGET LEVEL AND THE ACTUAL LEVEL must be increasing. Increasing means getting bigger, more positive, and you will recall that at the start of tracing the loop, the gap between the target and actual levels was a *negative* number. So if this number is increasing and becoming more positive, it must be becoming less negative, getting closer to zero.

The system is, once again, seeking the goal of being half full.

Read the last page again

Very few people get all that the first time around. So take a moment to read it again, to check that you really follow it. The key point is that, in describing the behavior of the loop rigorously, all the items are *signed quantities*, in that they intrinsically carry a plus sign or a minus sign. In general, when they carry a plus sign, we don't think about it or even notice it; in fact, in every example until this one, all the items have carried an implicit plus sign. This is the first example in which some items have carried a minus sign, and the mind-blower is the fact that when you *increase* a negative number (say –3), you make it more positive (it becomes –2), not more negative (it doesn't become –4).

Let's now suppose that I have inadvertently poured too much out and the ACTUAL LEVEL OF COFFEE IN THE CUP is now less than the TARGET LEVEL OF COFFEE IN THE CUP. The GAP BETWEEN THE TARGET AND ACTUAL LEVELS is therefore a positive number, and so I take a positive PHYSICAL ACTION; that's because of the S. This implies that I pour the coffee back in, which makes sense. The effect on the ACTUAL LEVEL OF COFFEE IN THE CUP is positive (the S again) and so this increases once more, as also makes sense. The increase in the ACTUAL LEVEL OF COFFEE IN THE CUP causes a decrease in the GAP BETWEEN THE TARGET AND ACTUAL LEVELS (that's the O), but that's intuitively much easier to understand while the ACTUAL LEVEL OF COFFEE IN THE CUP is increasing. The fact that the GAP BETWEEN THE TARGET AND ACTUAL LEVELS is getting smaller implies that, once again, the system is converging on its goal.

Phew! What is happening here is much more easily appreciated from a graph, showing a somewhat exaggerated form of the behavior of the actual level of coffee in the cup over time (Figure 6.3).

This graph vividly depicts the progressive over- and under-shooting of the actual level of coffee in the cup as it converges on the target. The target is specified by the dangle, the TARGET LEVEL OF COFFEE IN THE CUP, and dangles that have this role are known as *target dangles*; in contrast to the rate dangles that we met on page 80.

The behavior of all balancing loops

Balancing loops converge on targets or goals. Sometimes these are explicitly stated in terms of a target dangle, sometimes not; but whenever you see a balancing loop, the corresponding behavior is target seeking. Sometimes the target is reached smoothly, but if there are time delays in the system, the system may oscillate before the target is reached.

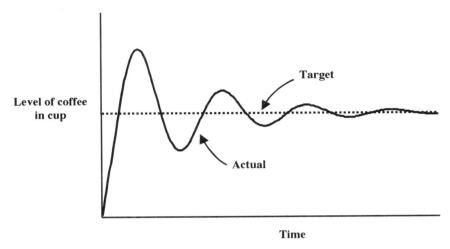

Figure 6.3

Once again, we have a wonderful unifying principle. All balancing loops seek goals, and the *same* causal loop diagram can result in a smooth progression to the goal (as shown on page 104) or an oscillatory one. The difference between these two behaviors is all about how quickly the system responds to the signal that the actual is different from the target. If the system responds essentially instantaneously, the behavior is usually smooth; if the system has time delays (as simulated by the assumption of being distracted in the coffee example), then the system will usually oscillate.

Strange showers

The coffee cup example is a sensible example of the smooth approach to a target, but it is rather artificial as regards oscillation; few of us are that clumsy. However, there are many everyday examples in which this oscillatory behavior is common.

A familiar one is the use of a shower in an unfamiliar hotel. You set the regulator at "warm," let the shower run for some time, and decide that the water is too cold. You then adjust the regulator to "hot," let the water run some more, and somewhat impatiently (it's cold standing there with no clothes on!) test it again. It's still too cold. So you push the regulator to "very hot" and it begins to warm up nicely. You jump under the shower and, a few seconds later, jump out from under the scalding hot water. You now have the problem that the regulator is behind a torrent of water hot enough to strip the skin off your whole body, so you find a towel, wrap it around your hand, and thump the regulator to "cold." After about three tries, the temperature is just right.

This is the causal loop:

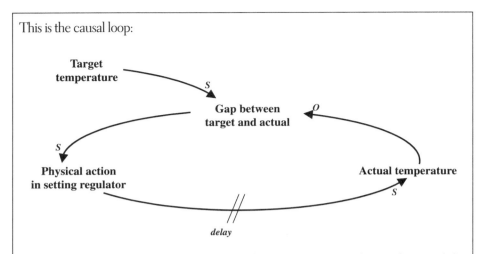

The two diagonal lines represent the time delay between setting the regulator and the actual temperature of the water coming out of the shower. If this delay is more than a few moments, we tend to get impatient! So we readjust the regulator setting, with the result that we make the system oscillate.

Balancing loops in business

Balancing loops are everywhere in business. Most of them look like Figure 6.4.

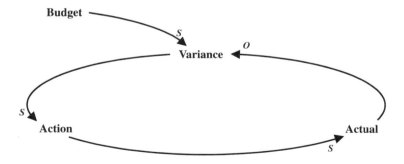

Figure 6.4

A BUDGET is set during the policy-making budgeting round and becomes the target to achieve. During the course of the year, the management accounts track the VARIANCE between BUDGET and ACTUAL. This comparison prompts whatever ACTION we determine is required to bring the actual results into line with the budget. That is what we do in practice: From a systems thinking perspective the budgeting system comprises a balancing loop, which acts to seek the goal of meeting the budget.

As a concrete example, Figure 6.5 is a diagram relating to pricing policy.

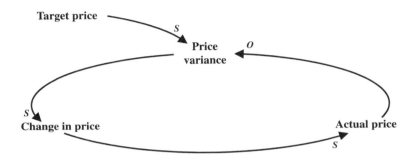

Figure 6.5

The action relevant to this case is a CHANGE IN PRICE, where this change can be either an increase (if the ACTUAL PRICE is lower than the TARGET PRICE) or a decrease (if the ACTUAL PRICE is higher than the TARGET PRICE). This single diagram covers both cases and the Ss and the Os work automatically either way. So if we define the PRICE VARIANCE as:

$$\text{PRICE VARIANCE} = \text{TARGET PRICE} - \text{ACTUAL PRICE}$$

then, if the TARGET PRICE is higher than the ACTUAL PRICE, the PRICE VARI-ANCE is a positive number. The S linking PRICE VARIANCE to CHANGE IN PRICE indicates that the bigger the (positive) PRICE VARIANCE, the bigger the (positive) CHANGE IN PRICE; and the S linking CHANGE IN PRICE to ACTUAL PRICE results in a price increase, to bring the actual price in line with the target price. Similarly, if the ACTUAL PRICE is higher than the TARGET PRICE, the PRICE VARIANCE is a negative number, causing the change in price to be negative, causing a decrease in the actual price, once again as required.

Figure 6.6 overleaf is another form of the same diagram in which the action is described as the INCREASE OR DECREASE IN PRICE, a form of language that explicitly recognizes that the action can be in either direction, depending on the circumstances.

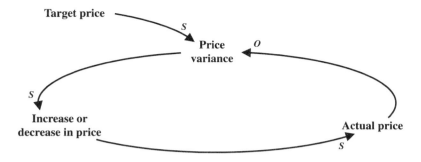

Figure 6.6

Sometimes we have specific words to represent the "increase in" or "decrease in" actions, so Figure 6.7 is an example of a balancing loop relating to managing the headcount and Figure 6.8 is one relating to assets.

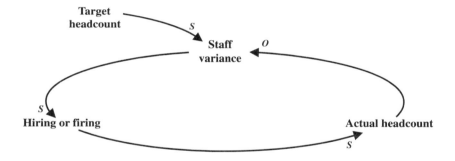

Figure 6.7

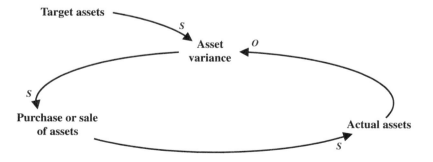

Figure 6.8

As a matter of best practice in drawing balancing loops, the action description should always include both the positive and negative words or phrases. Even though we prefer to think about hiring rather than firing, in principle both actions are possible, and either will be invoked depending on the nature of the variance in question.

Two more examples. Figure 6.9 relates to reward and remuneration policy, which captures the management of the ACTUAL REWARD STRUCTURE to be in line with the TARGET REWARD STRUCTURE in terms of a CHANGE IN REWARD STRUCTURE, which might be salary increases or decreases, or revised bonuses, holidays, or other benefits.

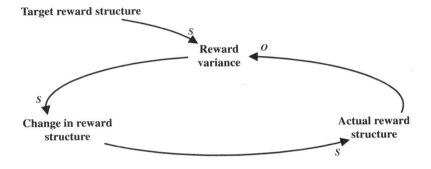

Figure 6.9

Figure 6.10 is a final example that introduces two new features.

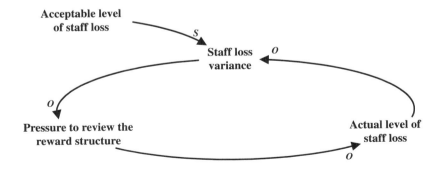

Figure 6.10

This diagram is all about the ACTUAL LEVEL OF STAFF LOSS, a situation that all businesses experience. Employees are not serfs, bound to their masters, but are employed under legal contracts that allow them to resign, for the most part, whenever they wish in accordance with the contractual notice period. Most businesses also accept that a certain level of staff turnover is normal and natural, even healthy, because it brings a flow of new people into the organization. So although many organizations do not have an explicit target for staff loss—which they do have for staff numbers, assets, and so on—they probably have an ACCEPTABLE LEVEL OF STAFF LOSS, this being the level of staff loss that marks the threshold at which there starts to be concern. So the first new feature of this diagram is the recognition of an implicit, rather than an explicit, target or goal.

What happens when the ACTUAL LEVEL OF STAFF LOSS exceeds the ACCEPTABLE LEVEL OF STAFF LOSS? What action do we take? To start with, when the STAFF LOSS VARIANCE is relatively small, we probably don't do a great deal; but as this variance gets bigger and is perceived as a trend rather than a statistical fluctuation, it results in progressive PRESSURE TO REVIEW THE REWARD STRUCTURE, the intention of which is to reduce the ACTUAL LEVEL OF STAFF LOSS. This assumes, of course, that it is the reward structure that is the key driver of actual level of staff loss; in reality, it may be merely one component of a more complex picture, so the action might be more realistically described as PRESSURE TO INVESTIGATE THE STAFF MORALE PROBLEM AND FIX IT.

That leads to the second new feature of this particular diagram: The closed loop is not the familiar two Ss and one O; rather, it is three Os, something we have not seen before. The number of Os is still odd, so the loop remains a balancing loop, but why three Os?

This requires some careful thought, remembering, as we saw on page 106, that items in causal loop diagrams are implicitly associated with plus and minus signs. The definition of STAFF LOSS VARIANCE is, as usual:

STAFF LOSS VARIANCE = ACCEPTABLE LEVEL OF STAFF LOSS − ACTUAL LEVEL OF STAFF LOSS

The management problem usually arises when the ACTUAL LEVEL OF STAFF LOSS over a period of time is consistently greater than the ACCEPTABLE LEVEL OF STAFF LOSS (although the other way round can sometimes be a problem), when the STAFF LOSS VARIANCE is a *negative* number. As is intuitively sensible, the larger this negative number, the greater the PRESSURE TO REVIEW THE REWARD STRUCTURE upward, increasing the overall value of the reward package to employees. A negative variance is driving a positive action, hence the O. Similarly, the

hoped-for effect of increasing the value of the reward package is to reduce the
ACTUAL LEVEL OF STAFF LOSS, hence another O here. And three Os result, as we
need, in a balancing loop. The opposite, but less likely, situation works too: If the
ACTUAL LEVEL OF STAFF LOSS is too low the STAFF LOSS VARIANCE is positive, driving the negative action of reviewing the reward structure downward, with the
result that staff are encouraged to leave, so increasing the STAFF LOSS RATE!

In general, balancing loops have three links around the closed loop, and
as long as the total number of Os is odd the loop is a balancing loop. This
implies that there is either one O or three: Zero or two Os make a reinforcing
loop. If there is one O, the most common location is the link from ACTUAL
[WHATEVER] TO VARIANCE, for this is driven by the definition of variance as:

$$\text{VARIANCE} = \text{TARGET} - \text{ACTUAL}$$

As long as the ACTUAL is a positive quantity—as it almost invariably is in a business context—then, for any given TARGET, the larger the ACTUAL the smaller
the VARIANCE, hence there is an O linking ACTUAL to VARIANCE. And usually
the other two links are both Ss, but not in every case; we have just seen an
example with two Os. How come?

The answer is, once again, because of language: It is our choice of words
that makes the last balancing loop contain three Os. This is perhaps clearer if
we refer not to STAFF LOSS, but to the equivalent, although rather less familiar, concept of STAFF RETENTION (Figure 6.11).

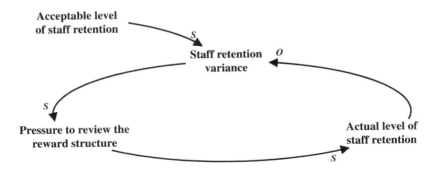

Figure 6.11

The structure of the Ss and Os around this loop is more familiar, but the
words probably aren't. Suppose you have an establishment of 100 staff and

you expect that 10 people leave each year, so your ACCEPTABLE LEVEL OF STAFF RETENTION is 90. Suppose that, for whatever reason, the number of leavers is 20, implying that the ACTUAL LEVEL OF STAFF RETENTION is 80. The staff retention variance is then 90 – 80 = 10, a positive number. This exerts a positive PRESSURE TO REVIEW THE REWARD STRUCTURE upward, to enhance the benefit package, so increasing the ACTUAL LEVEL OF STAFF RETENTION, hence the two Ss.

As we have seen before (see, for example, page 63), the use of Ss and Os around a closed loop is totally dependent on language. To my mind, for this particular example the language of staff loss is more natural than the language of staff retention, and a consequence of using this language is a balancing loop with three Os. No matter: The language makes sense and so does the loop.

Balancing loops are often linked

In business, balancing loops are all about meeting business goals and objectives. All businesses have multiple objectives and so managing a business is about managing many balancing loops together.

Figure 6.12 takes the headcount example in Figure 6.7 one step further and introduces to it the ACTUAL LEVEL OF STAFF LOSS, the effect of which is to decrease the ACTUAL HEADCOUNT.

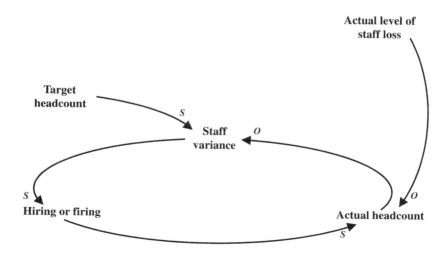

Figure 6.12

The ACTUAL LEVEL OF STAFF LOSS, however, is itself a component of our now familiar three-O loop (Figure 6.13).

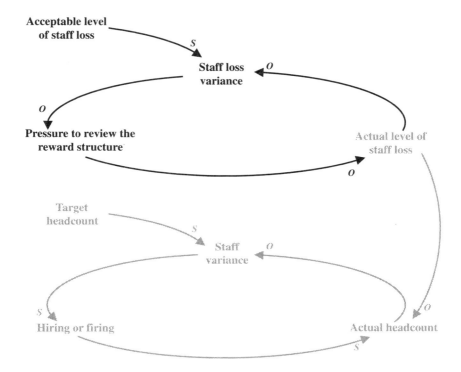

Figure 6.13

These two loops are linked together, as is indeed the case in real life, since we are managing both the headcount and staff losses together and simultaneously.

And in practice, there is (at least) a third balancing loop involved too. If we assume that the sole driver of the ACTUAL LEVEL OF STAFF LOSS is the reward structure, then the PRESSURE TO REVIEW THE REWARD STRUCTURE results in a change (usually upward) in the target reward structure as we revise our reward policies (see Figure 6.14 overleaf).

In this diagram the link from the PRESSURE TO REVIEW THE REWARD STRUC-TURE to the ACTUAL LEVEL OF STAFF LOSS is now shown dotted, because it has been replaced by the connection into the reward structure loop, since this controls the action that we actually take with the intention of controlling the ACTUAL LEVEL OF STAFF LOSS.

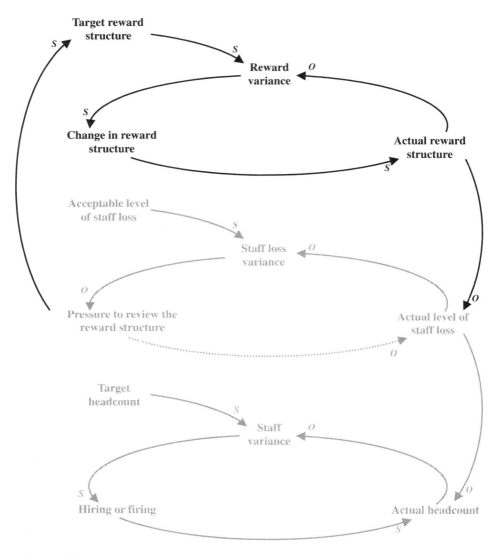

Figure 6.14

This is now a structure of three interconnected balancing loops, each of which captures a different aspect of managing staff. Through policy, among many other things, we set a TARGET HEADCOUNT and a TARGET REWARD STRUC-TURE, and various outcomes happen in the business as a result. One of these outcomes is the ACTUAL LEVEL OF STAFF LOSS, which we monitor and compare to the ACCEPTABLE LEVEL OF STAFF LOSS. If the resulting STAFF LOSS VARIANCE is OK, then fine; but if not, it triggers a resetting of the TARGET REWARD STRUC-

TURE and maybe some other things too. The continuous monitoring of actual outcomes (in this case, the ACTUAL LEVEL OF STAFF LOSS) against intended outcomes (in this case, the usually implicit, but nonetheless real, ACCEPTABLE LEVEL OF STAFF LOSS) triggers changes in policies (in this case the TARGET REWARD STRUCTURE)—or, if "policies" is in some contexts too grand a word, this comparison triggers some form of managerial action.

It is as if management is all about sitting at some form of enormously complex control panel, with all sorts of buttons, knobs, and levers, with names such as target headcount, target reward structure, and target assets, and, at a more operational level, hirings, firings, salary increases, and asset purchases. We sit at the control panel and move the target levers from time to time, fine tuning the business machine and taking the appropriate managerial actions to guide the business toward desired outcomes such as sales, profits, reputation, and share price. As we monitor the actual outcomes against the desired outcomes, we press this button, twiddle that knob, or pull this lever. As this example demonstrates, most of the buttons, knobs, and levers are attached to interconnected balancing loops, a theme I shall explore in more depth in Chapter 10.

Balancing loops and time delays

Ideally, in any balancing loop the actual converges on the budget or target in a nice smooth way (Figure 6.15).

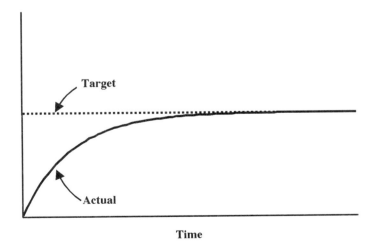

Figure 6.15

In practice, however, the road is sometimes a bit rocky. Most real systems are more like the strange shower (see page 107) than the steady pouring of a cup of coffee, because they are full of time delays: the time taken to measure the actuals and compute the variance, the time taken to produce the management accounts, the time taken to interpret the management accounts, the time taken to decide what action to take, the time taken to put those actions into practice, the time taken for those actions to have their effect. This can therefore result in the kinds of oscillation we saw on page 107 and the possibility that these oscillations can be aggravated by our impatience, or perhaps lack of awareness of the extent and impact of the time delays in the system we are trying to manage. Given the problem we all experience in getting the temperature of an unfamiliar shower right—where there is only one time delay to take into account—no wonder managing a business isn't easy.

A familiar context in which oscillations can very easily occur relates to inventory control and supply chain management. These systems are often associated with the maintenance of particular pre-determined levels of stock, which act as the targets, and the actions are usually the placing of purchase orders on suppliers to replenish stock that has been sold or issued from stores. With all sorts of time delays inherent in the reorder process, these systems are notorious for their tendency to oscillate and so appear to be out of control.

Changing the goal posts

Below is a graph showing the behavior of an inventory control system, with a target level of stock. Unfortunately, because of the time delays in the system, the natural behavior is oscillation—but an oscillation that eventually stabilizes on the target inventory.

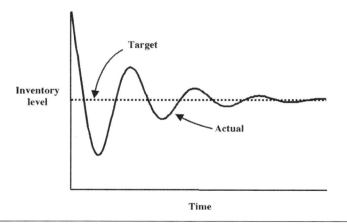

It so happens that the inventory control manager hasn't been trained in systems thinking. That initial rapid decrease in inventory starts making him worried that he will soon run out of stock, which is bad news for the factory and bad news for him personally. So he thinks, "Since the inventory is plummeting, I'd better increase the target levels, just a little, and reorder more than I might otherwise."

This is a graph of what happened next:

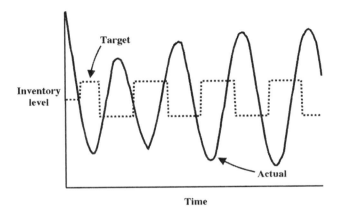

The manager's fear-induced changing of the target actually makes matters worse. This system really is out of control, and becoming progressively more so. Oh dear.

This graph, by the way, and all the others in this book, have been generated by a computer modeling tool that allows you to simulate the behavior of causal loops, as I'll explain in more detail in Chapters 12 and 13.

As this example shows, the dynamic behavior of many systems over time can be very complex and quite bewildering to understand. So the poor inventory manager's well-intentioned desire to bring the system under control is perfectly understandable, but in practice very misguided. His best policy was not to interfere but to do absolutely nothing and wait for the system to stabilize of its own accord. However, you have to be a wise person—and also have wise bosses—to do the right thing and let it be. Sometimes interfering, rushing to take vigorous and decisive action, is precisely the wrong thing to do.

Although the dynamic behavior of this system appears to be very complex, the underlying system isn't complex at all: It is merely that now familiar balancing loop of target, actual, variance, and action, with some time delays.

Dynamic complexity

This is a powerful example of another unifying principle of systems thinking. As they evolve over time, many systems behave in a bewilderingly complex manner. This is called *dynamic complexity*. As we have just seen, the underlying causal loop structure is often much, much simpler, and one of the ways in which systems thinking can help you understand complex dynamic behavior is by providing you with a means to go behind the observed complexity to reveal the often much simpler causal loops.

Most people find it hard to understand dynamic complexity and to see the underlying patterns and causes clearly. Somehow the human mind is much more able to handle *detail complexity*, the understanding of systems, at a single point in time, which are composed of very many elements.

Rather than playing a guessing game when readjusting the target stock levels, our bewildered stock control manager might have been better off discovering why his inventory control system was subject to time delays and working to reduce those. But sometimes it is very tempting to deal with symptoms rather than causes.

On a grander scale, much of government policy is about the management of balancing loops. For example, in the UK the nine members of the Bank of England's Monetary Policy Committee, chaired by the Bank's Governor, Sir Edward George, meet every month to determine the interest rate. Their main mission is to "deliver price stability, as defined by the UK Government's inflation target" (I quote from the Bank of England's website www.bankofengland.co.uk/mpc/), while keeping the economy vibrant, and the only instrument they can wield is the interest rate. From a systems thinking point of view, their TARGET is low inflation and a healthy economy, their ACTUAL is the set of macroeconomic statistics, reflecting the overall state of the economy a number of months in the past when the statistics were gathered, and the only ACTION they can take is to change the interest rate by a fraction of a percentage point. This they do from time to time, and then the effects of this interest rate change work their way through the entire economic system.

The nation's overall economic system is obviously complex indeed and the time lags are measured in months and years. Recognizing this, the Committee knows that the wisest way to intervene is to make very small adjustments at relatively long intervals. This gives enough time for any one change to work through, and no single change is ever large enough to have an unwarranted

effect. The alternative policy of making dramatic changes more often is much
more likely to make the economic system unstable, with disastrous results.

Business cycles

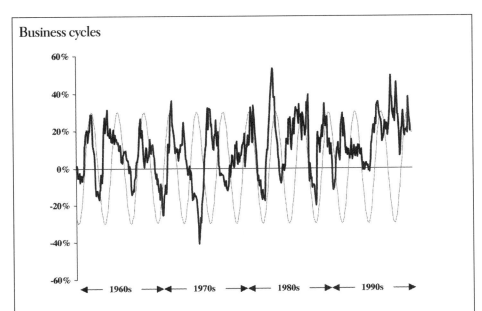

The heavy black line shows the year-on-year percentage change, over the four decades
from January 1960 to December 1999, in one of the key indicators of the US economy,
Standard and Poor's index of the stock market prices of 500 of the top US companies. Over
this time the index itself has, for the most part, steadily increased, but as comparison to the
light gray oscillation shows, its annual growth rate has bumped around. Many economists
talk of business cycles; systems thinkers will see the effect of a time-lagged balancing loop,
as US Inc. collectively strives to meet its growth targets.

What is the definition of variance?

As a finale to this discussion of balancing loops, you might like to try the quiz
overleaf. A health warning though: Many people find it a real brain-buster, so
it's not for the faint-hearted and you may prefer to go straight to the last section of this chapter on page 125. Nevertheless, if you do try it and succeed,
you can be very sure that you really do understand what causal loops are all
about.

Quiz time: What is the definition of variance?

An implicit assumption associated with this, now familiar, causal loop:

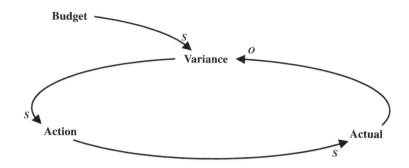

is that the definition of the variance is, in accordance with normal accounting convention:

$$\text{VARIANCE} = \text{BUDGET} - \text{ACTUAL}$$

Suppose, however, that we decide to define variance the other way around:

$$\text{VARIANCE} = \text{ACTUAL} - \text{BUDGET}$$

What does the causal loop diagram look like now? And, in particular, where are the Ss and the Os?

This is simply a matter of definition; nothing has changed in the real world. The basic structure of the loop must therefore be unchanged (Figure 6.16).

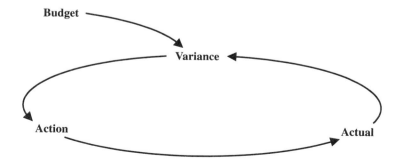

Figure 6.16

What has changed is the definition of the variance, which is now:

$$\text{VARIANCE} = \text{ACTUAL} - \text{BUDGET}$$

What does this do to the Ss and the Os?

If we look at the new definition, for any given BUDGET value, as the ACTUAL value *in*creases the VARIANCE *in*creases too, so that means that the ACTUAL and VARIANCE must be linked by an S. And for any given ACTUAL, as the BUDGET *in*creases the VARIANCE *de*creases—a direct consequence of that minus sign— so the BUDGET must be linked to the VARIANCE by an O.

That's it—the S and the O have flipped, that's the difference! So mustn't the causal loop look like Figure 6.17?

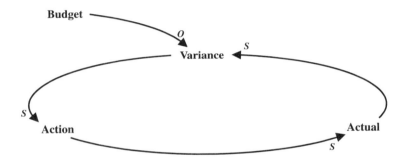

Figure 6.17

Most people leave it there, with a sigh of relief.

There's just one problem. Take a look at the loop and count the Os. And remember that the O linking BUDGET to VARIANCE should not be included in the count since it is outside the loop. In fact there are no Os in the loop of the last diagram; the loop is composed of Ss alone.

How does this loop behave? Because the number of Os in the loop is zero—an even number—it must be a reinforcing loop, characterized by expo-nential growth or decline. It is not a balancing loop at all.

Wait a moment though: Something can't be right. In reality, the loop was, and still is, a balancing loop, not a reinforcing loop. We can't have changed the real behavior of the system from a balancing loop to a reinforcing loop just as a result of changing an accounting definition. What has happened?

What has happened is that we haven't been thinking hard enough about

the Ss and the Os. Let's consider for a moment what is happening in reality
and make things concrete. Suppose that we're talking about headcount and
we find ourselves in a situation in which we have fewer staff (say, 10) than the
budget (say, 12) allows. In this case the variance, according to the new
definition:

$$\text{VARIANCE} = \text{ACTUAL} - \text{BUDGET}$$

is −2, a negative number.

What do we have to do to bring the actual back in line? We have to
increase the number of staff from 10 to 12; we have to make the ACTUAL bigger. The ACTION we have to take must therefore be a *positive* one, and so we
have a situation in which a negative VARIANCE is driving a positive ACTION.
These are in opposite directions and so the link between VARIANCE and
ACTION must therefore be an O. Completing the loop, the positive ACTION
causes, as required, an *increase* in the ACTUAL. This link is moving in the same
direction and so is, as before, an S.

Let's check this against reality. If our actual headcount is 10 and our budget is 12, the variance, according to the current definition, is 10 − 12 = −2.
This negative variance drives the positive action of hiring (the O), which in
turn has the desired effect of increasing the headcount (the S) so that the
actual becomes equal to the budget. The variance falls to zero and the system
stabilizes on the goal. That's all fine.

It works the other way too. Suppose that the actual headcount is 15 and the
budget is 12. The variance is now 15 − 12 = 3, a positive number. But since
the variance is linked to the action with an O, a *positive* variance drives a *negative* action. What is negative hiring? That has its own name: We call it firing,
a negative action indeed. This negative action serves to *decrease* the actual (in
accordance with the S) and the system converges once more on the budget.
The distinction between the positive action of hiring and the negative action
of firing is, of course, very similar to the coffee example, in which we distinguished between the positive action of pouring coffee into the cup and the
negative action of pouring the coffee out.

The causal loop diagram we now have is therefore as in Figure 6.18. How
does this loop behave? The loop contains a single O and so is, as expected, a
balancing loop, converging on the budget.

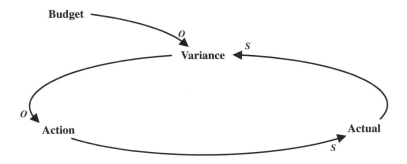

Figure 6.18

By changing the definition of variance from:

$$VARIANCE = BUDGET - ACTUAL$$

to:

$$VARIANCE = ACTUAL - BUDGET$$

we haven't changed reality, and so the structure of the two corresponding causal loop diagrams is necessarily the same. What has changed is the location of the Ss and the Os. The only one that is the same in both diagrams is the S linking ACTION to ACTUAL; all the other three have flipped from S to O or vice versa.

As we saw on page 63, it is all a question of language. Reality must be the same, however we choose to describe it, and if, for whatever reason, we choose different words, or in this case different arithmetical definitions, then this changes the Ss and the Os. Compiling causal loop diagrams therefore takes some care, but with a little practice you will soon feel very comfortable doing it. Some guidelines are given in the next chapter.

Time to reflect

The last two chapters have been demanding, but I trust you have found them worthwhile. Reinforcing loops and balancing loops are the two—and indeed the only two—fundamental building blocks of systems thinking, and on these two foundations everything else is built. Real systems are necessarily complex and the corresponding systems thinking diagrams—as you will see in the rest of this book—are also complex. However, this complexity can be tamed, since all systems thinking causal loop diagrams, no matter how complex, are built from two and only two building blocks: All real systems are networks of interconnected reinforcing and balancing loops. A deep understanding of these two fundamental loops is therefore enormously valuable in understanding the behavior of real, complex systems—from which wisdom springs...

Reinforcing and balancing loops — a summary

Many real systems are comprised of a large number of *interconnected elements* and exhibit very complex behavior as they evolve over time. A powerful method of capturing the interconnectedness of these elements, and of understanding their *dynamic complexity*, is by using *causal loop diagrams*. These show how the various elements in the system are connected by cause-and-effect relationships, the nature of each of which is depicted by the use of the symbols S and O. S implies that the elements connected by a specific cause-and-effect relationship move in the *same* direction (as customer satisfaction increases, sales revenue increases); an O implies that they move in *opposite* directions (as the workload increases, my ability to cope decreases).

Causal loop diagrams are comprised of a network of interconnecting *feedback loops*, associated with a (usually small) number of *dangles*, which represent the goals or outcomes of a system, or the external drivers of that system.

Single, closed feedback loops are of two and only two types. A *reinforcing* or *positive* feedback loop is characterized by having an even number of Os around the complete loop (with zero counting as an even number). We often recognize these loops as *virtuous* or *vicious circles*, for they exhibit *exponential growth* or *exponential decline*. The same cause-and-effect structure can behave in both ways—which behavior actually takes place in practice depends on how the feedback loop is initiated, and whether or not an actively spinning loop is subject to a sudden external shock.

A *balancing* or *negative* feedback loop is characterized by having an odd number of Os around the complete loop. These loops exhibit *goal-seeking* behavior, often toward an externally determined target or budget. Sometimes the approach to the goal is smooth, but if there are time delays associated with the feedback loop, they can exhibit overshoot and undershoot, causing the system to oscillate, possibly wildly.

7
How to draw causal loop diagrams

We have now looked at a host of causal loop diagrams, so the purpose of this chapter is to describe how to construct them. This is something of an art, since it is all about how to see the forest for the trees, how to know what level of detail to get into but also when to stop, how best to capture the essence of complex situations. Nonetheless, some useful guidelines do exist, so here are the 12 golden rules for drawing good causal loop diagrams.

Rule 1: Know your boundaries

One of the benefits of systems thinking is that it encourages a holistic view, taking everything of relevance into account. This could include literally everything, but that would be unhelpful; the trick is to stay relevant and to include everything of use, drawing the boundary there. It all depends on the system of interest so, referring back to the story of the elephant (see page 13), if the system of interest is an elephant, then we can draw our boundary around a single elephant; if our system is the study of elephants as social animals, the boundary is the herd; if the systems is the elephant as part of the ecosystem of central Africa, the boundary has to be the whole ecosystem.

The external boundaries of the system of interest are usually defined by the dangles, those elements of a causal loop diagram that determine targets, policies, goals, external drivers of a system, or outcomes. As an example, take another look at the central causal loop diagram of the back office case study, on page 36. This shows three dangles: the VOLUME AND VARIETY OF TRANS-ACTIONS as an external input driver; and the SERVICE QUALITY and COST as outcomes representing the results of the back office operation. If our objective is to understand the nature of the back office, then these dangles define the system boundary, because they specify what drives the back office system and what the system achieves.

If, however, our objective were different, it is likely that one or more of these dangles would be incorporated more fully, linked to their own consequences or driven by their own antecedents. A diagram representing the operation of the back office in the context of securities markets as a whole would identify the drivers of the VOLUME AND VARIETY OF TRANSACTIONS; SERVICE QUALITY would be embedded in the middle of a diagram looking at the overall interaction between the front and back offices; and COST would be an important central feature of a diagram looking at the bank's overall financial dynamics.

Why, then, does Figure 2.7 have these particular variables as dangles? Given that systems thinking encourages a holistic view, why shouldn't we trace the causality ever more richly?

You can if you want do, but as soon as you start doing this you might never stop. Everything is, quite literally, linked to everything else. The issue is one of pragmatism: Somewhere there is a boundary wide enough to incorporate the whole of the system of interest, without falling into the half elephant trap, but also without having to take into account the behavior of the entire cosmos.

So where is this boundary? There can be no general rules, because each system is different, but you know what they say about elephants: You may not be able to describe them, but you sure can recognize them when you see them! The same can be said of causal loop diagram boundaries: Once you've had some experience, you know when it feels right. Indeed, you can test this out on all the diagrams in this book. Do they feel right? Do they have a wide enough perspective, without getting bogged down in too much detail, or too much stuff genuinely extraneous to the system of interest?

Rule 2: Start somewhere interesting

Within the body of the diagram, everything is indeed connected to everything else, so, in principle, it doesn't matter where you start. If you trace the chain of causality, sooner or later you will cover the whole space. Although this is true, some places on the diagram are more "interesting" than others, and these are usually the places to start.

Here are some questions that you can ask to help determine a starting point:

➢ What are the key external drivers of the system?
➢ What are the key results of the system?
➢ What are the key items that relate to the problem we want to solve?

The first two questions will identify input and output dangles, such as POLICY OF COST CUTTING in the TV example and SERVICE QUALITY in the back office example. The third will throw the spotlight on matters such as the ABILITY TO COPE or the INCIDENCE OF ERROR, to take the back office example once more.

Once you have a few of these "interesting" items, you can start building the picture from there.

Rule 3:
Ask "What does this drive?" and "What is this driven by?"

The items within causal loop diagrams are all linked by chains of causality. Any two items—say, ABILITY TO COPE and SERVICE QUALITY—linked by an arrow are associated by a cause-and-effect relationship such that the item at the tail of the arrow (in this case, ABILITY TO COPE) is the driver of the item at the head of the arrow (SERVICE QUALITY); conversely, the item at the head (SERVICE QUALITY) is driven by the item at the tail (ABILITY TO COPE).

So if you have any one item, you can work forward around the diagram by asking "What does this drive?" (What does the ABILITY TO COPE drive or enable? SERVICE QUALITY, of course.) Likewise, you can work backward by asking "What is this driven by?" (What is it that drives SERVICE QUALITY? What about a concept like ABILITY TO COPE?)

Rule 4: Don't get cluttered

The problem you will inevitably face when you do this is that any one item might drive many others or be driven by many others; it is very rare for there to be a neat one-to-one relationship.

Suppose that you are looking at what drives the fundamental growth engine of your business and you are focusing in the first instance on PROFITS, a totally plausible starting point. Working backward, when you ask "What is this driven by?" you can cover pages and pages of flipcharts, as those who like using spreadsheets list the sales volumes and sales prices of every individual product in your catalog (analyzed by market, of course, if not by sales channel), only then to identify every single item of expenditure ever recorded in your general ledger.

I don't deny that the travel expenses to that master class on systems thinking did, eventually, affect profits; but they are not material. This is where you must exercise great restraint and resist all temptation to burrow deeper. Systems thinking looks "up" and "out," in contrast to the spreadsheet mentality that looks "down" and "in."

As another example, take the item SATISFIED CUSTOMER BASE. What drives this? This in fact is a good exercise to do in a small group. Ask this question and invite all the members of the group to write down their answer, in silence. Some people will write pages (from the quality of the products to the details of the competitors' advertising campaigns), others will write just a few bullet points, but let this be.

Then invite everyone to rank their own lists in order of importance, from the most powerful impact on the SATISFIED CUSTOMER BASE to the least.

You can now get these up on a flipchart—and stand back. You will probably find that there is no agreement at all, other than as you might expect from people's roles. Those in marketing tend to identify advertising, pricing, and promotions as the most important; those in new product development might choose product quality and innovation; those in production might go for product quality and technical specifications; those in HR might identify corporate culture and the training of the sales force; those in corporate strategy the activities of other companies in the industry and the company's overall competitive advantage.

Once again, I must agree that all of these—and a multitude of other factors too—do indeed affect the SATISFIED CUSTOMER BASE. What is happening here is not so much a proliferation of detail (as in the analysis of sales by product and channel) but a proliferation of mental models. Different people have genuinely and sincerely held different views on how the world works.

From the point of view of drawing clear causal loop diagrams, this diversity of mental models presents a very different problem from that of getting bogged down in general-ledger-style detail. In the general ledger case, a higher-level concept (such as TOTAL OVERHEAD) always embraces all the lower-level detail (such as the COST OF PREMISES, UTILITIES, and LOCAL TAXES), but in selecting what to include—or rather, exclude—from a list of alternative mental models, there is the danger that something really important might be omitted.

If you play safe and capture them all, you are likely to end up with a highly cluttered diagram in which everything really is connected to everything else, largely because everything is included! The forest gets lost in the trees and no one gets any benefit. However, if you select, say, ADVERTISING and ignore the CAPACITY TO INNOVATE, you might be discarding the most significant element.

Pragmatism demands that you are selective, but the process of selection raises the specter of inadvertently cutting your elephant in half.

So how do you decide what to include and what to exclude?

Once again, I won't give any general rules on the detail but a guideline on the process. Do this exercise as a small group (say, up to eight people) in one or more workshops, and work hard to build consensus on what makes most sense. That is exactly the process I used to compile the diagrams in this book. They did not just happen, they are the results of sometimes several weeks of observation, conversation, discussion, workshops, and testing things out. What I haven't shown here are the sacks full of diagrams I discarded, diagrams that were wrong, that people didn't recognize as reality, that missed the point, that were too cluttered, that were too high level, that just didn't feel right.

There is no doubt that the single most-used aid to systems thinking is the wastepaper basket, where all those diagrams that don't work end up.

So don't get cluttered. Don't fall into the analysis trap of burrowing down to ever deeper levels of detail. When the issue is one of different mental models, work in small groups to get a consensus view. And always check the result not only with the workshop group, but also with other interested people.

Rule 5: Use nouns, not verbs

If you look at all the causal loop diagrams in this book, you will find that *every* item is a noun or a noun phrase, rather than a verb or a verb phrase. So we have SERVICE QUALITY not DELIVER SERVICE QUALITY; ABILITY TO COPE not ENSURE WE CAN COPE; POLICY OF COST CUTTING not CUT COSTS. This is usually quite natural, with one major temptation, in the ACTION slot of balancing loops (Figure 7.1).

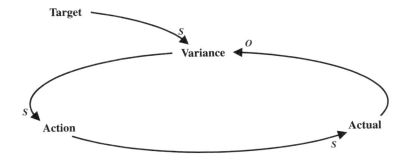

Figure 7.1

There is often a tendency to express the appropriate action as a verb (hire or fire) rather than as a noun equivalent (hiring or firing). If you can keep to nouns, even here, so emphasizing the action itself, you will find that your causal loop diagrams are clearer.

Rule 6:
Don't use terms such as "increase in" or "decrease in"

When drawing causal loop diagrams you will inevitably be tempted to include these two phrases in your descriptions. For example, in the causal loop diagram for the back office, you might consider the causality to be a link from the ABILITY TO COPE to, for example, an INCREASE IN THE ERROR RATE (with an O) or a DECREASE IN THE ERROR RATE (with an S).

However strong the temptation, resist it. That's what the arrows are for, especially the Ss and the Os. The causality is that the ABILITY TO COPE directly drives the INCIDENCE OF ERROR; whether this is increasing or decreasing depends on whether the ABILITY TO COPE is increasing or decreasing, and on the strength of the interaction. To use the phrase "increase in" within the description presupposes that the cause-and-effect relationship is always one of an increase, the question being a matter of degree as to whether this increase is modest or severe. The possibility that there might be a decrease is much less apparent and might inadvertently be overlooked.

If you do feel that "increase in" and "decrease in" are the most natural descriptions of a particular situation, try three alternatives. One is the complete phrase "increase or decrease in" itself; a second is "pressure on"; and the third, and arguably the simplest, is "change in." The benefit of these is that they do not presuppose directionality and so explicitly allow for both increases and decreases. In fact, there is one particular situation in which "change in" is usually the most natural description. This arises in balancing loops of the type in Figure 7.2.

If this loop is being used to describe, say, the policy on staff establishment, the target might be TARGET STAFF ESTABLISHMENT; the actual, ACTUAL STAFF ESTABLISHMENT; and the variance, STAFF VARIANCE. The ACTION would describe the action most appropriate to these circumstances, usually the actions of HIRING OR FIRING, where the inclusion of both hiring and firing recognizes that the action might be in either direction.

If, however, this loop is being used to describe pricing policy, we would naturally write TARGET PRICE, ACTUAL PRICE, and PRICE VARIANCE (or maybe

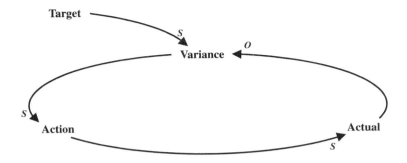

Figure 7.2

PRICE GAP), but what words would we use for the ACTION we would take to bring the ACTUAL price back into line with the TARGET price? To me, the most natural words here are CHANGE IN PRICE, or INCREASE OR DECREASE IN PRICE.

Why is this? As we saw on page 110, the explanation lies in the language: Whereas we do have words in English for "increase in staff establishment" (hiring) and "decrease in staff establishment" (firing), we don't have a single word specifically to represent the action associated with "increase in price" or "decrease in price." You might be thinking, "What about inflation or deflation, isn't that a word for the increase or decrease in price?" It is, but these terms tend to be used for changes in the overall macroeconomic price level. The business people I talk to don't use these words in relation to their own products and services, they say "change in price."

So the phrase CHANGE IN [WHATEVER] will sometimes be seen in the ACTION slot in a balancing loop, but if more specific words exist these will be preferable.

Rule 7: Don't be afraid of unusual items

Causal loop diagrams aren't accounting spreadsheets. I agree that you would not expect to find items such as the ABILITY TO COPE in the budget pack, but, although we rarely talk about such things, they are there, they do drive behavior, and they are important. One of the great benefits of systems thinking is that it legitimizes the discussion of topics that might otherwise be taboo.

You will also find that causal loop diagrams often contain phrases such as POLICY ON [WHATEVER], especially as a dangle, and PRESSURE ON [WHATEVER] to express various types of interaction and influence. These are particularly helpful in capturing complex concepts, as is a phrase such as the EFFECT OF

[WHATEVER] ON ATTRACTING AND RETAINING CUSTOMERS. In the case of advertising, for example, we all know that this effect is there, but few companies measure it. Likewise, one of the reasons that companies like to have well-trained staff is because they recognize the existence of the EFFECT OF HAVING GOOD STAFF ON ATTRACTING AND RETAINING CUSTOMERS. Very few companies measure that one either, yet it is very real, as anyone who has been at the wrong end of surly service knows all too well. In causal loop diagrams it is reality that counts, rather than our ability to measure. So if it's real, capture it.

Rule 8: Do the *S*s and the *O*s as you go along

The Ss and the Os are often hard to think about (look again at pages 121–5 if you need a reminder), because the seemingly simple question "Does 'this' increase as 'that' increases (implying an S) or not (an O)?" requires very clear thinking to answer. There is therefore a very strong tendency to think "I'll leave all that until I've finished." Don't. Do it as you go along.

There are two reasons for this. The first is that the question is itself a diagnostic of the diagram, for one of the reasons that the question is often difficult to answer is because one of the items being linked is wrong or poorly expressed, or maybe both are. As the diagram becomes progressively more perceptive, the S/O dilemma often just evaporates.

The second reason is that as you draw the diagram, complete with Ss and Os, this actual process helps you understand the structure and the underlying rationale and dynamic of what is happening in reality. Reinforcing loops are fundamentally different from balancing loops and these should make intuitive sense. But if you haven't captured the Ss and the Os as you go along, you can't identify which loops are which, so it all becomes a progressively more complex mess.

Rule 9: Keep going

When you start a systems thinking exercise you are usually full of confidence: "Of course I can do it, it's easy, isn't it?" You run a few workshops, learn a lot about the topic of interest, and start drawing. And then you get really stuck in and the shock hits. Your diagram is becoming more and more of a mess and you haven't got the remotest idea what is going on.

This happens on every systems thinking exercise, because it isn't easy.

Managing a real business is complex and so capturing the essence of all or part of this is necessarily complex too.

The complexity can be tamed, but only with diligence. Don't give up. Keep going. See what happens if you ignore much of the detail; see if you can identify a higher-level concept that embraces all the lower-level stuff. Remember that your most valuable tool is the wastepaper basket, and you will fill many of these before you get any diagrams that work. It's very easy to be misled by the diagrams in this book, all of which, I trust, make sense. However, don't be deluded by the "ones I prepared earlier." Many of these took weeks of effort and I can remember all the diagrams I drew that aren't in this book but ended up in the trash.

Rule 10: A good diagram must be recognized as real

Causal loop diagrams must represent the reality as perceived by the community who "own" the system of interest; it must reflect their mental models. Whenever you have a diagram that you think is heading in the right direction, check it with the team and see which bits correspond to reality, and which bits don't. Be alert to people using phrases such as "Mmm, I see what you mean, but I don't see it that way," because it may be that the diagram is not yet complete, or that it reflects your mental models rather than theirs. However, it may be that some people see the world one way and others another, so there will not be one causal loop diagram but maybe two or even three, corresponding to different sets of mental models held by different individuals or groups.

If you find yourself in this situation, work on two, three, or four diagrams in parallel, to capture the reality as perceived by each community. Then, when each diagram has been validated by the appropriate people, run a workshop at which members of each community present their diagrams to the other communities. The theme of this workshop is: "Are we living in the same world or in different worlds?" Let the communities present their own versions of the world as they view it and see what happens. There will be a great deal of discussion and debate, and you will hear people say things like "Really? I've never thought of things like that" and "But I see things this way..."

Ideally, after however long it takes, you will end up with a single, unified diagram that captures different elements of its various predecessors. And even more ideally, you will end up with a situation in which the workshop participants say, "At last, now I understand what you've been talking about! Isn't it great that we are all looking at the world the same way?" The mental models are now being shared.

If this ideal is not reached and no unified view results, at least the participants will know much more specifically where the differences are and why they exist. That will give everybody quite a lot to think about.

Rule 11: Don't fall in love with your diagrams

A well-drawn diagram, with a neat layout, tidy arrows, and a pleasing overall shape, is an immensely powerful means of communication and has much more impact than a scruffy scribble with the arrows all over the place and untidy marks where errors and rethinks have obviously been rubbed out. My regret with the diagrams in this book is that the printing process obliged me to be restricted to the use of black and white, so depriving the diagrams of the power of using different colors to distinguish key features (such as policies, or the main loop).

The care required to produce a good diagram, however, implies that it begins to assume, in the eyes of the originator at any rate, the status of great art. And because it is a work of art, the artist naturally has a profound reluctance to change it. So when someone says "What about...?" there is a very strong tendency to reply "I see what you mean, but..."

What is happening here is a tussle in your mind: The intellectual problem solver is thinking "Yes, that's a good point," while the tired artist is saying "I was up half of last night finishing that ******** diagram, and I'm blowed if I'm going to change it now!"

Nevertheless, change it you must. You wouldn't believe how many times I redrew the diagrams in this book; you really wouldn't.

Rule 12: No diagram is ever "finished"

In many ways this is the single most important rule: No causal loop diagram is ever finished. Not even the ones in this book. I'm sure you have spotted some improvements or enhancements, so do email me accordingly at dennis@silverbulletmachine.com!

The real world is complex, and any diagram, however insightful, will always emphasize some things and ignore others. But the world changes and what might have been less important a while ago might become more important later. Expect the diagrams to change. Like the world, causal loop diagrams are living things.

The 12 golden rules of drawing causal loop diagrams

Rule 1   Know your boundaries

Rule 2   Start somewhere interesting

Rule 3   Ask "What does this drive?" and "What is this driven by?"

Rule 4   Don't get cluttered

Rule 5   Use nouns, not verbs

Rule 6   Don't use terms such as "increase in" or "decrease in"

Rule 7   Don't be afraid of unusual items

Rule 8   Do the Ss and Os as you go along

Rule 9   Keep going

Rule 10   A good diagram must be recognized as real

Rule 11   Don't fall in love with your diagrams

Rule 12   No diagram is ever "finished"

Part III
Applications

In which we explore how the fundamental building blocks of systems thinking—the reinforcing loop and the balancing loop—combine to form insightful descriptions of some real systems.

"How can we grow our business?" is the key question of Chapter 8. In principle, every business contains a reinforcing loop as its engine of growth and so this should grow the business exponentially for ever; in practice, as we all know, this just doesn't happen. Why not? Because every reinforcing loop is surrounded by at least several balancing loops that, sooner or later, stop growth. Under these circumstances, is it wiser to "pedal harder" and fuel the reinforcing loop, or to "take the brakes off" by relieving the constraints of the balancing loops?

Chapter 9 examines two specific business problems and shows how systems thinking can be enormously helpful in determining wise policies. One problem is a development of the television story we saw in Chapter 3; the other concerns what happens when an organization outsources a mission-critical activity.

The most important policies, of course, relate to business strategy and this forms the subject of Chapter 10. Here we shall see how systems thinking can be a very powerful tool in taming the complexity of a situation every business faces, how to take the best possible decisions under conditions of uncertainty.

The final chapter of this part paints an even bigger picture. One of the greatest threats to humanity today is global warming, and Chapter 11 presents a systems thinking explanation, one that bears an uncanny resemblance to the systems thinking description of business strategy!

8
Stimulating growth

Chapters 5 and 6 examined in detail the two fundamental building blocks of systems thinking, the reinforcing loop and the balancing loop. In practice, it is very rare to find systems that can be described completely by only a single loop. Most real systems are best described in terms of networks of interacting, interconnected loops, some of which will be reinforcing loops, others balancing loops.

The purpose of this chapter is therefore to continue the exploration of what happens when the fundamental loops are linked together, following on from our discussion toward the end of Chapter 5. From a business perspective, the overall theme of this chapter is about growth. All businesses strive to grow, but as we all know it's not so easy.

In real life, exponential growth does not go on for ever

Let's return to one of the causal loops we explored in Chapter 5 (see page 75), the one describing the engine of business growth (Figure 8.1).

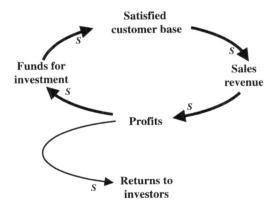

Figure 8.1

I have incorporated an additional feature, RETURNS TO INVESTORS, an output dangle representing the overall objective of the business.

Every business has a growth engine of this general form and, as we now know, the behavior of this loop is exponential growth or decline, without limit, for ever. Sadly real life isn't like that, but the conclusion is not that the loop does not show exponential growth; rather, it is that the loop, as drawn, is not yet a suitable representation of the real world. There are events happening in the real world that are not yet captured in the diagram.

One such event is market saturation, the fact that all markets are necessarily finite. One way of capturing this is to introduce two new items: TOTAL MARKET SIZE and MARKET SHARE (Figure 8.2).

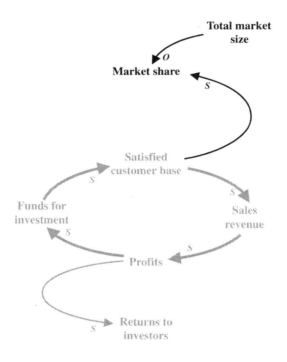

Figure 8.2

As the SATISFIED CUSTOMER BASE increases so does the MARKET SHARE, hence the S. But for any given SATISFIED CUSTOMER BASE, the larger the TOTAL MARKET SIZE the smaller the MARKET SHARE, hence the O.

Ss, Os, and arithmetic

Some of the relationships captured in causal loop diagrams are conceptual, for example the belief that as the back office WORKLOAD increases, the departmental ABILITY TO COPE is diminished. Other relationships are much more tangible, since they represent definitions or arithmetic relationships. We have already met one example, the definition of variance:

$$\text{VARIANCE} = \text{BUDGET} - \text{ACTUAL}$$

Market share is another, defined (in the current circumstances) as:

$$\text{MARKET SHARE} = \text{SATISFIED CUSTOMER BASE} / \text{TOTAL MARKET SIZE}$$

Whenever items are mutually related by arithmetic expressions of this type, it is very easy to determine which are the Ss and which are the Os.

In general, in a causal loop diagram the item on the left-hand side of the expression will be linked, separately and individually, to all the items on the right-hand side of the expression by arrows that point from each right-hand side item to the left-hand side item. If the right-hand side item has a plus sign (such as BUDGET in the expression for VARIANCE), or is the numerator (upper part) of a ratio (such as SATISFIED CUSTOMER BASE in the expression for MARKET SHARE) the link is an S; if the right-hand side item has a minus sign (such as ACTUAL in the expression for VARIANCE), or is the denominator (lower part) of a ratio (such as TOTAL MARKET SIZE in the expression for MARKET SHARE), then the link is an O.

A normal feature of most businesses, however, is that as the MARKET SHARE increases, it becomes progressively more difficult to attract new customers. This means that there is another link to introduce, linking the MARKET SHARE to the SATISFIED CUSTOMER BASE, with an O (Figure 8.3 overleaf).

We now have a structure of two interconnected feedback loops, with one input dangle and one output dangle. The lower loop is a reinforcing loop and strives to grow exponentially; the upper loop is a balancing loop that seeks the goal of the TOTAL MARKET SIZE.

What happens as the two loops operate together? At first, when the SATISFIED CUSTOMER BASE is small and nowhere near the TOTAL MARKET SIZE, the balancing loop has no effect and the reinforcing loop spins away, growing the SATISFIED CUSTOMER BASE exponentially. But as the MARKET SHARE gets steadily larger, so that the SATISFIED CUSTOMER BASE approaches the TOTAL MARKET SIZE, it

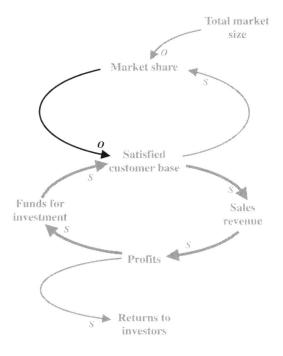

Figure 8.3

becomes progressively harder to attract new customers and so growth slows down.
The balancing loop is kicking in, braking the growth of the reinforcing loop and
applying the brakes progressively harder, until growth stops, at which point the
SATISFIED CUSTOMER BASE limits at the TOTAL MARKET SIZE (Figure 8.4).

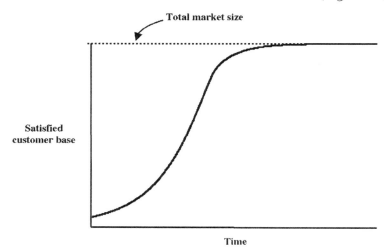

Figure 8.4

Limits to growth

The causal loop structure shown in Figure 8.3 — a reinforcing loop connected to a balancing loop — is a very common feature of many more complex diagrams.

As this example shows, and as we saw on page 98, the effect of the balancing loop is to arrest the growth of the reinforcing loop, and so this structure is known as *limits to growth*.

If the balancing loop has a target dangle, as in Figure 8.3, the reinforcing loop grows to the limit specified by the dangle, as we have just seen.

If there is no explicit goal-seeking dangle, the effect of the balancing loop is to act as a brake on the spinning of the reinforcing loop, and the behavior of the system over time will vary depending on just how the brakes are applied, for example whether or not the braking is smooth, and whether or not the intensity of the braking varies over time. This can give rise to a great range of dynamic behaviors, according to whether or not the reinforcing loop is winning over the balancing loop at any instant:

➤ If the braking is sudden and powerful, the action of the balancing loop might be to flip the reinforcing loop from exponential growth into exponential decline.

➤ If the braking is constant and relatively gentle, the system can show continuous growth, but at a rate less than would have happened in the absence of the braking effect of the balancing loop.

➤ If the braking becomes progressively stronger over time, the system will grow exponentially at first, then more slowly, and may then stabilize.

➤ If the braking varies over time, the system will grow sometimes, be stable sometimes, and decline at other times.

The limits to growth structure is one of several *archetypes*, commonly recurring structures composed of a small number of loops.

Growth to a limit is much more realistic behavior of a real business than is unconstrained exponential growth for ever, but there are many other factors beyond the total market size that might limit growth. For example, very few businesses can achieve 100 percent market share. Most countries have antimonopolist regulators who intervene to stop any one player having too big a slice of the total cake (Figures 8.5 and 8.6 overleaf). And there are always competitors or new entrants fighting you in the never-ending battle for customers (Figure 8.7 on page 145).

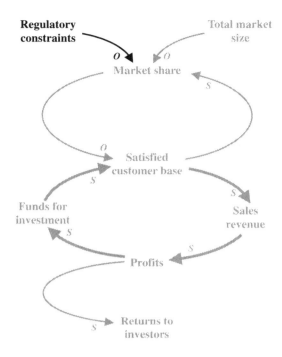

Figure 8.5

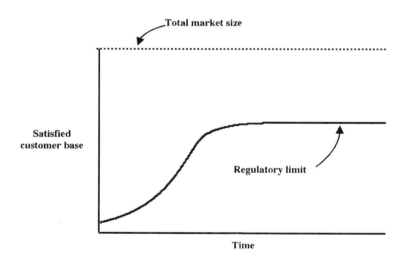

Figure 8.6

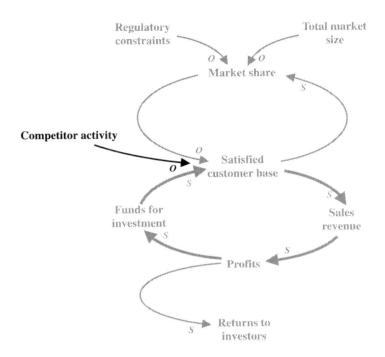

Figure 8.7

The three constraints discussed so far—the total size of the market, a regulator, the competition—are external. Every business, however, soon discovers that there are some other constraints that kick in way before the external ones stop the business from growing (Figure 8.8 overleaf).

These two new features capture a multitude of situations. As the business grows, as reflected by the increase in MARKET SHARE, the INTERNAL SIZE AND SCALE of the business increase and, as a result, the business becomes progressively difficult to manage. Any number of OPERATIONAL INEFFICIENCIES arise: systems become cumbersome, internal communications break down, someone decides to build a plush new head office. The cost of this inefficiency drives down PROFITS and limits growth: Do you see the balancing loop linking MARKET SHARE, INTERNAL SIZE AND SCALE, OPERATIONAL INEFFICIENCIES, PROFITS, FUNDS FOR INVESTMENT, SATISFIED CUSTOMER BASE, and back to MARKET SHARE?

But this is nowhere near the whole story. Some of the OPERATIONAL INEFFICIENCIES—a major failure in the supply chain, for example—might prevent the delivery of goods to a retail outlet, so depressing SALES REVENUE, as well as reducing PROFITS by virtue of the extra costs. And the resulting bad

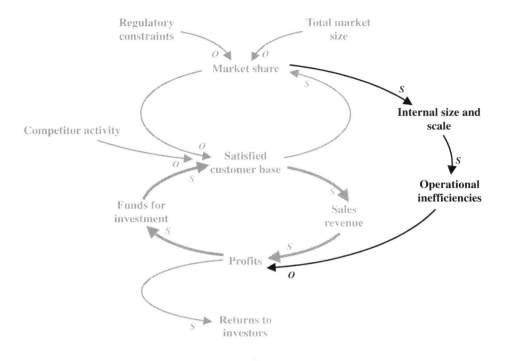

Figure 8.8

customer service might have an adverse impact on the formerly SATISFIED CUS-TOMER BASE. A more complete diagram is therefore as in Figure 8.9.

This diagram shows three internal balancing loops, all acting independently but together, which, individually and collectively, put the brakes on growth. If any one of these internal balancing loops comes to dominate the reinforcing loop, then growth is being limited by self-inflicted wounds, rather than by external forces. And if any one of these constraints kicks in particularly harshly—that major failure in the supply chain, maybe—then that might cause the reinforcing loop to flip from constrained exponential growth into free-fall exponential decline. Things are indeed becoming more realistic.

Breaking through the constraints

Figure 8.9 is not simple—but then neither is growing a business. Nevertheless, now you know how to look at causal loop diagrams, that complexity is becoming tamed.

The diagram is comprised of five interconnected closed feedback loops,

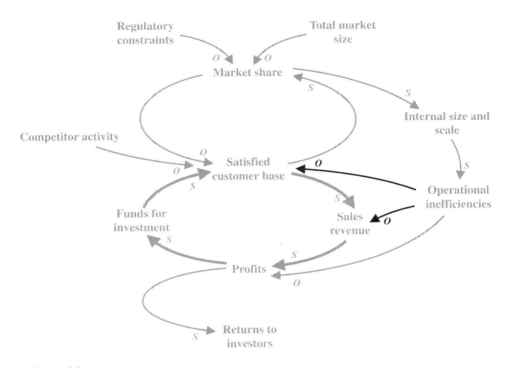

Figure 8.9

with four external dangles. And of these five feedback loops, one is a reinforcing loop and all the other four are balancing loops.

The sole, lonely reinforcing loop is the one linking SATISFIED CUSTOMER BASE,
SALES REVENUE, PROFITS, and FUNDS FOR INVESTMENT—the loop that drives the
engine of business growth. Once the loop starts spinning as a growth loop—usually by the initial injection of capital to kick-start the FUNDS FOR INVESTMENT—
then, in principle, the loop should spin away exponentially, for ever.

The reason that in practice it doesn't is as a result of the braking effects of
all those balancing loops, some of which are external, some internal. The diagram shows these loops generically; in day-to-day business terms, we experience them as individual problems to solve, actions on our already overflowing
to-do lists. Maybe it is recruiting more staff for the call center to improve service levels, maybe it is finalizing the negotiations for the new premises to
allow for expansion of factory capacity—all of these are examples of actions
being taken to relieve constraints to enable growth. And there aren't just three
internal balancing loops constraining growth, there are hundreds. But there
is, in general, only that one reinforcing loop, struggling to break free.

Not all of these balancing loops are actively acting as constraints simultaneously; rather, they usually kick in one after the other, and as soon as you have relieved one you come up against the next. Management is a continuing stoking of the fire of the business-driving reinforcing loop, while struggling to break through successive layers of constraint, giving—if you get it right—a growth path like that in Figure 8.10.

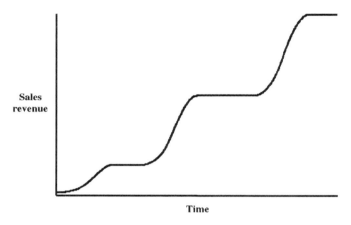

Figure 8.10

In this example, periods of growth are interrupted by periods of stability as successive constraints bite, but are eventually overcome. Fortunately, this business has been able to maintain stability between the bursts of growth. Most have a bumpier ride, as in Figure 8.11.

This, probably more common, example shows periods of growth, during which the reinforcing loop is dominant, interspersed with periods of decline, as different balancing loops not only arrest the growth but begin to flip the reinforcing loop from virtuous to vicious. While this is going on, managers battle against the constraints, but are able to relieve them before the business goes bust. The general trend is growth, although it's a struggle.

How well do you manage the constraints?

What are the three most important constraints limiting the growth of your business today?

What are you doing to alleviate them?

Once these are alleviated, what are the next three, lurking as yet unnoticed but just waiting to bite?

What are you doing now to stop that from happening?

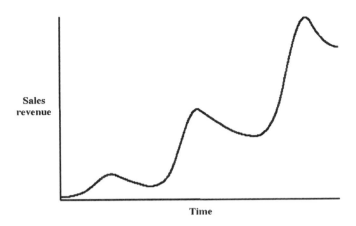

Figure 8.11

Wise managers see the constraints coming before they bite and have implemented policies to break through them. Their to-do lists are not overflowing, because they know the importance of directing their energies at just the right problems to solve. And, faced with the realities of constrained growth, they know when to fuel the fire of the fundamental, driving, reinforcing loop and when to turn their attention to relieving the constraints.

Eliyahu Goldratt

Eliyahu Goldratt is the author of the bestselling business book *The Goal*, written — unlike almost every other business book — not as a list of bullet points but as a novel, telling a story. The story is set in a manufacturing company and relates the day-to-day problems of managing the business. The moral of the story, however, is all about paying attention to bottlenecks and constraints. If you can identify and manage these, and then relieve them, the rest can, in essence, look after itself.

Over recent years Goldratt has further developed his Theory of Constraints and has published three more books: *It's Not Luck*, *Critical Chain*, and *Necessary but not Sufficient*.

The growth of urban populations

The context

Businesses are not the only things that grow: Individual organisms grow; populations grow; cities grow; nations grow, civilizations grow. However, none of these grows continuously, without limit. Sooner or later, growth ceases and the individual, the population, the city, the nation, or the civilization either stabilizes or starts to decline. So let's turn our attention away from business for a moment. Let's look at a much bigger picture: the growth of cities and the causes of the industrial revolution. As we shall see, this story also contains an important message for business.

Quiz time: What fueled the industrial revolution?

The industrial revolution, which began in Great Britain in the mid-1700s, transformed the world, shifting the global economy irreversibly from one based on agriculture to one based on manufactured goods and trading. What do you think fueled the industrial revolution?

Those with a literal frame of mind will answer "coal." In the coal-fueled steam engine, humankind discovered a controllable source of power liberating them from reliance on their own muscles, or those of pack animals. Those who think more expansively might answer "the enlightenment," the cultural shift in politics and the structure of society liberating people from the oppression of rapacious kings and despots. Systems thinkers, however, might answer "tea."

Tea? How on earth could the industrial revolution have been fueled by tea? That's nuts!

I agree that it's surprising and I don't deny that coal and the enlightenment—and a host of other things too—played their part. However, tea contributed more than you might think, so let me tell the story.

The dynamics of population growth

My starting point is to examine how populations in general, and urban populations in particular, grow. This of course is all about BIRTHS (see Figure 8.12).

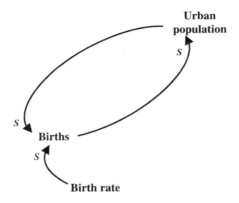

Figure 8.12

In general, the larger the URBAN POPULATION, the larger the number of BIRTHS; and the larger the number of BIRTHS, the larger the URBAN POPULATION. There are some time delays in there, to allow for children to reach maturity, but I haven't explicitly shown these to avoid cluttering the diagram. This is a familiar reinforcing loop, which will show exponential growth, the rate of growth being determined primarily by the BIRTH RATE, a statistic specifying, at any given time, the number of births per thousand in the population. There is in fact another factor influencing the size of the population, the average life span: As people live longer the population grows, independently of the number of births. For simplicity, I am ignoring this effect.

Another example of a one-way link

It is worth pausing for a moment to think about the Ss in this causal loop diagram. As the BIRTH RATE increases the number of BIRTHS increases too, so that's an S; as the number of BIRTHS increases the URBAN POPULATION increases, so that's an S too; as the URBAN POPULATION increases there are more adults, and so the number of BIRTHS increases, so that's the third S. That all makes sense.

However, what happens as we try the reversibility test? As the BIRTH RATE decreases the number of BIRTHS goes down, implying that these two items move in the same direction, confirming the S. Likewise, as the URBAN POPULATION decreases there are fewer adults, and we would expect the number of BIRTHS to go down too — once again, these items are moving in the same direction, confirming the S here as well.

However, as the number of BIRTHS goes down, the URBAN POPULATION doesn't. What happens is that the URBAN POPULATION continues to grow, but rather more slowly. We therefore have a situation in which the number of BIRTHS is *decreasing* but the URBAN POPULATION is continuing to *increase*, albeit more slowly, suggesting that this link is an O not an S.

In fact this link is indeed an S, for this is another example like the one we examined on page 66 in which a particular link on a causal loop diagram only works in one direction. There the context was pouring coffee into a cup, and the explanation was based on the fact that this is fundamentally a unidirectional process — the action of pouring coffee into the cup can only result in the cup become more filled, never less so. The explanation here is the same: Births are inherently unidirectional and can only increase the urban population. The real world works in one direction only, and so does the corresponding causal loop diagram. Such one-way links arise from time to time and the conditions under which they do so are described on page 289.

Populations, however, do not grow without limit, so there are some more factors to take into account. The most important of these is the number of DEATHS (Figure 8.13).

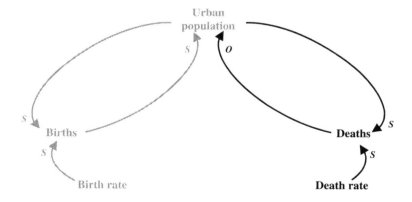

Figure 8.13

The greater the URBAN POPULATION, the greater the number of DEATHS; but since the number of DEATHS acts to deplete the URBAN POPULATION, this loop feeds back with an O.

> **Quiz time: How does this structure behave?**
> Figure 8.13 has a reinforcing loop, driving growth in the URBAN POPULATION by means
> of BIRTHS, interconnected with a balancing loop, depleting the URBAN POPULATION as
> a result of DEATHS.
>
> In what respects is this overall system structurally similar to the business growth system
> shown on page 142? In what respects is it different? What is the overall dynamic behavior
> of this system?

If you compare Figure 8.13 with Figure 8.3 on page 142 depicting how a business grows, you will find an important similarity: Both have the structure of a single reinforcing loop interacting with a single balancing loop. As we have seen, the action of the balancing loop is to put the brakes on the spinning of the reinforcing loop.

However, there is also an important difference. The business growth loop has one output dangle—RETURNS TO INVESTORS—which is the overall objective of the system, and one input dangle—TOTAL MARKET SIZE—the effect of which is to constrain the business growth loop to a limit, the limit (in that case) of the total market.

The diagram of population growth does not have any output dangles, since the population system does not have a purpose in the same sense that a business does. The population system, nevertheless, does have two input dangles—BIRTH RATE and DEATH RATE—but their action is different from the action of the input dangle TOTAL MARKET SIZE in the business growth example.

In the business growth example, TOTAL MARKET SIZE represents a physical capacity that the system cannot exceed, so acting as a target dangle, allowing the business system to reach this limit but go no further. In the population system, the BIRTH RATE and DEATH RATE do not represent physical capacities that cannot be exceeded; rather, they specify how strongly the reinforcing loop is spinning (the higher the BIRTH RATE, the faster the URBAN POPULATION is growing) and, simultaneously, how hard the balancing loop is putting the brakes on (the higher the DEATH RATE, the faster the URBAN POPULATION is being depleted). These dangles are therefore not target dangles, they are rate dangles, which as we saw on page 80 specify the rates at which loops are operating.

The dynamic behavior of the population system as depicted so far therefore does not show growth to any particular limit, because no limit is as yet implied. Rather, as discussed on page 143, this population system (assuming constant life spans) can show a wide variety of dynamic behaviors depending on the specific values attributed to the birth rate and the death rate at any time. For example:

> If over a period of time the birth rate is always equal to the death rate, the population will stay stable.
> If over a period of time the birth rate exceeds the death rate by a constant amount, the population will grow exponentially, the overall rate of growth being determined by the difference between the birth rate and the death rate.
> If over a period of time the death rate exceeds the birth rate by a constant amount, the population will decline exponentially, the overall rate of decline being determined once again by the difference between the two rates.
> If over a period of time the birth and death rates vary independently, the population at any time will be stable, growing or declining according to the specific circumstances, and a graph of the population over time will be an arbitrary-looking wavy line.

This is another example of a phenomenon that we have already seen several times: A very simple basic structure can show very complex patterns of dynamic behavior.

Figure 8.13, of course, underpins the story of the frogs and the lily-pad (see page 83). For many years the lily-pad population had been stable and the lily-pad remained at a constant size at the far end of the pond. Then some chemicals polluted the pond and triggered an increase in the "birth rate," but without affecting the "death rate." This caused the lily-pad to exhibit exponential growth, doubling in size every 24 hours.

Driving economic prosperity

Since urban populations are not tied to the land, they find other things to do with their time. They make things, they trade things, they engage in economic activity, they create ECONOMIC PROSPERITY. The generation of wealth is attractive. As it says in the story of Dick Whittington, who served as Lord Mayor of London on three occasions around 1400, "the streets of London are paved with gold." This, of course, is a magnet to country lads like Dick Whittington who want to make their fortune and take their share of the SURPLUS WEALTH.

Economic prosperity drives migration into cities, which in turn increases the urban population (Figure 8.14).

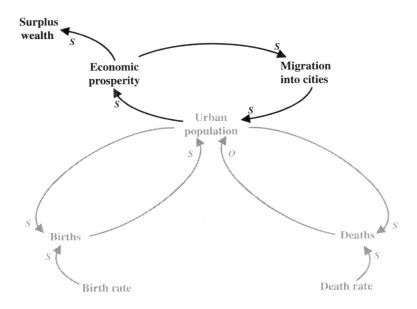

Figure 8.14

This introduces a second reinforcing loop, also driving up the urban population.

Urban growth doesn't go on for ever

As cities grow two other important things happen. First, the increasing urban population puts a progressive strain on local agricultural resources, until such time as there are too many mouths to feed. As the increasing need for food begins to exceed the food available, this increases the likelihood of famine, and once a famine strikes this not only causes an increase in the death rate but also diminishes the birth rate. The adult population is cut back hard from two directions as deaths increase and births decrease and, after a while, stability is restored, a stability in line with the available agricultural capacity (Figure 8.15 overleaf).

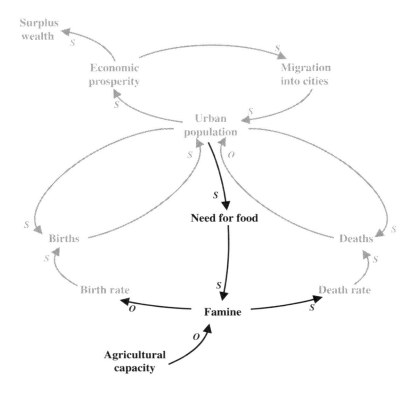

Figure 8.15

Structurally, this enhanced diagram consists of two interconnected reinforcing loops—one driven by BIRTHS, the other by ECONOMIC PROSPERITY—linked to three balancing loops—the original one driven by DEATHS and two new ones: one from the URBAN POPULATION, through the NEED FOR FOOD and FAMINE and back through the DEATH RATE; the other back through the BIRTH RATE. As a count of the Os quickly demonstrates, these are indeed balancing loops.

These three balancing loops collectively limit the growth of the two reinforcing loops, the limit now being determined by a new dangle, the local AGRICULTURAL CAPACITY. This is a capacity that the system cannot exceed and so it acts as a target dangle, defining the ultimate constraint on growth. This system cannot grow indefinitely, it must be constrained by the AGRICULTURAL CAPACITY.

However, there is one more feature we need to add, since there is a second important result of a growing URBAN POPULATION: OVERCROWDING and the associated DISEASE, contagious diseases such as measles and influenza, and diseases of pollution such as typhus and plague. And disease kills (Figure 8.16).

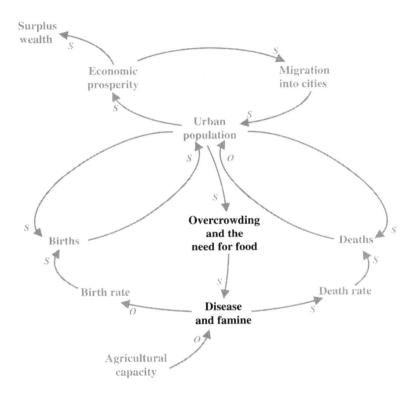

Figure 8.16

The growth of urban societies in western Europe was driven by this system for centuries. Cities would grow to a certain size and then either famine or disease (and sometimes also war) would cut back the adult population. Only if circumstances were to become favorable once more would growth start anew. Population growth was stimulated as agricultural productivity grew in the earlier 1700s and, in some fortunate places in western Europe, famine became less of a constraint. But disease would not go away.

Quiz time: How do you grow this business?

Suppose for the moment that it is 1750 and you happen to be the monarch of a small state in Europe. Times are good: Your lands are fertile, your cities are bustling, your subjects are content. As a hereditary monarch you have an eye to the long term, and as the 34-year-old parent of three healthy young heirs you have no anxieties about the succession.

You wish to implement some policies to grow the economic prosperity of your state and, as a benevolent but absolute monarch, you have the power to do what you want, although you wish to act with wisdom.

Do you:

A   Find a pretext to wage war with a neighboring state?
B   Invite that new-fangled economist, Adam Smith, to leave the cold of Glasgow and settle in your much warmer capital to try his theories out for real?
C   As the role model in society, initiate a fashion for drinking tea every morning and in the middle of the afternoon?
D   Introduce a totally new concept, the child benefit allowance, an "inverse tax" under which the state pays its subjects if they have children?

What would you do?

The wise monarch thought long and hard and, after due consultation with many distinguished advisers, announced option D, the new "inverse tax." Archivists have discovered a memorandum written shortly after the decision was made, recording the monarch's thinking:

Option A, to wage war against a neighbor, might reap the benefit of enhancing our agricultural capacity, but since we don't have any problems with the existing capacity, the inevitable depletion of our population in general, and the urban population in particular—especially all our fecund young males—does not seem a very wise move since our objective is economic prosperity. Our objective is not personal self-aggrandizement or waging war for war's sake. And there is always a risk that we might lose. History tells us that wars—especially those against nearest neighbors—have rarely enriched the victors, and have often devastated both victor and victim.

Inviting Adam Smith to be the first holder of our new government post of Chief Economic Adviser is an interesting suggestion, but it isn't clear what he might actually do. And recent history has given the appointment of expatriate

Scottish financial wizards something of a bad press. After all, it's not that long since John Law all but ruined Europe's most populous—and ostensibly most economically powerful—nation, France.

We discount option C as frivolous. What is tea anyway?

Option D is truly innovative and our preferred choice. Throughout our kingdom's long and noble history, our loyal subjects have been the main source of tax revenue to the crown, so for the crown to start dishing money out to them is nothing short of revolutionary. The thinking behind the idea, however, is smart. Its basis is the recognition that the main driver of economic growth is our population, and this is primarily driven by the birth rate. What better way of stimulating the birth rate than to pay people to have children? Subtle, eh? We recognize, of course, that this policy will take some years to have any effect and that the drain on the treasury will hit right away. No matter: We are not after a quick fix, the long term is by far the most important. And what about giving an extra bonus to those who live in cities, just to make sure that it's the urban population that grows the fastest?

The monarch implemented option D and continued the policy for 20 years. However, over that time she noticed something that she hadn't expected. For sure the birth rate did go up and, even more, the treasury went down. Although she stuck to her guns, overall the urban population just didn't budge! The economy grew a little, but nothing like as much as she had hoped. What did grow, unexpectedly fast, was the death rate. In fact, the cities had become really quite horrible, with disease rampant; the only buoyant part of the economy had become the interment business. As new babies were born, even more people seemed to be dying—if anything the urban population was declining.

The only exception was one city, a seaport engaged in trade with the Indies. That city had grown and grown and was overwhelmingly the biggest, most prosperous city on the continent. That was very fortunate, for the taxes on trade from that one city alone were supporting the whole "child benefit" program. What a stroke of luck!

So one day, the monarch traveled to the thriving seaport to try to understand why it alone had been so successful. At the formal reception, the mayor of the city handed her a cup of steaming, light brown liquid.

"What do we do with this?" she asked.

"You drink it, Your Majesty."

"Drink it?"

"Yes, Your Majesty, you drink it. It is delicious, but—I must admit—something of an acquired taste. It has become extremely popular in this fine city."

"Really? Oh well, if you say so. What is it called?"

"Tea, Your Majesty."

Tea is indeed a pleasing drink, but it's not just a pleasant taste. Tea also has medicinal properties: It contains tannin, and tannin kills bacteria. It is not as powerful as a modern antibiotic, but it is strong enough to relieve the constraint of disease a little, so allowing the birth rate to exceed the death rate just enough, and for long enough, to permit the natural exponential growth of the population system to power away. In fact, tea has a double benefit: the mild antibacterial property of the tea itself, and the fact that the water needs to be boiled, so killing water-borne bacteria. Remember, this all happened way before people had heard of "public health."

Amazingly enough this story is fundamentally true, although no one recognized it at the time. In the later 1700s one European society had acquired the habit of drinking tea, Great Britain. Alone in Europe, urban populations in Britain sustainably broke through the limit holding all other urban communities back, the limit imposed by the diseases of overcrowding. And remember that the death rate has to be reduced by only a little, since as long as it is sustainably less than the birth rate the population will grow exponentially. The populations in urban centers in Britain did just that.

In eighteenth-century Great Britain a few other conditions were also right: There was ample coal, there was a culture of trade and communication, and there was (for the times, anyway) an enlightened approach to politics and society. That is why the industrial revolution started in Britain, a revolution inadvertently fueled by tea.

The final causal loop diagram

Figure 8.17 is the final causal loop diagram in this story.

This is a "limits to growth" structure, which results in SURPLUS WEALTH. It is ultimately constrained by the AGRICULTURAL CAPACITY, which determines the point at which the total population is too large for its food supplies, so causing FAMINE. And since the AGRICULTURAL CAPACITY is finite, this represents a final, fixed constraint, which can be alleviated—but never totally removed—by increasing agricultural productivity or by finding new and different sources of food.

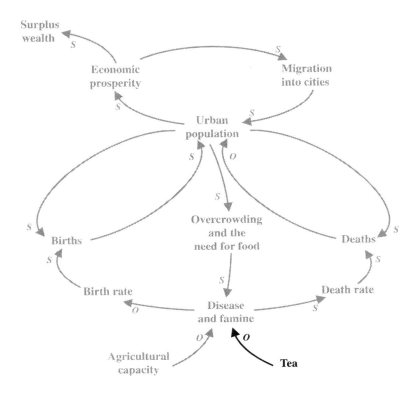

Figure 8.17

A second constraint is DISEASE, caused primarily by overcrowding. This can be alleviated by public health programs and by pharmaceuticals, either deliberately through the use of drugs such as antibiotics or totally accidentally by drinking tea. Unlike AGRICULTURAL CAPACITY, DISEASE does not have a finite capacity and so acts as a dynamic, rather than an ultimate, constraint. If the AGRICULTURAL CAPACITY is not a binding constraint, the URBAN POPULA-TION will increase or decrease in accordance with the BIRTH RATE and the DEATH RATE, which are themselves determined by FAMINE and DISEASE. So if FAMINE is not an issue and if DISEASE is alleviated, the URBAN POPULATION will grow and grow, as will SURPLUS WEALTH.

The moral of this story

This story, although couched in somewhat theatrical terms, is very real. It is all about how to stimulate growth in the real world, where growth is inevitably limited by any number of constraints.

The story highlights the difference between two types of policy that can be adopted to stimulate constrained growth.

One policy is to encourage the reinforcing loop, the fundamental engine of growth. In the story this corresponded to encouraging births (so stimulating the reinforcing loop through BIRTHS) and also to hiring Adam Smith (to encourage the reinforcing loop through ECONOMIC PROSPERITY).

Adam Smith

Adam Smith was born near Edinburgh in 1723 and is most renowned for his book *An Inquiry into the Nature and Causes of the Wealth of Nations*, first published in 1776, sparking a revolution in economics perhaps as profound as that in politics started that very year in Philadelphia. Although he did not explicitly know it, he was also a profound systems thinker. Much of his work, not only in economics but in social philosophy, was about how to orchestrate an "orderly society," which, in systems thinking terms, is all about how to design a self-organizing social system.

Smith's writings draw on two central concepts: the "inner man," which serves to restrain independent action (in systems thinking terms, the voluntary constraining of individual behavior, as described on page 16), and the "invisible hand," through which individual profit-maximizing behavior benefits society as a whole — in systems thinking terms, Smith is of course describing an emergent property of a well-structured economic system.

The other policy is to alleviate a constraint, as illustrated in the story by waging war (with the objective of capturing more AGRICULTURAL CAPACITY) and by drinking tea (inadvertently, but with the effect of reducing DISEASE).

Don't pedal harder, take the brakes off

Although the policy of making the reinforcing loop spin faster is both more obvious and often quite easy to implement, it is usually unwise. For if you push against a fundamental constraint, the constraint will usually push back—harder.

A far, far wiser policy is to alleviate the constraint, since once this is done the reinforcing loop takes off of its own accord and spins away under its own momentum, without the need for outside intervention. This is the same as the urban population in Britain growing as a result of drinking tea. No government told people to drink tea or to have more babies. People drank tea and continued to have babies, but fewer people died. So the population grew, all by itself. Provided that the loop is set off spinning as a virtual circle rather than a vicious one, remove the constraint and let it be.

In practice, this is often hard to do. Perhaps the right actions are seen as quick fixes and so are ignored; perhaps the right actions are not identified because people do not recognize that there is a constraint. Have you ever heard of a company that continued to spend buckets of money on advertising a product that was no longer competitive in the market? Is that relieving a constraint? Or pedaling harder?

When growth starts to become constrained, wise managers work on alleviating the constraints, not on pushing the reinforcing loops harder. That is because they have a deep understanding of the many causal loops operating within, and around, their businesses.

How to reduce your to-do list wisely

You and your colleagues are probably totally frenetic taking actions, running initiatives, directing programs, ticking off to-do lists. Take a moment to make a list of the most important of these actions and write this list in the left-hand column of the following table:

Action	Driving a reinforcing loop	Relieving a constraint	Other

Then for each tick the appropriate column.

If you have any ticks in the "Other" column, why are you doing these things?

If you have any ticks in the "Driving a reinforcing loop" column, for each of these:

➤ Is the corresponding loop constrained or not?

➤ If it is constrained, what are the constraints?

➤ How do you know?

➤ What actions need to be taken to alleviate these constraints?

➤ Would you be wiser taking these actions than the ones you are actually taking?

Does this help you reduce your to-do list?

9
Decisions, teamwork, and leadership

Chapter 8 threw the spotlight on the management of business growth and highlighted the dilemma between taking action to fuel the fire of the reinforcing loop, or action to relieve the constraints on a balancing loop. Fueling the reinforcing loop is usually the more obvious action and a tempting quick fix; relieving a constraint is often harder to spot and to do, but usually wiser.

In this chapter I will delve to a more detailed level and describe two case studies that show how systems thinking can illuminate policy decisions, so helping to distinguish between quick fixes and more robust solutions, thereby guiding wise action. The first case study is back in the television industry and builds on the story presented in Chapter 3; the second is about outsourcing and the resulting mutual dependence of buyer and contractor. Both these stories share two underlying themes: teamwork and leadership.

The talent problem

My first story is about how systems thinking helped a group of senior executives in the television industry address what they call the "talent problem." Although this example is set in the world of television, as you will see the story does apply much more widely. Also, the emphasis is not so much on exploring in detail how the system evolves over time, but rather on the determination of wise, robust policies—policies that enable steady growth, policies that relieve a damaging constraint. So there are no graphs, but lots of causal loop diagrams!

Most television businesses—indeed, most businesses in general—are always under pressure to control costs. On page 42, we saw the causal loop repeated in Figure 9.1.

This is formed of two intertwined reinforcing loops, which can show exponential growth or decline. The language used in the drawing is suggestive of decline, but you can readily see that the loops are able to act as mutually reinforcing virtuous circles rather than vicious ones.

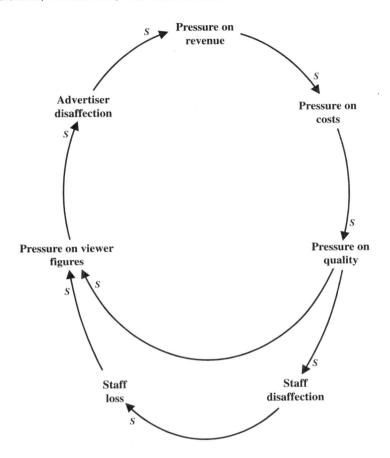

Figure 9.1

A specific issue that the management team felt was an especially powerful constraint on their business was the talent problem, the impact on their business caused by the possible loss of key talented people, either stars who appear on the programs or those important behind-the-scenes players, the pool of very experienced and capable scriptwriters, producers, and designers. In the UK this issue is relatively new. A few years ago the television industry had very few players and was dominated by the BBC (British Broadcasting Corporation). Mobility from one television company to another was rather unusual, for once someone joined the staff of a particular company, they tended to stay there for their entire career.

The familiar combination of deregulation and new technologies has changed all that. With many new channels on both radio and television, and with a mixture of distribution mechanisms such as terrestrial broadcasting, cable, satellite, and now the web, there are many more, and many new, companies in the industry and the talent can move around.

The obvious quick fix if a star threatens to move is to increase their salary and hope that they will stay. However, this might not be the wisest move. To explore this in more depth, a small team examined the issue using systems thinking. In doing this, we realized that there were three main perspectives:

➤ That of the senior executives, who are seeking to grow the business, but also to contain costs.
➤ That of the stars, whose loyalty to the company is now much more fragile.
➤ That of the younger members of the team, those who currently stand in the shadows of the stars but who aspire to become stars themselves.

Since wisdom is all about seeing a problem in a holistic manner and understanding the consequences of alternative possible actions, we thought it might be helpful to draw some causal loops capturing how the issue is perceived by each of these communities.

The senior executives' perspective

Our starting point is to recognize that many senior television executives are driven by very strong PERSONAL AMBITION. They want to succeed, and success in this business is, in many organizations, ultimately measured by the number of viewers who watch their programs (Figure 9.2).

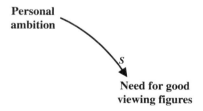

Figure 9.2

The increasing NEED FOR GOOD VIEWING FIGURES enhances the DEPENDENCE ON STARS, since it is the stars—the star scriptwriters, producers, designers, presenters, and actors—who draw the viewers. This in turn increases the FEAR OF LOSING STARS, so exerting an increasing PRESSURE TO ACCEDE TO

STARS' DEMANDS as, realizing their increased power, they negotiate for higher salaries and benefits. But if there is also a POLICY OF COST CUTTING, what happens? CONFLICT. Conflict in the mind of the executive who fears that saying "no" to the star will cause the star to leave, so eroding the viewing figures and damaging the executive's power base (Figure 9.3).

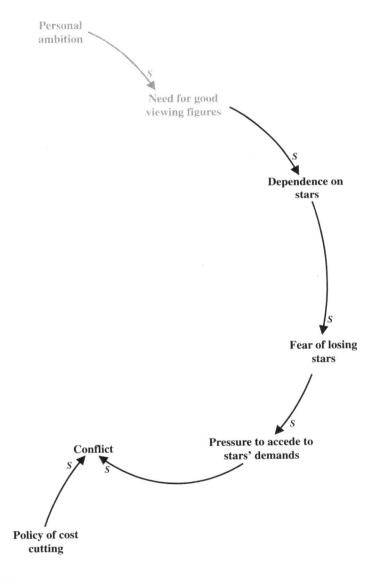

Figure 9.3

The quick fix of giving in to the PRESSURE TO ACCEDE TO STARS' DEMANDS is so tempting. I can do a deal now: No one else need know about it and by the time I have to argue it out with the managing director, the viewing figures will already have come through, so I'm bound to get away with it...

Unfortunately, matters rarely work out so neatly. How many organizations do you know where "no one else need know about it"? News of the special deals soon leaks out (Figure 9.4).

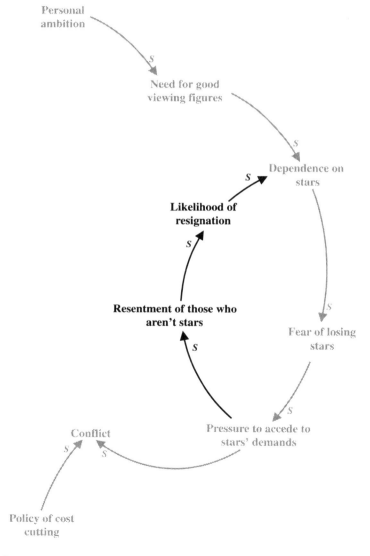

Figure 9.4

What better way is there of fueling the RESENTMENT OF THOSE WHO AREN'T STARS—the experienced people who haven't made it into the limelight, the assistants, the juniors, the younger staff? They may not be stars, but they still perform important functions and if this increases their LIKELIHOOD OF RESIGNATION—after all, it isn't only the stars who are mobile—then this reinforces the DEPENDENCE ON STARS. Leaping to the quick fix of yielding to the PRESSURE TO ACCEDE TO STARS' DEMANDS is undoubtedly good news for the stars, but rather bad news for everyone else.

That includes the poor senior executive. The CONFLICT hasn't gone away, but how can it be resolved? "If I yield even a little to the stars," thinks the executive, "I'll be under a lot of PRESSURE TO CUT COSTS ELSEWHERE, which will further increase the RESENTMENT OF THOSE WHO AREN'T STARS and aggravate the CONFLICT even more. The upshot of this is to increase my STRESS and that might interfere with my own personal performance. That means my NEED FOR GOOD VIEWING FIGURES is even more important so that I am politically safe…" (see Figure 9.5 overleaf).

No one ever said that the life of a senior television executive was an easy one and this diagram helps to explain why. All the loops—and there are a lot of them if you count all the different closed paths—are reinforcing loops, ratcheting each other up with each relentless turn. No wonder these people are stressed.

The problem, however, remains: What is the wisest policy to adopt under these circumstances? Figure 9.5 captures how the world looks to the senior executive, but that is not the whole story.

The star's perspective

Figure 9.6 on page 171 is the starting point for how a star sees the situation.

Stars also have a well-developed sense of PERSONAL AMBITION, which in their case manifests itself in a DESIRE TO BE A STAR. However, there are little stars and big stars, and so any star with driving ambition is never satisfied with the current LEVEL OF STARDOM. The DESIRE TO BE A STAR is in essence a desire to be a bigger star. The bigger star you are, the greater your PUBLIC VISIBILITY, which does wonders for your SELF-IMPORTANCE, fueling your DESIRE TO BE AN EVEN BIGGER STAR. This wonderful, self-indulgent reinforcing loop (perhaps, in this case, the description "virtuous circle" is not quite appropriate!) will be recognized by everyone who has had first-hand experience of a *prima donna*.

The higher the star's PUBLIC VISIBILITY, the greater their VALUE TO THE COMPANY; and the stronger the star's sense of SELF-IMPORTANCE, the stronger

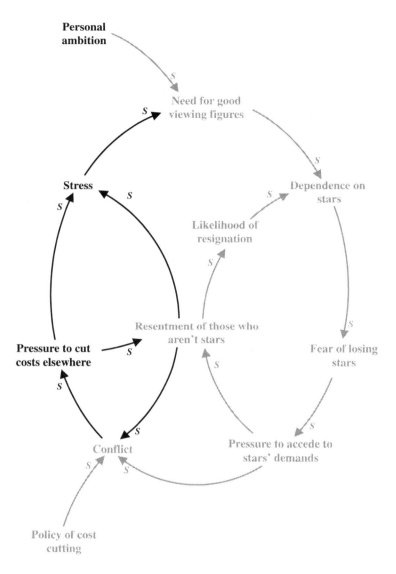

Figure 9.5

the star's belief in their INTERNAL BARGAINING POWER, especially if market conditions are driving an increase in the ATTRACTIVENESS OF ALTERNATIVE EMPLOYERS, as stimulated by DEREGULATION AND NEW TECHNOLOGY (Figure 9.7).

From the star's perspective, their increasing VALUE TO THE COMPANY ought to increase the WILLINGNESS OF THE COMPANY TO ACCEDE to their demands.

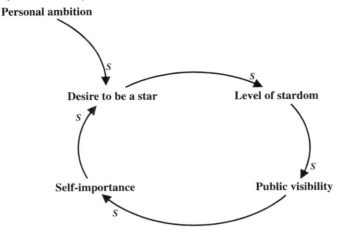

Figure 9.6

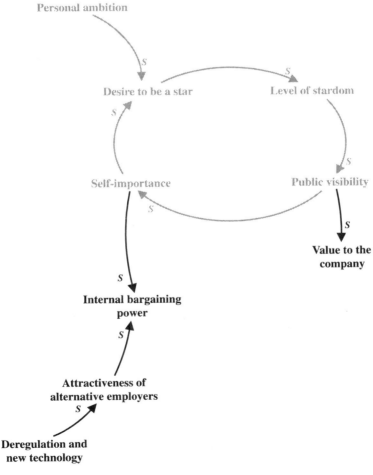

Figure 9.7

The tension between the star's INTERNAL BARGAINING POWER, as driven by the ATTRACTIVENESS OF ALTERNATIVE EMPLOYERS, and the WILLINGNESS, or otherwise, OF THE COMPANY TO ACCEDE creates a state of CONFLICT in the star's mind. Should I resign or not? How close to the brink can I push the company, without being pushed over myself? And how sure am I that things will be better elsewhere? This conflict is resolved if the company agrees to my demands or if the alternative possible employers aren't so attractive after all. But if the company is obstinate, or if I get a really good offer from the competition, that increases the LIKELIHOOD OF RESIGNATION.

Figure 9.8 is the final causal loop from the star's perspective.

This causal loop diagram contains only one feedback loop, the *prima donna* reinforcing loop at the top. Everything else relates to the associated

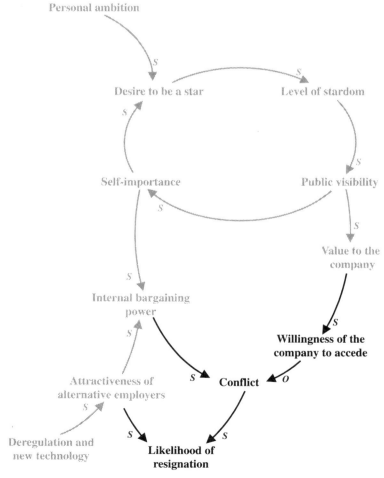

Figure 9.8

dangles: the goal of PERSONAL AMBITION, the external driver represented by DEREGULATION AND NEW TECHNOLOGY, and the outcome of the LIKELIHOOD OF RESIGNATION. The possibility that the star's CONFLICT between staying and resigning might balance out is indicated by the juxtaposition of the S and the O. If they do, the star stays; if they don't, then the LIKELIHOOD OF RESIGNA-TION increases accordingly.

As can be seen from the two causal loops drawn so far, the perspective of the senior executives is quite different from that of the stars; understandably so, because in this dispute they are on opposite sides of the fence. But we still haven't explored the whole story, for there is one more constituency waiting in the wings.

The perspective of the more junior staff

The company competes in the graduate market and strives to attract the best and the brightest. Those who do join are willing to learn, but they are ambi-tious too and want to be the stars of the future. Figure 9.9 overleaf is a causal loop diagram representing their perspective.

Does this diagram make sense?

You've seen a lot of causal loop diagrams now, so take a good look at this one and read the story directly from the diagram. Do you agree with the overall message? Do you agree with the Ss and the Os? How does the feedback loop behave? From the company's point of view, is this good news or bad news?

Starting at the top, the greater the PRESTIGE OF THE COMPANY, the greater the ATTRACTIVENESS OF THE COMPANY TO NEW RECRUITS, and the greater the com-pany's RECRUITMENT SUCCESS. Some time later, however, the ambitious young staff are seeking "star" opportunities, and the more successful the recruitment campaign of a few years previously, the greater the PRESSURE EXERTED BY YOUNG TALENT TO HAVE STAR SLOTS. The company, however, has only a given NUMBER OF STAR SLOTS available, as determined by the difference between the TOTAL NUMBER OF STAR SLOTS and the NUMBER OF INCUMBENT STARS. Given the ambition of the incumbent stars, it is most unlikely that they would step aside for the young talent, so the larger the NUMBER OF INCUMBENT STARS, the smaller the NUMBER OF STAR SLOTS AVAILABLE and the greater the

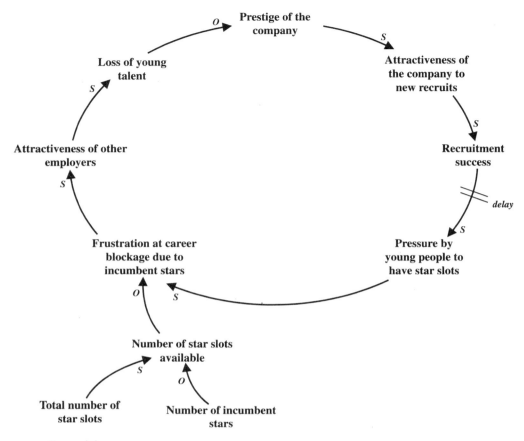

Figure 9.9

young talent's FRUSTRATION AT CAREER BLOCKAGE DUE TO INCUMBENT STARS. As the young talent become increasingly frustrated at waiting for the incumbent stars to retire, the ATTRACTIVENESS OF OTHER EMPLOYERS becomes progressively stronger. This drives a LOSS OF YOUNG TALENT and word of this exodus leaks back to the universities and colleges, damaging the PRESTIGE OF THE COMPANY.

This is a balancing loop, which will stabilize around the NUMBER OF STAR SLOTS AVAILABLE. This is doubly bad news for the company: It constrains growth and it also causes reputational damage.

What is the best policy?

These three causal loop diagrams capture the perspectives of the three major communities involved.

> **What would you do?**
> Take a look again at the three causal loops. What policies would you choose to adopt to solve the talent problem?

We have already agreed that the quick fix of acceding to the stars' demands is decidedly unwise. In fact, although the problem focuses on the stars, the wisest solution is not to be found from study of their causal loop. Rather, the solution emerges from examining the diagrams of the senior executives and the young talent.

The essence of the problem is the potential threat of "blackmail" by the stars, as indicated by the DEPENDENCE ON STARS shown in the senior executives' diagram. If this dependence can be broken, then the stars can no longer exercise a threat and the situation is stabilized. How can this be achieved?

The answer is to be found in the diagram of the younger talent, where we see that we suffer LOSS OF YOUNG TALENT as a result of their FRUSTRATION AT CAREER BLOCKAGE DUE TO INCUMBENT STARS. Isn't the smartest way of breaking the dependence on the incumbent stars to create as many opportunities as possible for young talent? As well as mitigating the DEPENDENCE ON STARS, this will also alleviate the FRUSTRATION AT CAREER BLOCKAGE DUE TO INCUMBENT STARS felt by the young talent. In addition, this has (at least) three beneficial side effects: It reduces the LOSS OF YOUNG TALENT; it arrests the erosion of the PRESTIGE OF THE COMPANY; and it also deprives the competition of an injection of well-trained staff, so diminishing their potential competitive advantage while preserving ours.

This policy of creating new opportunities for the younger staff clearly has many benefits, but it does have one downside. It recognizes that the company refuses to be blackmailed by stars—if a star chooses to resign as a result, so be it.

There are several ways of implementing this policy. One is to increase the variety and quantity of programs, so increasing the TOTAL NUMBER OF STAR SLOTS to be filled and ensuring that as many as possible of these are taken by younger people; another is to find ways in which the EXISTING NUMBER OF STAR SLOTS AVAILABLE can be more evenly shared across everyone. This requires the incumbent stars to make way for the younger talent, and the bigger egos will not rejoice at that. If that causes some stars to resign, the company will let that happen. So the sooner the "stars in waiting" can prove their mettle, the better.

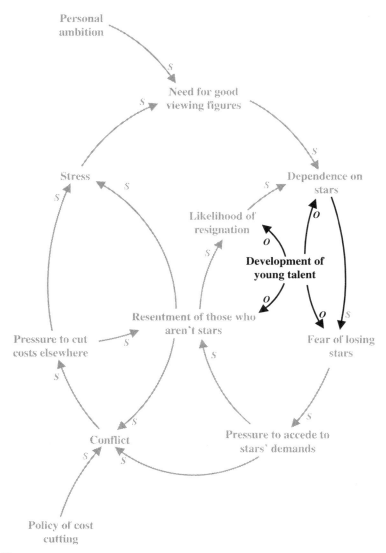

Figure 9.10

Figure 9.10 is a causal loop diagram from the senior executives' perspective incorporating a new item, DEVELOPMENT OF YOUNG TALENT, which stabilizes the system.

Figure 9.11 is a new diagram from the perspective of the young talent, which includes two new items, PROGRAM INNOVATION and SLOT REALLOCATION, both of which are driven by the policy of encouraging the DEVELOPMENT OF YOUNG TALENT.

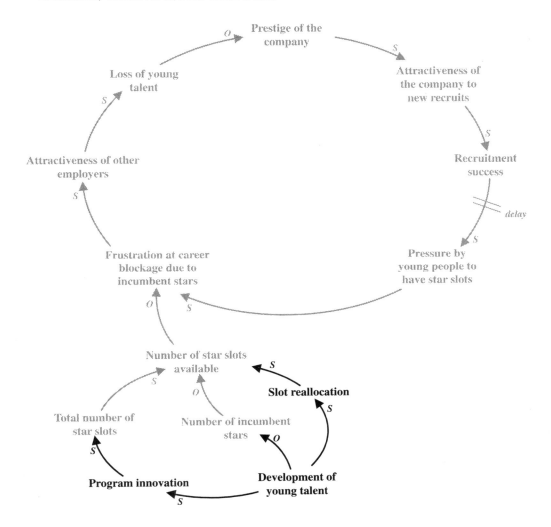

Figure 9.11

Clearly, this policy is not a magic wand in which everybody lives happily ever after. The price we have agreed to pay is the fact that the DEVELOPMENT OF YOUNG TALENT is not such good news for the incumbent stars. Figure 9.12 overleaf explains how the situation now looks to them.

At a stroke, the power of their three key cards—their INTERNAL BARGAINING POWER, their VALUE TO THE COMPANY, and the likely WILLINGNESS OF THE COMPANY TO ACCEDE to their demands—have been trumped.

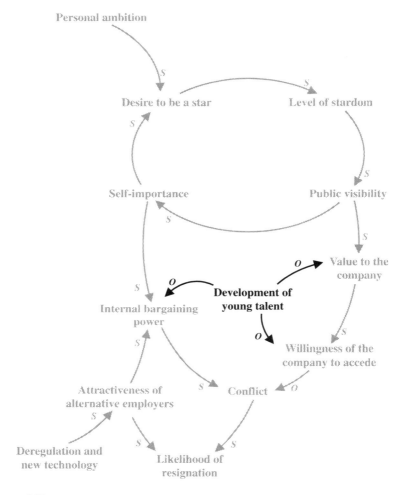

Figure 9.12

But that's all so obvious, isn't it?

With hindsight, of couse it's obvious; but then all good ideas, and all wise decisions, are "obvious" with hindsight. Nevertheless, when you're in the middle of
it all, with people pressing you to take decisions *now*, the phone ringing, the
budgets to finish, the meeting with the analysts in 20 minutes, and the general
harassment of everyday business life, maybe things aren't quite so obvious.

In my experience, causal loop diagrams can be challenged on two
grounds:

➢ That they are trivial and show nothing new.
➢ That the "insights" gained, in terms of understanding, policy formulation, and dynamic behavior, are self-evident and could easily have been determined without all the bother of drawing the diagrams.

The first point is, in one sense, quite true: Causal loop diagrams do not contain anything new. The purpose of drawing a causal loop diagram is to capture reality and, once drawn, the diagram must represent that reality. Accordingly, it cannot contain anything "new." Indeed, if the diagram does not conform to reality or fails to make intuitive sense, it is probably at best incomplete, at worst wrong. A good causal loop diagram therefore represents, and must be seen to represent, reality, and to do so succinctly and perceptively. This, however, is not the same as being trivial. Good diagrams, which throw a spotlight on to the most significant features and highlight the key relationships, require much careful observation, insightful understanding, and incisive thought to prepare.

The second point is cynical indeed. As I have just pointed out, with hindsight all wise policies are self-evident, obvious, no-brainers. But when we are faced with decisions, with those dramatic dilemmas that force us to choose between alternative "goods" or between equally unpalatable "bads," things aren't so easy. If they were, how would we explain all those unwise choices we make that, with hindsight, we regret?

Throughout history, wise people have taken good decisions without drawing causal loop diagrams. Nevertheless, those of us who do not quite rank alongside King Solomon could well find them helpful. Drawing and using good causal loop diagrams is all about seeing the forest for the trees. With hindsight this is easy, and the cynics disparage causal loop diagrams accordingly. But when you're in the middle of the wood in the dark, maybe it's not so trivial after all. Seeing the forest for the trees is so, so much easier after the forester has been around the wood and chosen the right trees to paint bright yellow. And that's what good, insightful causal loop diagrams do. When you compile a causal loop diagram you are that forester, distinguishing the important from the interesting but really not so important; throwing the spotlight on to the truly significant; identifying the right trees while avoiding all the half elephant traps.

My metaphors are running away with me, but I'm sure you know what I mean. Is it a coincidence that one of the founding fathers of systems thinking is the aptly named Jay Forrester?

Jay Forrester

Jay Forrester has had a remarkable career, playing a major role in the development of computers, in the geopolitical events associated with the Cold War, in the development of social policy, and in management education. He is also one of the founding fathers of system thinking, and especially of the use of computers for simulation (see pages 21 and 273).

Born on a cattle ranch deep in America's prairies, near Climax, Nebraska, in 1918, Forrester took a degree in electrical engineering from the University of Nebraska, and then joined the Massachusetts Institute of Technology as a graduate student. While working on a project to build Whirlwind, the world's first digital computer to operate in real time, he invented, and gained a patent in his own name for, a novel way of storing information. The very earliest computers used vacuum tubes to store information and then another form of device called an electrostatic storage tube. These were clumsy, big, power hungry, and slow. Forrester revolutionized the architecture and performance of digital computers, since his invention was ferrite core memory, a random access computer memory device consisting of a huge array of rings made out of a special magnetic material called ferrite. First developed in 1949, this form of computer memory remained the industry standard until the introduction, during the 1970s, of today's silicon chip memory technology.

In the early 1950s, Forrester was the director of the US government's SAGE project, a highly complex air defense system using a network of Whirlwind computers to control radar monitoring sites across North America and to track aircraft flight paths. SAGE began operation in 1958 and remained a critical component of the US's military strategy throughout the peak of the Cold War, until its replacement in 1983.

Forrester joined MIT's Sloan School of Management in 1956, where he was instrumental in setting up the project that led to the publication of *The Limits to Growth* (see page 23) and in building the computer simulation model that underpinned the project's quantitative analysis. His department, which he directed until 1989, continues to be the worldwide center of excellence for systems thinking and system dynamics. Forrester is still very active: In 1998 he was appointed Professor Emeritus at MIT, and his current main interests are in the fields of macroeconomic modeling and education.

Mental models

Causal loop diagrams must represent reality—but whose reality? We all see reality rather differently. What is important to you might be less important to me; what you might consider as the best action to take might be different from my choice. This is not a question of right and wrong, it is simply a manifestation of the fact that we all see the world differently.

What are the top three things we need to do right now?

Next time you are at a meeting, just before the meeting closes say to the group, "That was a good meeting. Why don't we all individually write down on a sheet of paper the top three things we need to do, in order of importance?"

Then, when each member of the group has written their own list, go round the group and collect each individual's views on a flipchart. Unless the group has already explicitly agreed what these are, I reckon the likelihood that each individual will have identified the same three things in the same order is zero — absolutely zero. Certainly there is likely to be some overlap, because the members of the group have all been at the same meeting. But differences will be inevitable. One person might identify the most important action as putting a project team together; someone else might say that it is to communicate the results of this meeting to those not present.

This is not a result of people not paying attention, nor is it the influence of some malicious demon sent to infect the group with discontent, nor is it the result of poor chairmanship. It is the inevitable result of different people having legitimately different views of the world.

These differences are important, because they underpin our attitudes and our actions, and one of the games we all play is to second-guess how our colleagues will react in any particular situation. If you are discussing budgets, for example, someone who sincerely and passionately believes that advertising is the single most powerful way of stimulating sales will argue vociferously to increase the advertising budget; someone else, who holds the equally valid, but different, belief that the best way to increase sales is to recruit more sales people, and to ensure they are all expertly trained in knowledge of the product, will argue equally strongly to allocate the funds to recruitment and training.

In principle these two beliefs are irreconcilable, since they are based on totally different concepts of how the world behaves. The advocate of advertising believes the strongest driver of sales revenue to be advertising; the advocate of recruitment and training thinks otherwise. These two people have different views — different mental models — regarding the cause-and-effect relationships underpinning how best to grow sales revenue and, as a result, they would draw different structures in a causal loop diagram seeking to capture that particular "reality" (Figures 9.13 and 9.14).

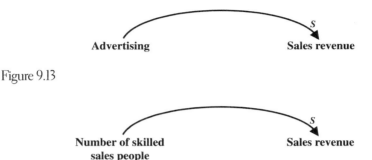

Figure 9.13

Figure 9.14

Overall, of course, both of these factors (and a host of others too) influence sales revenue. However, different individuals can hold different views on their relative importance and, if faced with a choice between one and the other, will make different choices. Mental models strongly influence decisions and behavior.

As you will have gathered by now, systems thinking in general, and drawing causal loop diagrams in particular, is an enormously powerful way of making mental models explicit. Indeed, all the causal loop diagrams you have seen so far (and all the others to come) are not so much representations of reality in an absolute sense; rather, they are representations of (for the most part) my mental models of how I believe the world behaves.

Peter Senge

As noted in the box on Jay Forrester, MIT (Massachusetts Institute of Technology) in Cambridge, near Boston, is the world center of excellence for systems thinking. One of the current leaders in the field is Peter Senge, the Director of Organizational Learning at MIT's Sloan School of Management. In his business bestseller *The Fifth Discipline*, Senge stresses the importance of mental models as fundamental drivers of behavior. If we wish to understand and appreciate the behavior of others, he cogently argues, we need to understand and appreciate their mental models; and, by the same token, if others are to understand and appreciate us, they have to understand and appreciate our mental models.

However, few of us go around saying, "My mental model concerning the fundamental drivers of sales revenue is all about advertising" (or whatever); rather, our mental models are revealed in bits and pieces, sometimes obviously, sometimes less so, by what we say and — more accurately — by what we do.

This makes the process of articulating and sharing mental models something of a protracted guessing game. Systems thinking, and drawing causal loop diagrams, can make this process much more specific and effective.

"Systems thinking" and "mental models" constitute two of the five disciplines referred to in the title of Senge's book. The other three are "personal mastery" (being very good at what you do), "shared vision" (having a full and mutually shared understanding of each other's mental models), and "team learning" (the emergent property — see page 14 — of a team to be far more powerful when acting together than when acting as individuals).

Senge strongly advocates — and I agree — that much of the dysfunction arising between people results from a failure to understand one another's fundamental beliefs, one another's deeply held mental models. Rather than listening to and respecting the other person's mental models, we seek to ram our mental models down the other person's throat and we get very frustrated when the other fool doesn't get it (Figure 9.15).

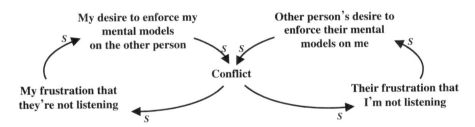

Figure 9.15

Two reinforcing loops, perfectly synchronized, escalate the conflict exponentially until the whole thing breaks down.

The wisest policy? Stop forcing and start listening.

Despite the fact that causal loop diagrams are visual, they play a very helpful role in listening, since in examining someone else's causal loop diagram you are in fact listening to their thinking; and anyone examining one of your diagrams is listening to you.

Teamwork

I mentioned teamwork in Chapter 1, in connection with the system-level concepts of emergence and self-organization (see pages 14–16), two topics to which I will return in a few pages. In the meantime, here is a rather different slant on the same theme.

What is a high-performing team?
Try this:
A high-performing team is a group of people whose mental models are naturally in harmony, especially as regards fundamental values.

Mental models and teams are intimately related, because, in my view, the highest-performing teams have a very deeply shared set of mental models. Members of the team are not in doubt about how others will act, they do not have to keep checking on each other, they know. Building a team of this quality rarely happens quickly, but it can be done over a period of time if people communicate and listen, if they discover that they aren't going against their most fundamental natures in agreeing.

Choosing the team
In 1805, before setting out on the naval expedition that was to culminate in the Battle of Trafalgar, Vice-Admiral Lord Nelson had a meeting in London with his boss, the First Lord of the Admiralty, Lord Barham. During the meeting, Barham handed Nelson the Navy List — containing the names of all the officers in the Navy at that time — and invited him to choose his own team. As he handed the List back, Nelson said, "Choose yourself, my Lord. The same spirit actuates the whole profession. You cannot choose wrong."

Although Nelson's language is somewhat archaic, his meaning is crystal clear. Given a free choice of colleagues to accompany him, he was content to take anyone. This was because he knew them all individually, had trained many of them, worked with them, spent hours and hours with each of them discussing strategy, deciding tactics, sharing ideas on how to manage a ship, how to lead a team. Over a period of time, they had crafted their mental models into an unforced, unified whole: "The same spirit actuates the whole profession." No wonder Nelson's captains were referred to as the "band of brothers."

The telephone directory test

You are with your managing director discussing the composition of a team to deliver an important new project. The MD hands you the internal phone directory and invites you to choose the members of the team that you will lead. Do you hand the directory back with the words, "You choose, Bob. They're all a great bunch and we all think the same way. Whoever you choose, we'll be a great team"?

Why not?

Mental models run very deep. They underpin our actions, behavior, and choices. The extent to which mental models naturally overlap determines whether or not a group of people is merely a group of people or a high-performing team. Causal loop diagrams make mental models explicit and one of the most powerful ways of building a team is to compile a shared mental model, one to which all the members of the team say, "Yes, I see the world that way too."

How sustainable is this relationship?

"Hey, wouldn't it be great to go to the theater this weekend?"

"I'm not sure... I was thinking of something a bit quieter, more intimate. How about going out for dinner somewhere really nice?

"That would be good, yes. But I would really like to see the new Tom Stoppard play — his plays are always great fun!"

"Yes, he's a great guy. But sometimes I have to concentrate so hard it makes my brain hurt. I fancy something less exhausting. What about dinner?"

They lapse into silence.

"If you love me, you'll give in and come to the theater."

"But if you love me, you'll give in and come to dinner."

And they both think, "Why does this happen time and time again? Wouldn't things work better if we naturally and spontaneously wanted to do the same thing?"

Let me conclude this discussion of teamwork by linking it back to some of the principal features of systems, as systems, that I introduced in Chapter 1, in particular the features of emergence, self-organization, feedback, and energy flow. From a systems standpoint, teamwork is an emergent property of a system comprised of the individual players, as the system self-organizes to show enriched order, enhanced coordination, and higher performance. This is achieved by a variety of internal feedback mechanisms and a flow of energy through the system as a whole. Furthermore, we know that the essence of a system is the connectedness between its component parts, rather than the individual properties of those component parts themselves.

This all sounds pretty abstract, theoretical, and academic. So let me make it practical, pragmatic, and helpful. If we wish to build a team, we are in fact engaging in the design of a system. The critical design principle is therefore to create the right connections between the component parts.

In the cases in which we are interested, of course, the component parts are all people. How do you build connections between people?

Talking is one way, in both senses of the term. It is indeed one way of building connections between people, but it runs the danger of being a one-way method of connecting, as the talker rams their ideas into the no-longer-paying-attention mind of the erstwhile listener.

Listening, in fact, is a much better way of building connections. "Active" listening is better still, a form of listening in which the listener makes it abundantly clear to the speaker that the message being conveyed is being heard, understood, and reflected on. "Passive" listening, in which the listener merely sits there, leaving the speaker to wonder whether or not anything has got through, just doesn't work. Once again in systems terms, active listening explicitly transmits information of successful receipt of the message from the listener back to the transmitter of the message. What else is this but another, though very subtle, example of feedback? And as we saw in Chapter 1, feedback is an integral feature of self-organizing systems.

But what are we taking about and actively listening to? As we know from our own experience, if discussions with colleagues stay at the level of whether or not I have done the action points I was assigned at last week's meeting, then this does not build high-performing teams. Communication at the level of the business transaction does not achieve this result. We have to get to a deeper level—the level of the mental model and, behind that, the level of the true person.

Many of us find that rather uncomfortable: We don't want to speak personally and we much prefer to keep the conversation away from ourselves. Reference back to Chapter 1, however, will identify that there is another essential requirement of self-organizing systems. As we saw on page 16, the behavior of an individual component of the system is constrained. In this case, the constraint is an obligation on each individual team member to be willing to listen and to become committed to the values and objectives of the team — in short, to become more connected. And building connections between people requires a huge amount of time, effort, and energy, as the following anecdote demonstrates.

A story about teamwork

In 1993, I attended one of the regular meetings of the UK consulting partners in the firm then known as Coopers & Lybrand. There were about 100 partners in the room, all highly educated, articulate, self-confident, and successful. The theme of the day was teamwork and the agenda was the usual stuff: "state of the nation" presentations, break-out groups, and plenaries.

Toward the end of the day, Malcolm Coster, the boss of the consulting firm, gave his "rah-rah" address, something he did very well since he was a good speaker, always holding the audience's attention; charismatic, even. The territory he was covering was familiar: how we should all work together more, share leads, use each other's staff. As Malcolm was talking my eyes drifted around the room and I watched the faces of many of my fellow partners. While I did this, similar thoughts kept coming into my mind. "Who's that fellow over there?" "What's the name of that woman sitting next to Tony? I don't think I've ever seen her before." "Who are all those people from Edinburgh and why are they sitting in a huddle?"

At the end of the presentation Malcolm asked for questions. There was the usual silence, which went on for rather longer than usual; he clearly hadn't planted any. So I put my hand up.

"Dennis?"

"May I ask a question, please? Not of you, Malcolm, but of everyone here? Thanks. I reckon there are about 100 of us in the room today. Is there any person here who knows the names of all the other 99?"

I paused and looked around the room. No one put up a hand — no one.

"If we don't even know one another's names, how on earth can we operate as a high-performing team?"

The need for energy in building and maintaining high-performing teams is no accident; it is, in fact, a direct consequence of systems theory. As we saw on page 15, self-organizing systems are necessarily open systems and require a continuous flow of energy in order to maintain order and cohesiveness. In the context of teamwork, that is what leadership is all about: the active, continuous, pumping of energy into and through the team, especially when the going gets tough. No wonder being a leader isn't easy. Not only does it require very careful, subtle attention to building and continually maintaining the interconnectedness between the individual team players, but it also requires that oh-so-draining giving of energy.

But that, of course, is exactly what Nelson did to build his band of brothers.

Outsourcing, partnering, and cross-boundary conflict

We usually refer to teamwork as something that applies within our own organization. Indeed, some organizations take this so far that the definition of "my team" is "us" and everyone else is "the enemy"—especially our competitors. Drawing such caricatures is commercially naïve today, when businesses are becoming increasingly interdependent. Advocating an attitude of "us and them," "we win, you lose" is in many circumstances counterproductive, but such attitudes remain very common.

One of the most adversarial situations in business is the tendering of contracts, for example when an internal function is outsourced. One instance of this is when a utility company—say, a water company, an electricity company, a gas supplier, or a railway company—which in the past might have had its own internal engineering function, wishes to appoint a subcontractor for the maintenance and renewal of its pipe, wire, or rail network. Since the utilities, although privatized in many countries, are still largely local monopolies, they have very strong buying power; by the same token, since there are many companies that can do the engineering work, any individual contractor is in a relatively weak position.

The utility invites, say, 12 engineering companies to tender and makes them jump through all sorts of hoops, many of which are contractual. The climate is usually one of low mutual trust and the game played by the utility is: "How can we screw down the contractors to commit to the lowest cost?" By the same token the contractors are thinking: "How low can we pitch the price to get the contract, so that once we have won and the utility is committed, we can ramp the price up from the inside by claiming all sorts of variations on the original contract?"

After a time-consuming and exhausting tendering process, one of the contractors is selected and, since it probably underbid, it is looking for every opportunity to make more money so that the contract ends up profitable. Of course the utility knows this and so is on the lookout, seeking to block the contractor at every attempt. This game is played out until the next tendering round. Suspicion and mistrust rule; everything is referred back to the detailed wording of the contract; the lawyers end up as the winners.

Is this the smartest way for the utility to get value for money?

How the world looks to the buyer

The buyer—a utility in this particular case, but in more general terms any organization that has outsourced a particular activity—needs to satisfy shareholders and also customers. The PRESSURE ON THE BUYER TO MEET SHAREHOLDERS' EXPECTATIONS usually translates into a PRESSURE ON THE BUYER TO DELIVER A PREDICTABLE PROFIT STREAM, because this implies a stable and reliable dividend to shareholders, as befits the needs of investors in a "safe" industry like a utility. Also, the PRESSURE ON THE BUYER TO SATISFY CUSTOMERS translates into a REQUIREMENT FOR HIGH TECHNICAL AND SERVICE QUALITY STANDARDS, a matter of fundamental importance in utilities such as water, electricity, gas, and the railways (Figure 9.16 overleaf). The company also has a POLICY OF OUTSOURCING, driven perhaps by regulatory pressures, perhaps by a belief that this will reduce costs in the long term, perhaps because it is perceived as the fashionable thing to do. However, the action of outsourcing a hitherto internal service creates a DEPENDENCY OF THE BUYER ON THE CONTRACTOR, since if the contractor were to fail the damage would be to the buyer.

The most recent, highly visible, example of this in the UK concerns the rail crash mentioned on page 87. It turns out that Railtrack, the owner of the railway tracks in the UK, subcontracted inspection and maintenance to a number of engineering companies, one of which, Balfour Beatty, had the contract for the stretch of line that failed at Hatfield. Was Balfour Beatty negligent in its performance of the contract? Or was Railtrack negligent in its supervision of the contract? Doubtless, the inquiry will find out. Whatever the outcome, there can be no doubt that the more mission critical the function a buyer chooses to outsource, the greater the DEPENDENCY OF THE BUYER ON THE CONTRACTOR (Figure 9.17 on page 191).

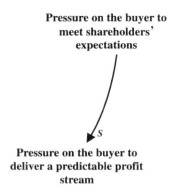

Pressure on the buyer to meet shareholders' expectations

s

Pressure on the buyer to deliver a predictable profit stream

Requirement for high technical and service quality standards

s

Pressure on the buyer to satisfy customers

Figure 9.16

As Railtrack discovered not only to its cost but that of many others too, the greater the DEPENDENCY OF THE BUYER ON THE CONTRACTOR, the greater the RISK TO THE BUYER OF COST ESCALATION AND QUALITY PROBLEMS, as the contractor seeks to exploit its position, perhaps by putting prices up at every opportunity, perhaps by cutting corners. These factors all combine to put considerable PRESSURE ON THE BUYER TO CONTROL OUTSOURCED COSTS AND QUALITY (Figure 9.18 on page 192).

This creates quite a dilemma: The buyer is totally dependent on the contractor to deliver quality work at the agreed costs, but, because the work has been outsourced, the buyer has relinquished the right to managerial control. Before the function was outsourced, of course, issues of cost and quality were

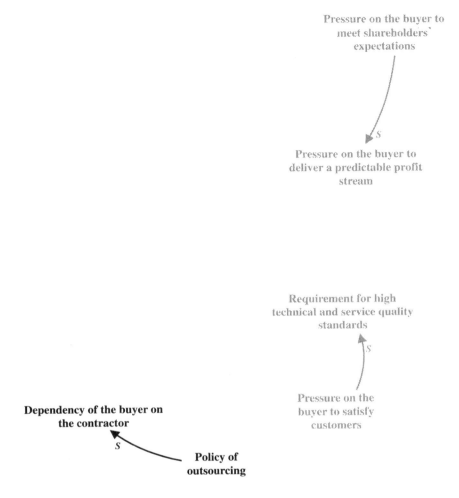

Figure 9.17

managed through internal processes. However, now that the function has been outsourced, a process that used to be exercised by internal management is replaced by one of contract law. Several months after the fatal crash, on the BBC television program *Panorama*, Steve Marshall, Chief Executive of Railtrack, was asked what the board of Railtrack had spent its time doing since the privatization of the railways. He answered, "We've spent most of our time negotiating contracts."

Before reaching for the lawyers, however, the most likely outcome of this dilemma is for the buyer to demand increasingly more detailed reports on what

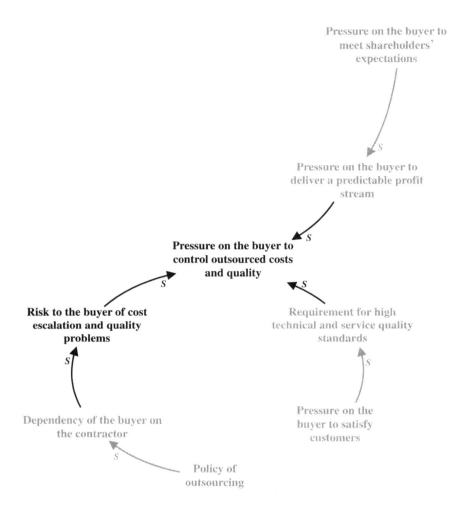

Figure 9.18

the contractor is in fact doing: reports on scheduling, reports on activities carried out, reports on compliance with standards. The buyer will also seek to have its own inspection teams verify the nature and quality of the contractor's work, supervising the quality control measures that the contractor is itself carrying out.

As the PRESSURE ON THE BUYER TO CONTROL OUTSOURCED COSTS AND QUALITY increases, this drives a PRESSURE ON THE BUYER TO INTERFERE WITH THE CONTRACTOR'S INTERNAL PROCESSES. This, of course, is unwelcome to the contractor and as the level of this interference increases, this progressively erodes the QUALITY OF THE BUYER–CONTRACTOR RELATIONSHIP (Figure 9.19).

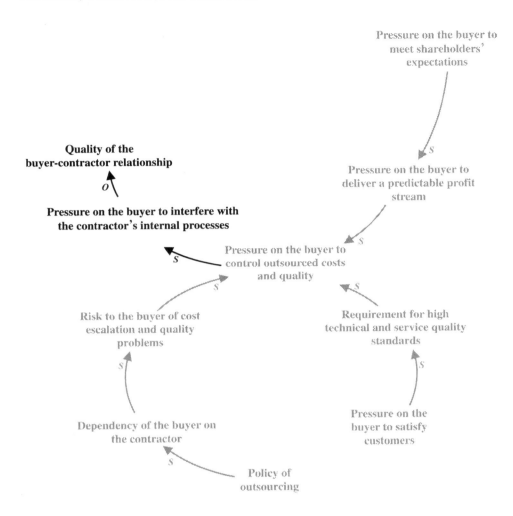

Figure 9.19

One possible consequence of a deterioration in the buyer–contractor relationship is the incentive that this gives to the contractor to be difficult and inflexible, especially as regards work that the buyer wishes to be carried out, but that was not defined in absolute, precise detail in the original specification. This results in more meetings, more arguments about what was and was not in the contract—all the games a contractor can play as the PRESSURE EXERTED BY THE CONTRACTOR ON THE BUYER TO INCREASE MARGINS builds up.

From the buyer's point of view this is bad news. Major costs are no longer as predictable as they should be and there is an increasing RISK TO THE BUYER

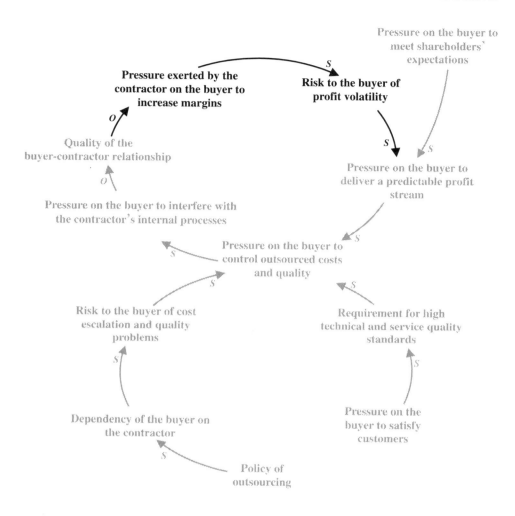

Figure 9.20

OF PROFIT VOLATILITY. However, since the buyer is still under PRESSURE TO MEET SHAREHOLDERS' EXPECTATIONS, this puts even more PRESSURE ON THE BUYER TO DELIVER A PREDICTABLE PROFIT STREAM. This in turn increases the PRESSURE ON THE BUYER TO CONTROL OUTSOURCED COSTS AND QUALITY even more, and so we have a damaging vicious circle (Figure 9.20).

One way to manage this is to have many subcontractors, so avoiding too high a DEPENDENCY OF THE BUYER ON (any single) CONTRACTOR. This can work for outsourced services such as cleaning or catering, but it is not so easy with IT, engineering, or construction. What is the wisest policy for the buyer to adopt in order to avoid a perpetual feud with the contractor on the one hand, or being blackmailed into paying increasingly higher prices on the other?

How the world looks to the contractor

Meanwhile, how does the contractor see things? The contractor also has share-holders to satisfy and the PRESSURE ON THE CONTRACTOR TO MEET SHAREHOLD-ERS' EXPECTATIONS gives rise to the normal PRESSURE ON THE CONTRACTOR TO DELIVER PROFITS. For a contractor, this is all about winning new contracts and keeping existing contracts profitable. The PRESSURE ON THE CONTRACTOR TO DELIVER PROFITS therefore drives the PRESSURE ON THE CONTRACTOR TO WIN NEW CONTRACTS, which in turn puts PRESSURE ON THE CONTRACTOR TO BID LOW to make sure that contracts are won. Once a contract has been won, the effect of the PRESSURE ON THE CONTRACTOR TO DELIVER PROFITS, combined with the consequences of winning new business by bidding low, results in PRESSURE ON THE CONTRACTOR TO SEEK VARIATIONS AND CUT CORNERS (Figure 9.21).

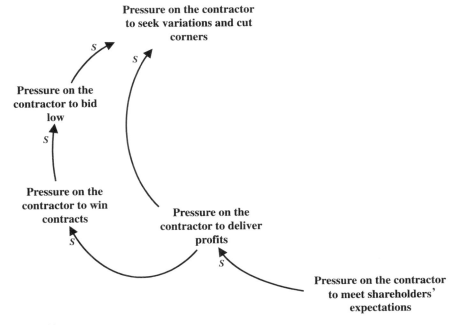

Figure 9.21

The result of the PRESSURE ON THE CONTRACTOR TO SEEK VARIATIONS AND CUT CORNERS is inevitable: CONFLICT, leading, as we have seen from the pur-chaser's standpoint, to the erosion of the QUALITY OF THE CONTRACTOR–BUYER

RELATIONSHIP. From the contractor's point of view, however, this can be a dangerous game, because it increases the RISK TO THE CONTRACTOR OF LOSING THE CONTRACT as well as any FURTHER BUSINESS.

The contractor's attitude to this risk will influence the WILLINGNESS OF THE CONTRACTOR TO COMPROMISE. If the contractor eases off, this reduces the PRESSURE ON THE CONTRACTOR TO SEEK VARIATIONS AND CUT CORNERS and the situation stabilizes; if it hardens, the adversarial nature of the relationship is enhanced. The WILLINGNESS OF THE CONTRACTOR TO COMPROMISE is itself influenced by the current PRESSURE ON THE CONTRACTOR TO DELIVER PROFITS, and the CONTRACTOR'S PERCEPTION OF THE BUYER'S DEPENDENCE. If, for example, the contractor is doing well from other contracts and is weak relative to the buyer, the contractor is likely to be flexible; on the other hand, if the contractor is having a difficult commercial time and the buyer is heavily dependent on the contractor, the contractor can be difficult without running too much risk of losing the contract (Figure 9.22).

This diagram has only one closed loop, a balancing loop, representing the fact that it is the contractor who tends to stabilize the situation, balancing the

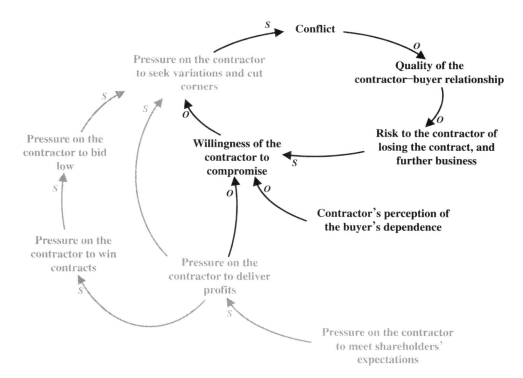

Figure 9.22

PRESSURE ON THE CONTRACTOR TO MEET SHAREHOLDERS' EXPECTATIONS in the context of the RISK TO THE CONTRACTOR OF LOSING THE CONTRACT, as assessed by the CONTRACTOR'S PERCEPTION OF THE BUYER'S DEPENDENCE. The buyer can, and often does, influence these by letting the contractor know just how many others could do exactly the same job, both better and more cheaply, and by threatening to terminate the contract. Nevertheless, in the end it is usually the contractor who determines whether or not to raise the stakes.

As a result the situation stabilizes as an armed truce, with the contractor always seeking to test how far the buyer can be pushed, and the buyer threatening to use other suppliers and in a permanent state of anxiety that the contractor will do something horribly wrong and upset the buyer's own customers.

How much simpler life used to be before we outsourced!

Is there a better way?

> **A better way**
> Take another look at the causal loop diagrams representing the buyer's viewpoint and the contractor's. Do they make sense? Do they ring true? Can you identify a single policy that works well from both perspectives?

One way of resolving conflict is to identify some policies or actions that work well for everyone involved. That way, both parties can agree to a common set of actions that benefit both—a true win–win game. A powerful way of identifying such policies and actions is by drawing causal loop diagrams from the perspectives of both parties and seeing if there are any policies that straddle both beneficially.

In this case there are two fundamental problems to overcome. First, the objectives of the buyer and contractor are different and in conflict: The buyer wants to save costs and the contractor wants to make profits. Since the contractor's profits increase the buyer's costs, this appears to be an inevitably adversarial win–lose game. In fact, as we all know, things are more complex. The buyer does not have cost minimization as the sole, ultimate, over-riding objective. The buyer has to deliver some sort of service—safe water, a reliable railway, or whatever—and so must meet these needs as well. And the contractor is not looking to make profits at the expense of, say, winning repeat business (which is far less costly than winning new business) or damaging its reputation. Overall, the contractor wants to do a good job and the buyer wants a good job done, so maybe there is some common ground after all.

The second problem—especially in construction and engineering—is the management of uncertainty. Much of the argument about contract variations arises from disputes over who should bear the cost of something that wasn't explicitly defined in the original contract. The contractor argues that the buyer should have thought of it in the first place and, having failed to include it in the specification, should bear the cost of having to fix it; the buyer argues that the contractor should have anticipated that there might be a slab of concrete five feet underground where the contractor's gang has to dig a trench and should have taken that possibility into account in the costings.

In fact, both sides know that specifications are never totally complete and that unexpected things happen on projects. So rather than argue about the blame and the cost, why not anticipate that these things will happen and devise constructive methods of problem solving, in which both sides can share the pain and the gain?

Figures 9.23 and 9.24 (pages 199–200) show how the same policies—about the buyer's and contractor's mutual willingness to align objectives, and the buyer's willingness to commit to share benefits—work beneficially from both parties' perspectives.

The BUYER'S WILLINGNESS TO COMMIT TO SHARE BENEFITS is a strong signal to the contractor that the variation game is not the only way to make the contract profitable. From the contractor's point of view, it encourages a more realistic bid in the first place and creates a climate in which the buyer and contractor seek to solve problems, rather than argue about variations. From the buyer's point of view, the risk of cost escalation, and hence profit volatility, is reduced, although it is likely that the costs originally committed to will be higher. Nevertheless, it could well be in the buyer's interests to commit to higher costs that are more likely to be stable, than to lower costs that then escalate.

More fundamentally, the BUYER'S AND CONTRACTOR'S MUTUAL WILLING-NESS TO ALIGN OBJECTIVES enhances the quality of the relationship, moving it away from an adversarial win–lose conflict to one of win–win partnering.

Both these policies are underpinned by the BUYER'S WILLINGNESS TO COMMIT TO THE LONGER TERM, a willingness made real by committing to work with the contractor as partners with shared objectives, in principle, for many years. This commitment is in the gift of the buyer and it is not a quick fix. But is it the wisest policy?

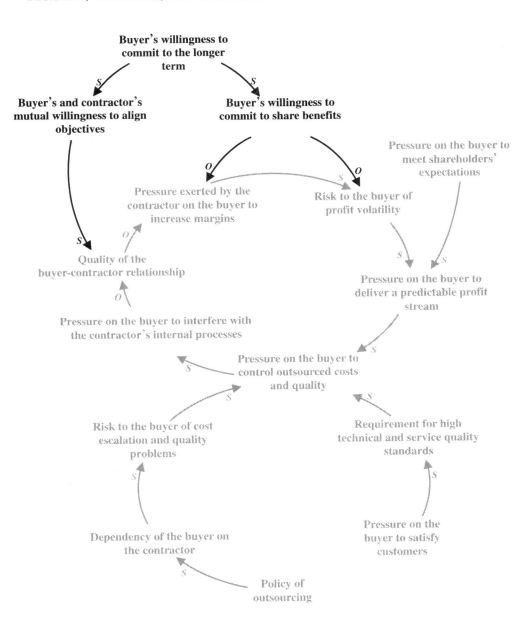

Figure 9.23

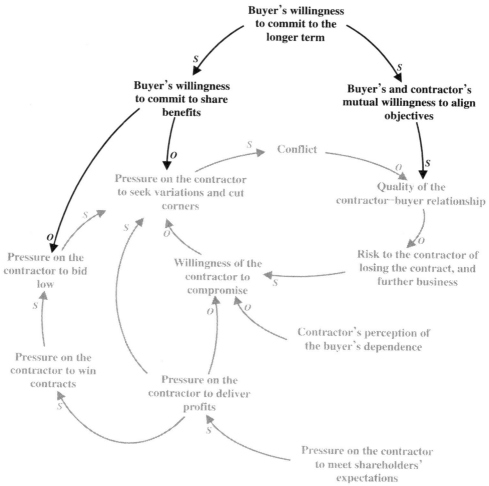

Figure 9.24

It is indeed the buyer that has the opportunity to take the initiative to realize the wise solution, because, in this relationship, it is the buyer that has the
power. In most buyer–contractor relationships the parties are not equal. Power
usually lies with the buyer and, depending on how the buyer chooses to exercise that power, the relationship is more or less adversarial. A wise buyer, however, does not exploit this power, but rather uses it to agree a redefinition of
the relationship away from master–servant to one of peer–peer, so transforming it from win–lose to win–win.

Teamwork is not necessarily something that happens solely within a single
organization, it can also cross boundaries, and indeed erase them.

The systems perspective

As with the case study on managing talent, let me conclude this case study with some reflections from a systems perspective.

In this case, our objective is to take two separate systems — that of the buyer and that of the contractor — and attempt to combine them into a higher-level system, one that can exhibit the emergent property of a win–win game. This will not happen by itself, by accident, and we know enough about the theory of systems to recognize that the solutions must involve enhancing the connectedness between the two component systems. We also know that, for emergent behavior to arise, there must be some appropriate feedback mechanisms, that there will be constraints on the behavior of the component parts of the system, and that there must be an energy flow through the system.

It can therefore be no surprise that the key feature of the solution is the BUYER'S AND CONTRACTOR'S MUTUAL WILLINGNESS TO ALIGN OBJECTIVES; this, surely, indicates a deep level of connectedness. However, for this to happen the behavior of the two parties has to be constrained. As we have seen, the solution depends on the BUYER'S WILLINGNESS TO COMMIT TO SHARE BENE-FITS, so constraining the buyer's tendencies to wish to take the contractor for every penny it has. Likewise, the contractor must curb the PRESSURE ON THE CONTRACTOR TO SEEK VARIATIONS AND CUT CORNERS, so constraining the contractor's tendencies to argue over every single point that was not absolutely explicit in the original specification. The feedback, of course, is the mutual awareness of whether or not both parties are adhering to the rules of the game — we all know, when conflict breaks out, how easy it is to claim that "the other guy started it."

What about the flow of energy through the system to maintain its emergent features? Once again, this comes down to leadership. Very often, those at the top can believe that they have reached agreement on a new way of operating but things get bogged down in the middle, for example when one of the contractor's more aggressive site managers has a row with one of the buyer's equally belligerent quality inspectors. It takes a great deal of energy to ensure that the intentions of the bosses continue to be aligned and continue to have effect throughout the two organizations.

Nevertheless, as we saw in the story about Nelson, that is precisely what leadership is all about.

10
Levers, outcomes, and strategy

This chapter goes up a level and is primarily about business strategy. The centerpiece of the chapter is a generic causal loop diagram that can apply to all businesses and contribute to the very core of strategy formulation.

Levers

Management is all about taking actions, making decisions, being wise. Each wise decision results in an action, or possibly an explicit agreement not to act, and each action manifests itself in some change to the status quo. As we saw on page 117, in many ways management is like driving some huge machine: Managers decide what to do; they set the controls of the machine; and the machine does whatever the controls determine. For sure, most of the parts of the "machine" are human and do not respond in any sense "mechanically"; nonetheless, there is a powerful analogy of the management team sitting at a master control panel, pulling this lever, twiddling this knob, setting that switch.

Each *lever* has a *name*, for example the "staff headcount" lever, which determines how many people you employ; the "sales channel" lever, which determines the ways in which you access your market; the "spend on IT" lever, which determines your annual spend on IT. At any time, each lever is associated with two *lever settings*. The first is the *actual setting*, representing the actual current value of the lever, or its description if a numerical value is not appropriate. So, for example, the staff headcount lever might have "As of today, we employ 3,000 people" as its actual setting; the sales channel lever might be described as "Today we reach our markets by using direct mail and telesales"; and the actual setting of the spend on IT lever might be "Our current expenditure on IT is £1.5 million per month."

In addition to the actual setting, each lever is associated with a *target setting* specifying what the value of that lever *should be*, rather than what it actually is. These target settings represent, at a higher level, management policies, which become reflected, at a lower level, as budgets. So the target values of the staff headcount lever might be "By the end of this year, we aim to have 3,200 staff"; the sales channel lever might be "Our policy is to reach our markets by using direct mail and telesales"; and the spend on IT lever might be "Our budget IT spend is £1.3 million per month." In the first case, the actual staff headcount is behind the year-end target and so a recruitment campaign is probably in place; in the second case, the actual setting of the sales channel lever is in harmony with the target setting and so the situation is stable; in the third case, the actual monthly spend on IT is more than the budget and this could trigger cost cutting.

Some organizations distinguish between budgets and targets, the budget being "that which must be achieved" and the more stretching target being "that which it would be nice to achieve." This suggests that each lever might in fact have three settings: the actual, the budget, and the target. In the interests of seeing the forest for the trees, however, and also recognizing that from a strategic point of view we are more interested in management policies than the minutiae of departmental budgeting, let's work on the basis that the levers have just two settings, actual and target.

What are the levers in your business?
Pause for a moment and think through the decisions and actions taken in your business. What are the levers that are pulled or pushed for each of these? What are their names? And what are the current values for the target settings and the actual settings?

This question is harder than it looks and it can result in a very long list. However, the list can be structured, since you will discover that the levers can be grouped into a relatively small number of hierarchies, which will reflect your organization's budgeting structure. The staff headcount lever, for example, might have an actual setting of 3,000, but this will be composed of lower-level levers such as "staff headcount in marketing," "staff headcount in finance," and "staff headcount in manufacturing" in accordance with your formal organizational structure. And these of course can be subdivided as "staff headcount in York factory," "staff headcount in Basingstoke factory," and all the rest.

Progressive subdivisions correspond to the domains of progressively more local management; their scope is correspondingly more limited and their time horizons progressively shorter. The most important levers, of course, are at the highest level, representing fundamental strategic policies, set by the board, for example what the overall staff headcount should be, what channels to market to deploy, or what the total IT investment should be. More junior levels of management are then responsible for the various actions required to bring these policies into reality: hiring, firing, and training; creating new channels to market; buying new IT equipment and building new systems.

What is strategy?

There are any number of definitions of strategy and the business books are full of them. In the current context, and in a very pragmatic sense, strategy can be defined in terms of the target settings of all your levers.

Any business, at any time, has its levers positioned at particular target settings. Strategy formulation is the process by which the senior management team decides how these lever target settings should be reset, if at all. Once these policy decisions are taken, the implementation of the strategy is the execution of all the corresponding actions, so that the actual settings of the levers can come into line with their target settings.

Strategy is all about resetting levers. Determining where a lever should be set, and then taking the corresponding actions, are — quite literally — the only things a manager can actually do.

Outcomes

Outcomes are the results of being in business. Outcomes also have *names* and *settings*; similarly, the settings come in two flavors: the *target settings* representing what we would like to achieve and the *actual settings*, which are what we are in fact achieving.

What are your business's outcomes?

Take a moment to list your business's outcomes. For each outcome, what are the corresponding target and actual settings?

The list of outcomes is generally much shorter than the list of levers, and usually comprises items such as:

➢ Sales volume.
➢ Sales revenue.
➢ Profits.
➢ Returns to investors.
➢ Market share.
➢ Rate of winning new customers.
➢ Share price.
➢ Reputation.
➢ Service quality.
➢ Throughput.
➢ Staff morale.
➢ Credit rating.

Items such as sales volume can be analyzed into as much detail as you wish — by product, by channel, by market—but, in aggregate, these all represent a single concept; similarly, items such as staff morale can be broken down into concepts such as staff loss rate, absenteeism, and so on. And as we saw with the levers, the outcomes can be structured into hierarchies. Also, even outcomes that are generally considered to be undesirable (such as the staff loss rate) have target values (most organizations see a modest level of staff turnover as beneficial, so very few would set their target loss rate at zero), as well, of course, as actuals (the staff loss rate that is happening right now).

How are the levers and the outcomes connected?

Compare the lists of levers and outcomes
Do you notice anything special, odd, or interesting?

In this comparison, most people notice that the list of levers is usually considerably longer than the list of outcomes, even at the policy level. What fewer people notice, but which to my mind falls into the category of "very interesting," is the fact that *the items on both lists are different: No outcome appears in the list of levers, and no lever appears in the list of outcomes.*

So, for example, there is no lever named "sales volume," "profits," "share price," and the rest. There are indeed many levers that *influence* these outcomes—the advertising lever, for example, influences sales volume; the overhead cost levers (there are lots of these) influence profit; and the public relations activity lever influences the share price. However, all of these are influences rather than direct drivers. You can spend as much money as you like on advertising, in the sincerely held belief that this will stimulate sales; the actual sales outcome, however, is in the gift of the market. Short of having all your family go to the shops to buy your product, at the end of the day all you can do is sit there and hope that the advertising has the effect you wished for.

Sometimes when people do this comparison they do find the same item on their lists of both levers and outcomes, and this may have happened to you. However, if you look back over the lists, you usually find that something has been misclassified. "Staff headcount," for example, might appear on your list of outcomes, but is this really an outcome, a goal of your business? Are you really trying to grow the headcount of your business for its own sake? I would be surprised. Staff headcount, in most businesses I know, is a means to an end—to provide a service, to operate machines and equipment—while the end, the outcome, is the result of all this endeavor, as measured in terms of sales and profits (for a commercial organization) or in terms of concepts such as throughput and service (for a non-commercial organization).

Likewise, "sales" sometimes appears on the list of levers. I guess we all wish it did. If any of us could magic up a lever with "sales" written on it, so that all we have to do is pull this lever and sales would *directly* result, then we would all be very happy indeed. Even in businesses that employ direct sales forces, the levers you actually pull are all about engineering face-to-face interactions with prospective customers: call rates, contact lists, and the rest. Short of illegal coercion, the actual sale is the gift of the customer—and if the customer doesn't want to buy, there is nothing you can do.

So a profound truth is the fact that *there is no action that any manager can take that can directly affect any outcome.* There really is no action that any manager can take, directly, to affect sales, profits, staff morale, the share price. Rather, the actions that managers take, the levers that they can actually pull, operate on the outcomes only indirectly, through cause-and-effect relationships that might be complex logically and may involve time delays.

> No lever is connected to any outcome directly; likewise, no outcome is connected to any lever directly. Rather, levers and outcomes are connected indirectly, as regards both logic and time.

That is worth thinking about. The statement is *not* saying that levers and outcomes are not connected at all; far from it. Rather, it is saying that they are connected, but that the connections are indirect, perhaps involving subtle cause-and-effect relationships, and maybe there are also time delays involved. A good example of this is the connection between the "advertising" lever and the "sales volume" outcome. The connection is both indirect and subtle. Few of us really understand precisely how advertising works, and even fewer of us can reliably state, "If we spend this amount on press advertising this weekend, I guarantee that the sales volume in the following five days will be [whatever]." The nature of the cause-and-effect relationship is not explicit and is rarely expressed as an algorithm or an equation.

For sure, most of us believe that advertising does influence sales, but the nature of the connection is indirect—whatever the marketing director might claim. What happens, for example, if competitors advertise their product even more forcibly over the same weekend? Or if there is some product scare? And how long does it take for advertising to influence a sale, especially for products like cars, washing machines, and holidays, which are not impulse buys or everyday items that you might reasonably expect to be purchased the day after your television ad was screened? We can—and do—pull the advertising lever, but in the hope or belief that something beneficial will happen to sales, eventually. We may compile all sorts of evidence to convince us that this is the case: awareness studies of audience recall, fancy econometric analyses, even fancier transfer function analyses. Nevertheless, however good the anecdotal or statistical evidence that advertising works the way you want it to, the actual, real, hard link between advertising expenditure and sales volume, revenue and profits—the true link between the lever you actually pull and the outcomes you want—is indirect, in both logic and time.

The link between the "advertising" lever and the "sales" outcome is a good example of a fuzzy link (see pages 65 and 133), one that we believe is present but is not readily expressed as a formula or algorithm. Many important links are of this nature, but there are also many links, especially those defining accounting relationships, that can be expressed more exactly. One aspect of the link between the "advertising" lever and the "profits" outcome, for example, can be defined in terms of the cost of advertising, which contributes to the total cost of running the business, which in turn influences the profits figure. This trail is well defined and, although there may be many steps along the way (if the advertising takes place overseas we may have to account for exchange rates, for example), each is simply a matter of carrying out the appropriate computation.

The fundamental fact remains, however, that there is no direct link between the "advertising" lever and the "sales" outcome, or between the "advertising" lever and the "profits" outcome, or indeed between any lever and any outcome. No manager can take any action that influences an outcome directly.

Why managing a business is difficult

As a manager, the *only* thing you can do is to operate on the levers—to decide their target settings and take corresponding actions to bring the actual settings into line.

As a manager, the *only* thing you want is a complete set of favorable outcomes, continuously.

However, no lever is directly connected to any outcome, either in terms of logic or time.

So the only thing you can actually do in practice is to pull the levers toward the target settings you believe in, close your eyes, and hope that the outcomes will come out right.

There's nothing else you can do.

That's why managing a business is difficult.

You don't, of course, close your eyes—but I'm sure you follow my imagery! In fact, you are continuously monitoring how the actual outcomes are measuring up against the target outcomes. And if things are off track, you take action accordingly. But what sort of action? You reset levers—that's the only thing you can do. Perhaps you change the setting of the "price" lever downward, hoping to encourage volume; perhaps you move the "promotions" lever upward with the same objective in mind; perhaps you ease the "training expenditure" lever to save money and bring the "profits" outcome more into line. Every action you take is, and can only be, the resetting of one or more levers. Obviously, resetting a lever often results in a dilemma in which one desired outcome might be increased but another diminished. For example, spending more on advertising might indeed increase sales (eventually), but it increases costs and so depletes profits (right now) as well. What is the overall effect and how long does it take to come through? Managing a business is indeed difficult.

Levers, outcomes, and systems thinking

The last few pages have been full of systems thinking. The most obvious is the last paragraph, which identified that the monitoring of target outcomes against actual outcomes triggers the resetting of one or more levers. This is, of course, a balancing loop (Figure 10.1).

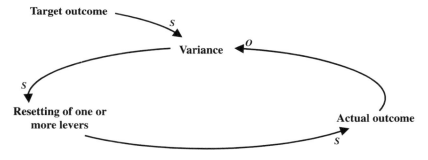

Figure 10.1

However, by far the more important reference to systems thinking is buried in the statement: "Rather, the actions managers take, the levers that they can actually pull, operate on the outcomes only indirectly, through cause-and-effect relationships that might be complex logically and may involve time delays." For, as the next few sections of this chapter will show, systems thinking can help you trace what these indirect connections are and how they evolve over time. Taming this kind of complexity is precisely what systems thinking is very good at doing.

Levers, outcomes, and loops

Our starting point is to capture some levers and outcomes as causal loops. Given the total number of levers and outcomes in any real business, capturing them all would give rise to a very cluttered diagram. In the interests of clarity, let's focus on just two outcomes—MARKET SHARE and RETURNS TO

INVESTORS—and a single lever, STAFF HEADCOUNT. As we shall see, additional levers and outcomes are easily incorporated later.

Figure 10.2 is a causal loop that captures the outcomes.

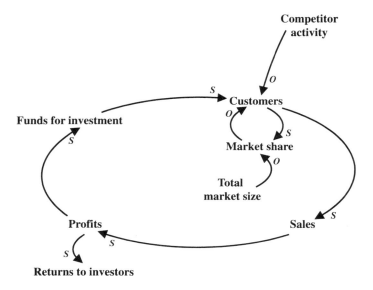

Figure 10.2

The two most important outcomes of MARKET SHARE and RETURNS TO INVESTORS are *actual* outcomes, measuring the actual overall results of the business; we'll see how the target outcomes—the intended market share and the required returns to investors—can be incorporated on page 226.

This loop is of course the now familiar reinforcing loop driving the engine of business growth. As we saw in Chapter 8, in practice the natural exponential dynamic of growth is constrained by many factors, both internal and external; for the moment only two of these constraints are shown, those relating to TOTAL MARKET SIZE and COMPETITOR ACTIVITY. All businesses have at least one engine of business growth of this type and the objective of all businesses is to make it spin faster.

There are, however, no levers that managers can pull that directly affect the two key outcomes of MARKET SHARE and RETURNS TO INVESTORS. If we assume the business we are considering is a service—software development, say—then one of the most important levers is the STAFF HEADCOUNT, a term that in this case I am using very broadly to encompass not only the numerical headcount, but also training and management development. Let's further suppose that the senior management team has agreed that the major current constraint on growth is the headcount, comprising the sales force as well as the software developers, and that to alleviate this constraint there is a need to increase both the staff numbers and their skills. This results in a decision to reset the staff headcount lever to a new target setting, the NEW TARGET HEADCOUNT. Comparison of the NEW TARGET HEADCOUNT to the ACTUAL HEADCOUNT gives rise to a STAFF VARIANCE. This is the trigger for invoking the actions of HIRING, FIRING, AND TRAINING, so as to bring the ACTUAL HEADCOUNT into line with the policy represented by the NEW TARGET HEADCOUNT. This is of course a balancing loop (Figure 10.3).

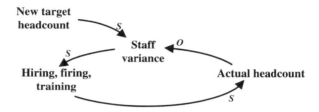

Figure 10.3

The target setting of the headcount lever, the NEW TARGET HEADCOUNT, is an input policy dangle, which we will leave dangling for the moment. We shall soon see how it is determined (see pages 226–31).

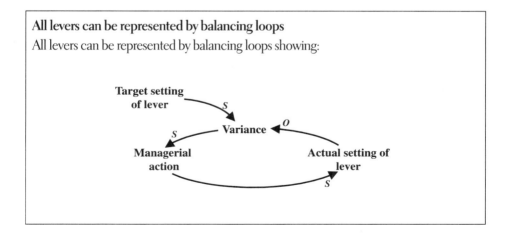

> ➤ The TARGET SETTING OF THE LEVER is determined by policy.
> ➤ The ACTUAL SETTING OF THE LEVER is determined by current reality.
> ➤ The MANAGERIAL ACTION is whatever is required to bring the actual setting into line with the target setting.

If we put these two loops together on the same page, we get Figure 10.4.

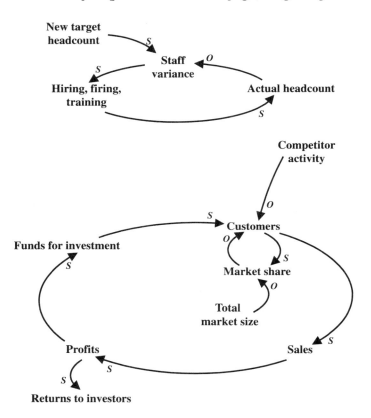

Figure 10.4

The actions that managers are taking are all around the balancing loop: taking the decision to reset the target value of the staff headcount lever to the NEW TARGET HEADCOUNT, and carrying out all the corresponding actions of HIRING, FIRING, TRAINING to bring the ACTUAL HEADCOUNT into line with the NEW TARGET HEADCOUNT. The fruits of success of all this activity, however, take place in the reinforcing loop, culminating in the growth of the two most important outcomes, MARKET SHARE and RETURNS TO INVESTORS.

At the moment, however, the two halves of the diagram are not connected. This is indeed a vivid representation of the principle that levers and outcomes are not directly connected, both logically and in time.

Nevertheless, the connections are there—but where?

Connecting the loops

One way of determining where the connections are is to select any item on the balancing loop, and any item on the reinforcing loop, and ask the question: "Is there any chain of cause-and-effect relationships between the chosen item on the balancing loop and the chosen item on the reinforcing loop, in either direction? If so, what is it? And how can we represent it succinctly?" If there is a chain of causality, we can capture it; if not, we can move on to explore the relationship, if any, of the same item on the balancing loop with the next item around the reinforcing loop. By doing this systematically for all the items in the balancing loop, testing the connections to all the items in the reinforcing loop, we can ensure that we cover all possibilities.

Let's take, for example, the item NEW TARGET HEADCOUNT in the balancing loop. Is this linked in any way to, for example, the item CUSTOMERS on the reinforcing loop? How does the aspiration of having, say, 300 more software developers influence the existing customer base or attract new customers? Maybe if there is a great deal of good press coverage, hyping up the growth plans, this might increase the firm's reputation, and this might get its name on some tender lists; that is a possibility. And good publicity may also help the share price.

However, one of the skills in drawing insightful causal loop diagrams is to distinguish the important from the incidental, to see the forest for the trees. A chain of causality from NEW TARGET HEADCOUNT through PUBLICITY and EFFECT OF PUBLICITY ON ATTRACTING NEW CUSTOMERS and then to CUS-TOMERS is a possibility, but in my view a weak one in this case. My judgment is not to include it here, but I can imagine other cases where it might be important. This, of course, is the manifestation of my mental models about this particular circumstance.

In fact, I do not see any appropriate links between the policy lever of NEW TARGET HEADCOUNT and any of the items on the reinforcing loop, so let's try another item in the balancing loop—say, the ACTUAL HEADCOUNT.

That is more promising, because I can see that there is a link between the ACTUAL HEADCOUNT and PROFITS. Clearly, there are all sorts of costs of employment—salaries, benefits, employment taxes—and the larger these costs, the smaller the PROFITS. On the same tack, pulling the action levers of HIRING, FIRING, TRAINING also incurs lots of costs—advertising, commissions to agencies, outplacement and redundancy costs, training costs—so let's lump all these together under the title COSTS OF THE CHANGE PROGRAM. This introduces two additional links to the diagram, both going from the balancing loop to the reinforcing loop, by way of an aggregate cost category, the TOTAL HR COSTS (Figure 10.5).

These links feed into the reinforcing loop with an O and so the effect is to act as a brake, which makes sense. And the diagram also makes the important point that the TOTAL HR COSTS are made up of two main components: the ACTUAL STAFF COSTS, which represent the total costs of the steady-state staff headcount that we have on board at any time, and the more transient COSTS OF THE CHANGE PROGRAM, these costs being specifically attributable to the current level of activity associated with the action levers of HIRING, FIRING, TRAINING.

Are there any more links from the ACTUAL HEADCOUNT?
Go back to the ACTUAL HEADCOUNT in the balancing loop and test this against all the other items in the reinforcing loop. Are there any more links? If so, how would you describe them?

There is indeed another link—in fact, it is the single most important link in the diagram. It connects ACTUAL HEADCOUNT with CUSTOMERS. Let me explain my mental model about what this link means and you can check my view against your own mental model.

Our business is software development and, as a service business, the success we have is attributable to the quality of the software we develop. The smarter our software, the better our project management in estimating and delivery, the more professional our sales process, the more successful the business will be. However, all these are themselves underpinned by people: If the caliber of our staff is poor or if we are too small so that key people are overstretched, then the business will fail. Fundamental to our business is the

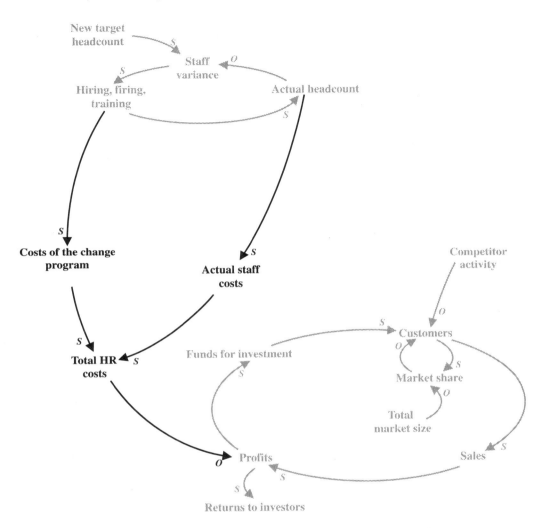

Figure 10.5

relationship between our people, as represented by the ACTUAL HEADCOUNT, and our CUSTOMERS. Good people keep our customers happy, so encouraging the opportunities for repeat business and increasing the likelihood of winning new business.

There must therefore be a link between ACTUAL HEADCOUNT and CUSTOMERS, since it is this link that keeps us in business. The link, however, is fuzzy: There is no equation that I can write down to express it, nor is there an accounting definition I can use. No matter—let me invent some words to

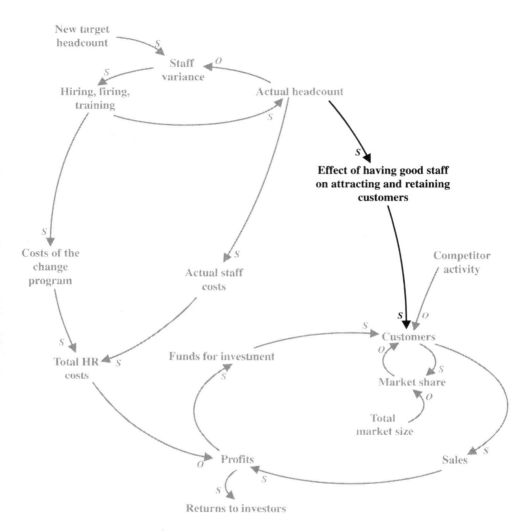

Figure 10.6

express the concept I have in mind. Let me call it the EFFECT OF HAVING GOOD STAFF ON ATTRACTING AND RETAINING CUSTOMERS. It may be fuzzy and intangible and I may not be able to measure it very well. But that doesn't stop it from being real (Figure 10.6).

This triggers another link, from the action lever of HIRING, FIRING, TRAINING into the EFFECT OF HAVING GOOD STAFF ON ATTRACTING AND RETAINING CUSTOMERS.

> **An S or an O?**
>
> Do you think that there is a link between HIRING, FIRING, TRAINING into the EFFECT
> OF HAVING GOOD STAFF ON ATTRACTING AND RETAINING CUSTOMERS? If so,
> what does it represent? And is it an S or an O?

I believe that there is a link and that it's an O. A change program usually disrupts the effectiveness of an organization. Experienced staff are tied up on recruitment and training and so are obliged to spend less time on customer-facing activities; if staff are being laid off, there is not only a distraction of effort but a dip in morale too. The action lever of HIRING, FIRING, TRAINING represents the activity that actually takes place to accomplish these actions, and my mental model is that this links to the EFFECT OF HAVING GOOD STAFF ON ATTRACTING AND RETAINING CUSTOMERS with an O. The greater the level of this activity, the less effective the organization will be at looking after customers (Figure 10.7 overleaf). Anyone who has ever experienced a merger knows this all too well.

If this last O is a surprise and you believe it should be an S, you may be failing to distinguish between the change program itself and the end result of the program, once it has been accomplished. The overall intention of HIRING, FIRING, TRAINING is of course to increase the EFFECT OF HAVING GOOD STAFF ON ATTRACTING AND RETAINING CUSTOMERS, so this is indeed an S type of link. But this is the result of the program, not a feature of the program itself—the program itself is disruptive. The disruption of the program itself is captured by the O—the end result is in fact not a link from HIRING, FIRING, TRAINING, but is derived from the ACTUAL HEADCOUNT as enhanced after the change program has been completed, and the link from ACTUAL HEADCOUNT to the EFFECT OF HAVING GOOD STAFF ON ATTRACTING AND RETAINING CUSTOMERS is already there, with the correct S. In the balancing loop, the action—in this case HIRING, FIRING, TRAINING—is a transient, and usually disruptive, activity, which exists only for as long as the action is taking place. The beneficial steady state is captured in the actual.

The last link

> **The missing link**
>
> There is one more link between the balancing loop and the reinforcing loop. Can you spot it?

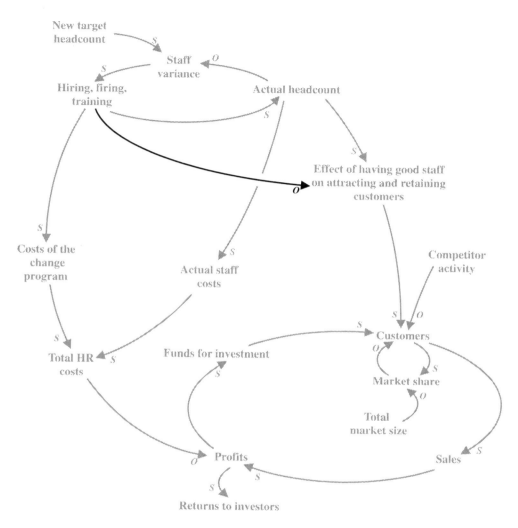

Figure 10.7

The diagram so far has two links from the balancing loop to the reinforcing loop, with opposing effects. The link through TOTAL HR COSTS and into PROF-ITS has an O and so is braking the reinforcing loop's spin, whereas the link through the EFFECT OF HAVING GOOD STAFF ON ATTRACTING AND RETAINING CUSTOMERS has an S and so is fueling the loop. That makes sense, since the management issue is to balance these two effects.

There is, however, one more crucial link between the two loops. But this link goes from the balancing loop to the reinforcing loop: It links FUNDS FOR

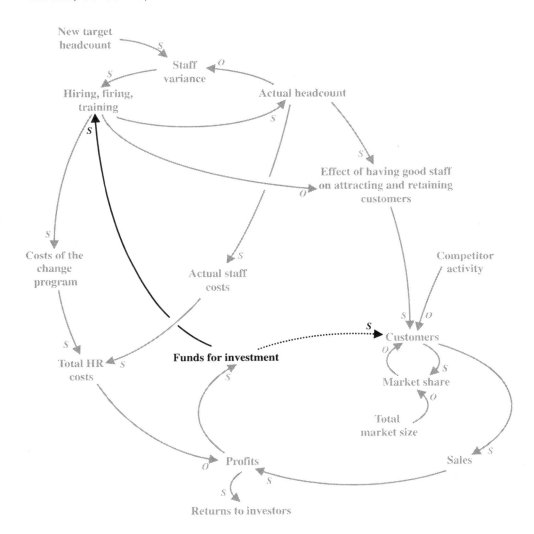

Figure 10.8

INVESTMENT to HIRING, FIRING, TRAINING, and this link is an S.

In this story so far, and in fact in all the stories of business growth in the preceding chapters, I have glossed over an important issue: the nature of the link between FUNDS FOR INVESTMENT and CUSTOMERS. Intuitively, this link exists and so it is correct to show it in all the diagrams so far. Nevertheless, this has glossed over *how* the investment actually works. It doesn't happen by itself; it happens because managers decide to invest funds in particular programs to help stimulate the acquisition of new customers and the retention of existing ones, as has been tacitly assumed by the single arrow linking FUNDS FOR INVESTMENT to CUSTOMERS in all the diagrams so far.

However, in the current case, just what is this program to help stimulate the acquisition of new customers and the retention of existing ones? It must be the program of HIRING, FIRING, TRAINING, which is financed by this investment. There is therefore a link from FUNDS FOR INVESTMENT to HIRING, FIRING, TRAINING, which *replaces* the link from FUNDS FOR INVESTMENT to CUSTOMERS. Conceptually these links are identical, but now we have the balancing loop shown explicitly we can identify what the link really means. Figure 10.8 captures this, but reminds us of the replaced link by showing it as a dotted line.

Does this diagram make sense?

Take a good look at Figure 10.8. Does it make sense? Where is the reinforcing loop? And how does it interact with the original balancing loop?

I trust that it does make sense because, as we will see shortly, this diagram is a basic building block of a generic strategic causal loop diagram. The reinforcing loop is still there too, but it follows a new path: starting at CUSTOMERS, then SALES, PROFITS and FUNDS FOR INVESTMENT; from there to HIRING, FIRING, TRAINING and on to ACTUAL HEADCOUNT; then back, by way of the EFFECT OF HAVING GOOD STAFF ON ATTRACTING AND RETAINING CUSTOMERS, to CUSTOMERS. There are Ss all the way. This is the original reinforcing loop, but enriched by stating explicitly not only what the FUNDS FOR INVESTMENT are being spent on—namely HIRING, FIRING, TRAINING—but also why the funds are being spent—to enhance the EFFECT OF HAVING GOOD STAFF ON ATTRACTING AND RETAINING CUSTOMERS. All this is:

➤ Driven by the input policy dangle of the NEW TARGET HEADCOUNT.
➤ With the outcomes of MARKET SHARE and RETURNS TO INVESTORS as constrained by:
   — the external factors of COMPETITOR ACTIVITY and TOTAL MARKET SIZE, and
   — the internal ones of TOTAL HR COSTS and the distracting effect of HIRING, FIRING, TRAINING on the EFFECT OF HAVING GOOD STAFF ON ATTRACTING AND RETAINING CUSTOMERS.

> **There is only one driving link from the balancing loop to the reinforcing loop**
> A notable feature of this diagram is that there is only *one* driving link from the balancing loop to the reinforcing loop—just a single, solitary link that connects the management actions with the objective of making the reinforcing loop spin faster. There are some other links too, but these all act as brakes.
>
> That driving link is crucial. Without it the reinforcing loop would grind to a halt and might possibly start spinning the other way into a spiral of decline. However, it is this link that is the fuzzy one—the EFFECT OF HAVING GOOD STAFF ON ATTRACTING AND RETAINING CUSTOMERS. Although it is fuzzy, it is the most important.

What about the other levers?

> **The other levers**
> The diagram so far shows the interaction between the reinforcing loop of business growth and the balancing loop associated with the lever for staff headcount. What would the diagram have looked like had we chosen, say, the organization's policy in relation to brand image?

What about the diagram in Figure 10.9 overleaf?

The story here is driven by a desire for a more modern brand, a corporate name change, or an identity "makeover." This creates a NEW TARGET BRAND IMAGE, which is significantly different from the ACTUAL BRAND IMAGE, so creating a BRAND IMAGE GAP, which initiates a REBRANDING PROGRAM.

This, of course, incurs significant COSTS OF THE CHANGE PROGRAM, which will be financed by the FUNDS FOR INVESTMENT. In addition, the steady state branding—both the old and the new—incurs ACTUAL BRANDING COSTS, contributing to the TOTAL BRANDING COSTS.

Why are we doing all of this? Because we believe in a concept that might be called the EFFECT OF BRAND IMAGE ON ATTRACTING AND RETAINING CUSTOMERS. If we didn't believe in that, we wouldn't spend all that money, would we? And, as usual with change programs, there is likely to be a downside of the change program itself, as senior managers spend an enormous amount of time debating the new name and the colors of the new logo, while customers wonder just what that strange, new, unpronounceable name really means.

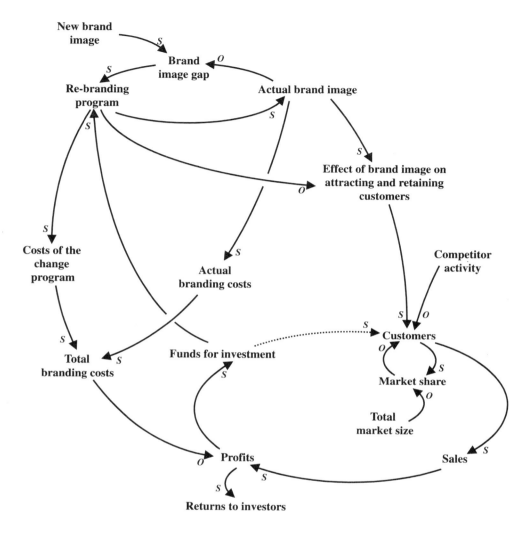

Figure 10.9

What are the differences between this diagram and the previous one?

Other than some specific changes in a few of the names — so HIRING, FIRING, TRAIN-
ING has been replaced by REBRANDING PROGRAM — there are none. These name
changes are appropriate since the two policy contexts are different, but from a structural
point of view the two diagrams are identical.

As I'm sure you have guessed, the diagrams would still be identical had I chosen pricing policy, asset policy, ethical policy, or whatever. This diagram is truly generic.

Whatever the lever, it will be associated with a balancing loop. Within that loop, any variance between the actual setting of the lever and the target setting will trigger management action. This will be some form of change program, which will last as long as required to bring the actual setting into line with the target.

The overall objective of this will be to create an actual setting of the lever that has a beneficial impact on the business growth engine, usually by having a positive effect on attracting and retaining customers.

The actual setting of the lever will incur operating costs, as will the change program, and these collectively feed back into the growth engine to deplete profits. The change program itself is also likely to have a detrimental effect.

The change program is financed by the funds for investment and, since this is usually a single fund, each of the various levers competes for these limited funds. One of the most important management decisions—and one that requires much wisdom—is the allocation of these funds across competing interests. This decision determines which of the various levers will be actioned more vigorously and which less so, with the overall intention of fueling the exponential growth of the business, so as to grow the desired outcomes as effectively as possible.

A general business model

As we have already seen when we listed the key levers and outcomes, the number of outcomes is usually significantly fewer than the number of levers; in general, a single growth engine is being controlled by many different levers. Since the interaction between any one lever and the growth engine is similar, we can capture a more realistic business model, as in Figure 10.10 overleaf.

This shows a business with two outcomes—RETURNS TO INVESTORS and MARKET SHARE—and driven by four levers representing STAFF POLICY, BRANDING POLICY, PRODUCT POLICY, and ASSET POLICY. Each of the associated balancing loops has been shown as a single symbol and the key interactions from each balancing loop to the central reinforcing loop have been summarized as a single aggregate COST and a GROWTH DRIVER, this being an abbreviation for the effect of the given lever on attracting and retaining customers.

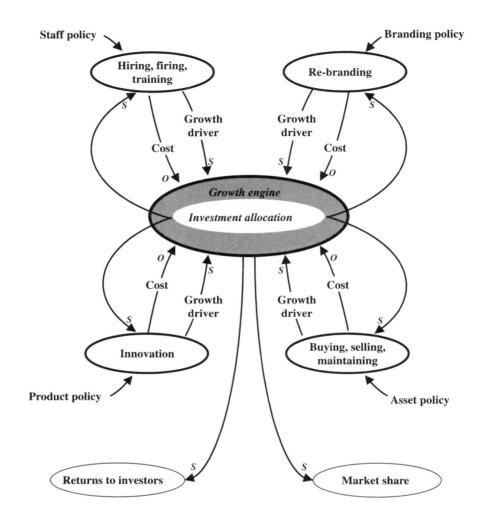

Figure 10.10

Central to the growth engine is the INVESTMENT ALLOCATION representing the decision on how best to allocate the funds for investment, generated by the business engine, across the various levers.

How does your organization take that investment allocation decision?
Every business takes this decision, so how does yours do it? Is it a power play? Or is it done with a wise understanding of each of the growth drivers associated with this diagram?

No business has only four levers, even at this level of aggregation, but no matter. I am sure you can see exactly how a multi-lever business could be portrayed on such a diagram, as well as a business with several different growth engines.

However, it is not just a diagram, since it is also a bridge into the ability to build a computer simulation model, so that you can—quite literally—build a "control panel" with "levers" determining the various lever settings. The model itself captures the logic of the causal loop diagram and so enables the dynamic behavior of the business to be simulated, resulting in graphs like the ones shown on pages 79, 142, and 149. As I mentioned on page 7, the computer modeling of causal loop diagrams, transforming the necessarily static paper-and-pencil picture into a dynamic "movie," is, appropriately enough, called system dynamics, a subject that I will explore in some depth in Chapters 12 and 13. Because the generic structure of the behavior of each lever is identical, building a strategic system dynamics model is not as difficult as you might think. In principle, you need build only two generic modules, one for the growth engine and one for the generic structure of a lever. The lever module can then be replicated and adapted for each lever and tuned with the appropriate data.

Tuning the data for each lever is in fact a much more demanding task than building the logic of the lever module. Central to each lever is that crucial, but very fuzzy, item the EFFECT OF [THIS LEVER] ON ATTRACTING AND RETAINING CUSTOMERS. This is not the type of item you see in accountants' spreadsheets, but it is very much the type of item found in wise strategists' system dynamics models. System dynamics models are very tolerant of fuzzy variables (see page 65), because systems thinking recognizes them as fundamentally important, even if the accountants don't yet measure them.

Performance measures

There is a great deal of truth in the saying "If you don't measure it, you can't manage it," and the objective of all performance measurement systems is to measure the things you need to manage.

Do they really do this?

The essence of systems thinking is to tame complexity, to see through the forest to the right trees, to identify and distinguish what is important from the rest. The items that are captured in causal loop diagrams are therefore precisely those that you need to manage. However, if you look through many of the diagrams in this book, some items are to be found in most businesses' accounting and measurement systems—items such as SALES and PROFITS—while many are not, particularly growth drivers like the EFFECT OF GOOD STAFF ON ATTRACTING AND RETAINING CUSTOMERS.

So do business measurement systems measure only those items that are easy to measure and ignore the rest? Or do they—or indeed should they—measure those items that are genuinely important, even if they are hard to measure? Another of the benefits of systems thinking is that the process of compiling causal loop diagrams identifies those items that should be measured, and wise organizations then set about solving the problem of how. Those that succeed reap the benefits.

The big picture

In this section I would like to tie up two loose ends identified by the dangles in the diagrams that we have been looking at so far.

First, the matter of target settings of the levers. In all the diagrams so far, the target settings of the levers—representing, for example, the NEW TARGET HEADCOUNT or the NEW TARGET BRAND IMAGE—have been input dangles specifying the goals of the balancing loops. Where do these targets come from?

Secondly, there is the issue of target settings of the outcomes, which have been absent from all the diagrams so far. All the outcomes, such as RETURNS TO INVESTORS and MARKET SHARE, have been actual outcomes representing the actual results of the business's operations, rather than targets.

In fact, these two loose ends may be tied up together in the same causal loop diagram (Figure 10.11). In general, the DECISION TO CHANGE THE TARGET SETTING OF ONE OR MORE LEVERS is the action determined as a result of the VARIANCES between the TARGET OUTCOMES and the ACTUAL OUTCOMES.

In this diagram, which is a balancing loop driving the ACTUAL OUTCOMES toward the TARGET OUTCOMES, the business engine represents the totality of the previous diagrams, which in effect have a single input dangle, representing the collective target settings of all the levers, and a single output dangle, representing the collective values of all the actual outcomes.

In practice, in most businesses the balancing loop in Figure 10.11 operates at three levels, depending on the timescales involved. Over the shortest

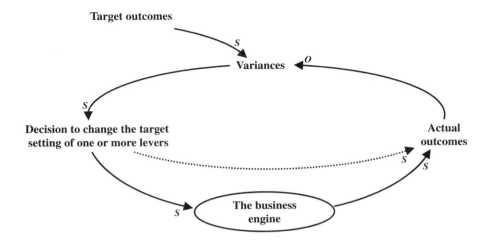

Figure 10.11

timescale, within an accounting year, and in particular as the organization nears the end of the accounting year, the TARGET OUTCOMES are THIS YEAR'S BUDGETS TO DATE, the ACTUAL OUTCOMES are THIS YEAR'S ACTUALS TO DATE as shown in the most recent period's management accounts. The action driven by the VARIANCES is the identification of SHORT-TERM FIXES, such as cutting

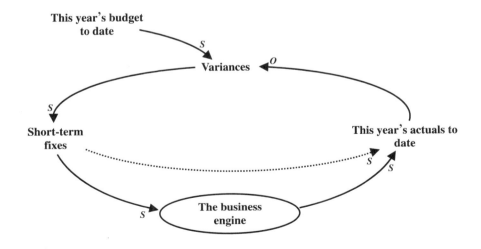

Figure 10.12

the training budget (a short-term resetting of the staff headcount lever), or a new sales promotion (a short-term resetting of the marketing mix lever), or whatever, so that the business is steered with the intention of bringing the actual year-end out-turn into line with the budget's aspirations (Figure 10.12).

In the medium term, a similar diagram represents the process of determining next year's budget too (Figure 10.13).

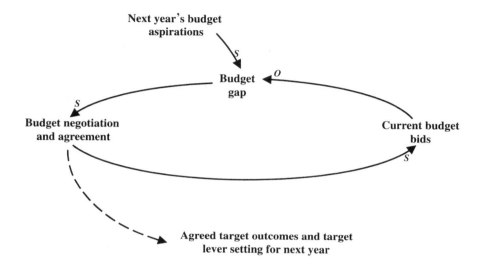

Figure 10.13

Different businesses operate this process in different ways. Those that go "top-down" start with NEXT YEAR'S BUDGET ASPIRATIONS; those that go "bottom-up" start with CURRENT BUDGET BIDS from each of the budgeting departments. Either way, all organizations go round the loop, negotiating, arguing, and bargaining, until a truce is reached, as recognized by "the budget," which determines both the target outcomes and also the target lever settings for the business for the following year. And once the target lever settings have been agreed these are compared to the actual lever settings, as shown in Figure 10.12. The bottom arrow in Figure 10.13, by the way, is shown as dotted to indicate that it is a flow of information, rather than a description of causality; by the same token there is no S or O, since the question "As the BUDGET NEGOTIATION AND FINAL AGREEMENT increase, do the AGREED TARGET OUTCOMES AND TARGET LEVER SETTINGS FOR NEXT YEAR increase or decrease?" doesn't really make sense. This is a feature of higher-level diagrams, which necessarily deal with broader concepts.

Structurally, the same diagram also applies at the strategic level, where the time horizon is much longer. The words are rather different, but the diagram, both in structure and in concept, is the same (Figure 10.14).

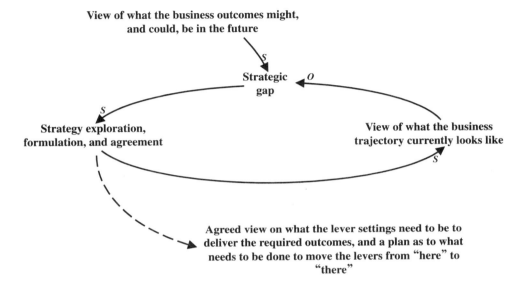

Figure 10.14

This diagram suggests that the process of STRATEGY EXPLORATION, FORMU-LATION, AND AGREEMENT is fundamentally driven by a mismatch between a VIEW OF WHAT THE BUSINESS OUTCOMES MIGHT, AND COULD, BE IN THE FUTURE and a VIEW OF WHAT THE BUSINESS TRAJECTORY CURRENTLY LOOKS LIKE. Since, as we have seen, the only actions a manager can take relate to resetting the levers, the result is an AGREED VIEW ON WHAT THE LEVER SET-TINGS NEED TO BE TO DELIVER THE REQUIRED OUTCOMES, AND A PLAN AS TO WHAT NEEDS TO BE DONE TO MOVE THE LEVERS FROM "HERE" TO "THERE."

However, where does the VIEW OF WHAT THE BUSINESS OUTCOMES MIGHT, AND COULD, BE IN THE FUTURE come from? To my mind, there is one and only one driver of this, the AMBITION, VISION, AND IMAGINATION of the senior man-agement team (Figure 10.15 overleaf).

The last three diagrams can be brought together to give a truly "big pic-ture" (Figure 10.16 on page 231).

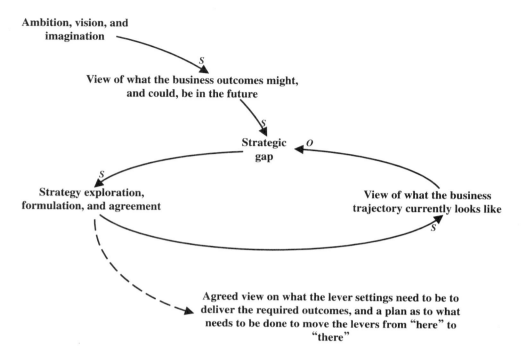

Figure 10.15

How does our organization determine strategy?

Figure 10.15 highlights three different approaches to strategy formulation:

➢ *Approach 1*: The collective VIEW OF WHAT THE BUSINESS TRAJECTORY CUR-
RENTLY LOOKS LIKE is "Well… don't know, really… probably OK" and there isn't
much AMBITION, VISION, AND IMAGINATION. The STRATEGIC GAP is correspondingly small.

➢ *Approach 2*: The business is approaching a crisis and the collective VIEW OF WHAT
THE BUSINESS TRAJECTORY CURRENTLY LOOKS LIKE is "We will be in one hell
of a mess." Although there isn't much AMBITION, VISION, AND IMAGINATION, the
STRATEGIC GAP is significant, but driven by crisis.

➢ *Approach 3*: There is tremendous AMBITION, VISION, AND IMAGINATION and the
business is in good shape. The STRATEGIC GAP is large, but as a result of the power of
the VIEW OF WHAT THE BUSINESS OUTCOMES MIGHT, AND COULD, BE IN
THE FUTURE.

Which approach does your organization follow?

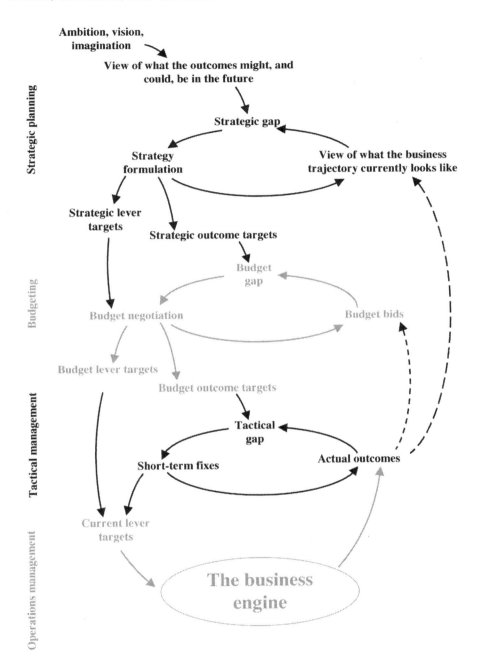

Figure 10.16

Encouraging ambition, vision, and imagination

As Figure 10.16 illustrates, the fundamental driver of business strategy is the organization's—or indeed a leading individual's—AMBITION, VISION, AND IMAGINATION. The more vigorous these are, the more powerful the VIEW OF WHAT THE BUSINESS OUTCOMES MIGHT, AND COULD, BE IN THE FUTURE. Conversely, the more limited these are, the duller the strategy, as articulated most forcefully in business guru Gary Hamel's most recent book, *Leading the Revolution*: "Giving planners responsibility for creating strategy is like asking a bricklayer to create Michaelangelo's *Pietà*."

There is a school of thought that sees qualities such as vision and imagination as intrinsic features of personality, with which only very few people are born. I certainly agree that there are some people who are amazingly charismatic, people who are true visionaries; but I certainly do not agree that the rest of us are unable to contribute. In my view, we all have the ability to envisage powerful pictures of the future, we can all stimulate our imaginations, we can all have great ideas. All of these characteristics can be enhanced by having the will to try as well as knowledge and confidence in the appropriate tools and techniques.

So let me conclude this chapter with a brief overview of a method to help encourage ambition, vision, and imagination in the context of strategic planning. As I mentioned on page 204, there are umpteen books on strategy and even more methods, tools, techniques, analytical approaches, and pro-forma charts. The method I will describe here is based on *scenario planning*.

The mental model underpinning scenario planning is the belief that no one can predict the future. For the faint of heart, this might imply that there is no point whatsoever in making any long-term plans—the future will always conspire against you. The best that can be achieved is therefore a series of day-to-day decisions, reacting to circumstances as they arise. This "do nothing" approach is regarded by many—including scenario planners—not only as an abdication of management, but as logically flawed too. Some decisions necessarily take a long time to implement and come to fruition. If you want to open a new market, build a new major factory, or develop a new drug, then the time that this will take goes far beyond anyone's ability to predict the future with certainty. Such decisions, however, must be taken.

Another reaction to the problem of prediction is the belief that "I can make the future happen." I may not be able to predict things in general but, as far as my business is concerned, "I'll do it my way." Those who take this view are often very powerful, dominating individuals, and sometimes they can indeed exert their influence—but equally, sometimes they can't.

Scenario planners steer a middle course. Decisions have to be taken, even though the future is uncertain. There are some things I can control, but there are many I can't. The best thing to do is therefore to take decisions now in the context of having examined a *range of plausible, alternative futures*, so that I have tested the decisions in the light of these possibilities. By doing so quite rigorously, I can minimize the likelihood of being caught unawares by unforeseen circumstances and maximize the opportunity of "catching the next wave."

Gods, gamblers, grinders, and guides

Another way of thinking about how planning methods map on to different personal styles and beliefs is shown on the grid below. The vertical axis represents the dominant style, distinguishing between control and empowerment; the horizontal axis, the dominant beliefs, distinguishing between prediction and exploration.

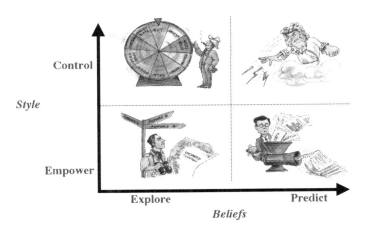

Those who believe that they can predict the future and who are controllers behave as *gods*. They have enormous self-confidence and they know the answers. They don't need any planning methods at all—these just get in the way of being decisive.

Those who are less confident in their ability to predict but who are also controllers are the *gamblers*. They know that they will not win on every bet, so they like to know the odds. Gamblers therefore ask for, and appreciate, financial analyses.

Those who prefer a style of empowerment but believe that they can predict are *grinders*. They just love analyses, methods, data, and techniques, since they are always searching for the "right" answer. Grinders are beloved of consultants, because they will always pay huge sums for the latest business school fad.

In the last quadrant are the *guides*. Unlike grinders, guides do not believe that there is a "right" answer waiting to be "found" if only they knew the right technique. Rather, they know that the future cannot be predicted and so they seek to guide their organization wisely through uncertainty. Guides find scenario planning to be a very powerful aid.

The central feature of my approach to scenario planning is the completion of a table with the structure shown in Figure 10.17. The columns represent various worlds, the first column being *today's world*, and the remaining columns a number of alternative *future worlds*. The three rows represent, respectively, *context, levers,* and *outcomes*.

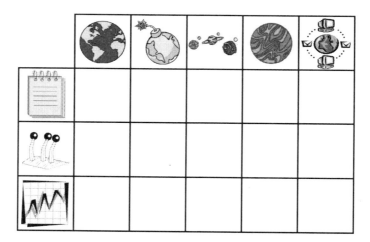

Figure 10.17

Let's look at the first column, *today's world*. The middle and bottom cells in this column require no further explanation – they contain, respectively, the names and current settings of all your levers, and the names and current settings of all your business outcomes, exactly as described in the earlier part of this chapter.

Your business, however, exists in a *context*—the context of today's world. The context cell therefore contains a description of just what that context is.

This is best documented as a structured list of bullet points, each of which is a particular, specific feature of today's business context. The emphasis of the description is not so much on the features of your business, since many of those are captured in the names and settings of the levers and outcomes. Rather, the emphasis is on external features of the environment in which your business operates such as the political context; the nature of the industry structure; the activities of competitors; social factors such as demographics; and technical factors such as the technological trends affecting your business and your customers.

These descriptions require considerable thought, effort, and clarity of mind. They need to pass the "Martian test," so that if you were to send a Martian an email of the description on his way over, on landing he would instantly recognize what he saw. Also, the descriptions need to be quite detailed. The metaphor here is that the picture being painted is not broadbrush, like a Gauguin or a Matisse; rather, it is like a Canaletto, or a Dutch Old Master, with fine detail, meticulously depicted. So don't be surprised if you compile several hundred individual items, clustered under headings like "industry structure," "political context," "demographics," and the rest, as suggested in the last paragraph.

How to be creative

The process described so far populates the cells in the first column of the scenario planning table, that of today's world. The next step is where imagination comes in, since this is the key skill in defining sets of descriptions for a number of alternative, plausible future worlds—descriptions of how the context in which your business operates might look in five, ten, or twenty years' time.

Things that are new have at least one feature that is different

Imagine something simple that you are familiar with—say, the game of chess. Imagine further that you have compiled a complete description of chess, in the form of bullet points, at a sufficient level of detail to pass the Martian test, so that a Martian, when landing, could identify the game of chess and distinguish it from a game of football, a game of cards, or a board meeting, from your description alone.

Now imagine that you have a similar description of another game—say, checkers. How do you distinguish between these two different games? They are very similar — both have black and white pieces; both are played by two players, on a board, sitting by a table; the board is identical, being checkered, eight squares by eight; both games can be played by adults and by children, by men and by women. The differences between chess and checkers lie at a lower level of detail: The characteristics of individual pieces are different and the rules of the moves are different.

Now imagine a game that doesn't exist. "That's crazy," I hear you say, "How can I imagine a game that doesn't exist?"

You've just had a clue how to do this. Take a game that already exists, such as chess, and list its features. Then take one of those features and make it different. As soon as this happens, the resulting game must be different from chess, because you have changed a feature. And you never know, it might be new too. So, for example, take the feature of chess that "all squares are identical," meaning that there are no "special" squares, like those in snakes and ladders or Scrabble, so that when you land on a particular square something happens.

What would happen if one (or more) squares in chess were special? You could be immune from being taken; or it might be that two pieces can occupy the same square; or it might be that if these two pieces are the king and queen of the same side, they can produce a baby — a prince, say, (that could be a knight) or a princess (a new piece, maybe like a little queen, able to move in any direction, but for only two squares)…

The process outlined in the last box is an enormously powerful method to help stimulate your imagination, to enhance your creativity, to enable you to come up with stunning new ideas. The power of the method is attributable to two fundamental features:

➤ Creativity and innovation in business never take place on a "greenfield" site, on totally unfamiliar territory. On the contrary, they take place on very familiar territory indeed, territory that you have usually helped develop and on which you have been successful. So any process of idea generation that starts with a blank sheet of paper is missing a vital ingredient—the knowledge that you already have.

➤ Secondly, the method recognizes that, once a new idea has been found, the difference between, say, the new product and existing products is in the *detail* of its features, as the chess example demonstrates.

The starting point of this process is therefore not a blank sheet of paper, but rather a comprehensive description of what you already know, compiled as a list of bullet points that would pass the Martian test. Once this list has been compiled, the next step is to select a feature and ask the question: "How might this be different?" This forces the conversation toward differences and it is here that innovation lies. It must be true that "that which is new must be different" and we all agree that "that which is different is not necessarily new." However, it might be, and it is one hell of a good place to start.

This process is called *InnovAction!*™, as described in detail in another of my books, *Smart Things to Know about Innovation and Creativity*. If you would like to see some examples of this process in action you will find many there, but you already know enough to see how it can apply to scenario planning. The process of compiling the detailed contextual description of today's world gives you the starting point, since if a feature of today's world is that "the industry structure is comprised of four major global players, sixteen large companies in the UK, and a host of small operations," or whatever, this alone provides a great springboard for imagining how things might be different.

What if the four major players merge? What if the sixteen UK majors fragment? What if the small operations club together? All of these are possible and might happen. If they do, how would that affect our business if we were to stay more or less the same? Would we be stronger or weaker? And if we would be weaker, what would we have to do now to become stronger? Maybe we should initiate merger discussions and so change the setting of our "mergers and acquisitions" lever; maybe we need to develop some new products to move into less congested markets, so changing the setting of the "product development" and "channel" levers. This indeed is the stuff of strategy.

By taking each feature of today's world and asking "How might this be different?" you can generate many, many plausible views of how the future might look, especially if this is done in workshop style with around 12 people; indeed, a series of one- or two-day workshops is ideal. The result is literally hundreds and hundreds of possible different features. For a while this looks like an unstructured mess, but a stage is reached at which different themes cluster together, forming groupings that can be regarded as self-consistent. This in turn leads to agreement on a range of contextual descriptions that represent possible, alternative future worlds.

With some tidying up, this completes the entire first row of the scenario planning table. We have generated insightful descriptions of a range of alternative future worlds, descriptions consistent with, but different from, the description of today's world.

An important feature of this process is that there is no judgment made, either of the likelihood of a particular world evolving or of desire. The test is plausibility, the possibility that it might happen, rather than the likelihood or hope that it will happen.

Back to levers and outcomes

The stage we have reached is that we now have a complete set of contextual descriptions across the top of the table shown in Figure 10.1, representing all the chosen worlds, and we have the levers and outcomes as in today's world.

The next step is to ask the question, for each of the alternative future worlds, "If the levers remain at their actual settings as in today's world, will the outcomes be 'good' or 'bad'?" This is a test of today's lever settings in each of the future worlds. At one level, it is a question of imagination and intuition: Can we imagine how the business would perform under a status quo policy framework in any given future context?

A few of us can do this intuitively, but most of us can't. The levers and outcomes are disconnected in logic and time and the whole thing is context dependent. That is why a systems thinking approach can really help, because it provides a rigorous analytical framework to think all of this through. And it is even better when it is supported by a computer simulation model, since this can be used to trace the evolution of the business as the future evolves from today's world to any one of the chosen future worlds. Indeed, the scenarios that give scenario planning its name are the stories telling how today's world might evolve along a number of alternative paths, each of which leads to one of the chosen alternative future worlds.

Suppose you decide that, in a given future world, the outcomes of your business, with the levers set as in today's world, are "bad." What do you do next? You reverse engineer the lever settings. You set out to discover what the lever settings have to be in order to give "good" outcomes. And that is where the ambition comes in, because this might require setting the levers to very different positions from where they are now, or indeed invoking new levers altogether—totally new products, new markets, or a new approach altogether. In fact, these "new" levers have been there all along—it just so happens that their target and actual settings are currently zero. Once again, this process of reverse engineering the levers can be done intuitively, or by reference to causal loop diagrams, or with computer simulation support.

So after examining each world you end up with a completed table. You have descriptions of today's world and a variety of alternative future worlds; you have "good" outcomes along the bottom row in each world; and in the middle row you have identified what the lever settings have to be in order to give those good outcomes.

Then the fun starts, because it is at this point that you can start making decisions. And it is at this point that different organizations adopt different styles. Some take a low-risk approach and seek to identify a group of lever settings that are the same, or closely so, in as wide a range of possible future worlds as possible. This implies that if the levers are set to those values, the future might evolve in a wide variety of different ways, but the business is still relatively secure. Other organizations take a much riskier, but no less valid approach: The management team decides that there is an overall goal to strive for and they go for it. The scenario planning exercise might indicate that this will be strongly successful if the future evolves in a particular way, reasonably successful under certain other circumstances, and a disaster under others. No matter. The upside is attractive and the team has the ambition, vision, and imagination to go for it. And they do—but with wisdom, rather than with rashness.

The scenario planning process has provided insight as to the external conditions that will make this strategy a success and those that bode ill. So as the future evolves for real, the organization tracks what is happening, getting as early a warning as possible as to whether the conditions are evolving favorably or not. If things are favorable, fine; if not, maybe the strategy has to be reconsidered. Nevertheless, this is no knee-jerk reaction to a particular external event; rather, it is a well-considered recognition that we don't control everything.

The outcome of the exercise is therefore fourfold:

➤ It creates a compelling view of the future, as depicted by the chosen future world.
➤ It determines what the lever settings have to be in the chosen future world, so specifying the target lever settings that should be set now.
➤ Comparison of these strategic target lever settings with the current actual lever settings identifies the management actions that need to be taken to close the gaps.
➤ The exercise will have built insight, enthusiasm, and commitment.

11
Public policy

Systems thinking also applies to matters of public policy

Most of the examples so far in this book have related to business, dealing with matters such as how to grow a business smoothly and the formulation of strategy. Systems thinking, however, is by no means restricted to business and for-profit organizations. Much of Jay Forrester's pioneering work related to public policy, as documented, for example, in his books *Urban Dynamics* (1969), which examines issues such as inner-city decay, and *World Dynamics* (1971) which addresses global issues such as population growth and pollution. *Schools that Learn* (2000), the most recent book by Peter Senge and his team, is all about education.

In this chapter, I therefore take the opportunity to show how systems thinking can be used to explore an issue that is very much in the arena of public policy. Global warming—the progressive rise in the temperature of the earth, by just a fraction of a degree each year—is of fundamental importance to everyone on the planet. It also recently hit the headlines, with US President Bush's rejection of the "Kyoto Protocol." Drawn up in 1997 under the auspices of the United Nations, this Protocol committed the 39 signatory nations (which included the US, the UK, France, Germany, Japan, the Russian Confederation, and China) to reduce the emissions of so-called greenhouse gases from cars and industrial plant, which environmentalists, and also many scientists, believe are a major cause of global warming. Like all such treaties, the Protocol required ratification by individual governments and in 2001 the US refused. Since the United States is the world's largest single contributor of greenhouse gas emissions (25 percent of the world's total), President Bush's refusal to limit them is potentially of great significance.

Was President Bush's decision wise? Or has he helped condemn the planet?

After reading this chapter, you will, I trust, be able to take an informed view. The next several pages present some causal loops representing my mental models on how this complex system behaves. You may disagree. Fine—perhaps this will encourage you to draw your own causal loops and, if you do, please let me know!

Back to population

The starting point is the dynamics of human population growth. As we saw in Chapter 8, the growth in a POPULATION can be represented by a pair of inter-connected feedback loops: a reinforcing loop driven by the BIRTH RATE, and a balancing loop driven by the DEATH RATE. Figure 11.1 is a more generalized version of Figure 8.13 on page 152, where the POPULATION now refers to the total global population, of all ages, in both rural and urban environments.

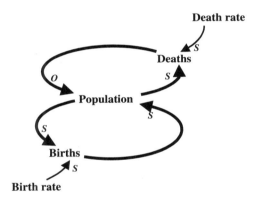

Figure 11.1

The reinforcing loop grows exponentially but is restrained by the balancing loop. Since the BIRTH RATE and the DEATH RATE are rate dangles rather than target dangles, this system does not converge on a target but rather grows, declines, or stabilizes according to the dynamic behavior of the BIRTH RATE and the DEATH RATE. Along with the natural process of ageing, the major factor influencing the DEATH RATE is the incidence of DISEASE (Figure 11.2 overleaf).

As the POPULATION grows, so does the level of economic activity of all types: not just the urban-based activities of manufacturing and trading, but also rural activities such as agriculture. Some of this activity is required for survival, such as food production; some is driven by the human DESIRE FOR WEALTH (Figure 11.3 overleaf).

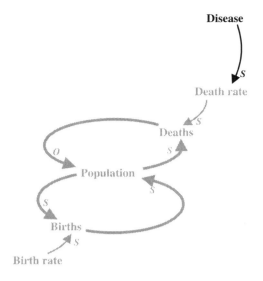

Figure 11.2

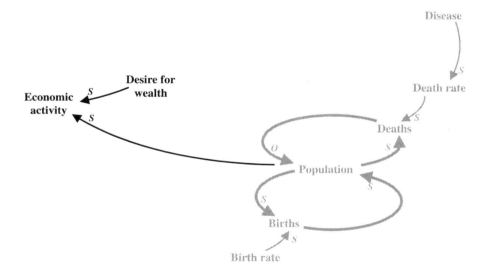

Figure 11.3

What are the consequences of economic activity?

ECONOMIC ACTIVITY does indeed create wealth and improve standards of living, but that is not the only consequence. As ECONOMIC ACTIVITY increases, so
does RESOURCE CONSUMPTION. While there are plenty of resources to go
around, that's fine; but these resources have a finite RESOURCE CAPACITY, and
when the resources—land, water, oil—are not so abundant, this leads to COM-
PETITION FOR SCARCE RESOURCES, which in turn leads to FAMINE and WAR.
These drive up the DEATH RATE, so arresting the inexorable exponential
growth of the reinforcing loop. In addition, as RESOURCE CONSUMPTION
increases so does POLLUTION, not only in terms of the creation of waste products, but also in terms of a broader definition of pollution that includes overcrowding and the general spoiling of living conditions. This, of course, drives
the incidence of DISEASE (Figure 11.4).

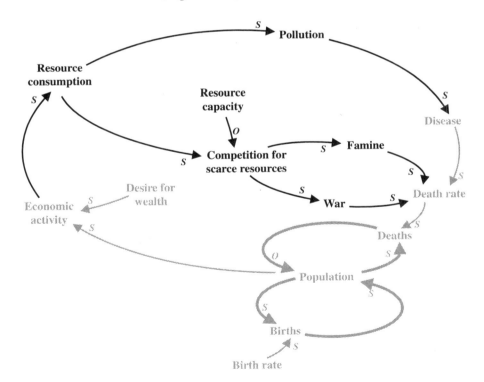

Figure 11.4

What is the structure of this system and how does it behave?

This structure is a single reinforcing loop—that linking POPULATION and BIRTHS—being slowed down by four balancing loops operating together. One from POPULATION to DEATHS and back to POPULATION, represents the natural ageing process; the three others, through DISEASE, FAMINE, and WAR, all increase the DEATH RATE beyond the level associated with natural ageing.

These four feedback loops have been recognized throughout human history. Indeed, the Four Horsemen of the Apocalypse, dramatically portrayed in Albrecht Dürer's woodcut of 1498, are famine, pestilence, war, and death (Figure 11.5).

Figure 11.5

The only ultimate constraint on growth is the target dangle, RESOURCE CAPACITY, and when this is not binding the population grows, declines, or stabilizes according to the relative impact of these four horsemen. For centuries, despite the terrible havoc wreaked by the four horsemen, the BIRTH RATE kept just ahead of the DEATH RATE, so that the global population grew, but very slowly. In the year 1000 the global population has been estimated at around 300 million; by 1800 it had risen to about 1 billion (Figure 11.6).

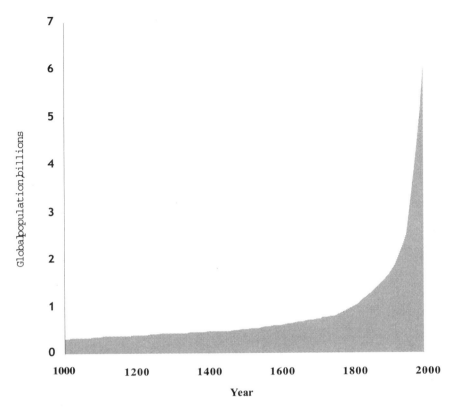

Figure 11.6

However, since 1800 the population has grown very much more quickly, and increasingly so: from around 1 billion in 1800 to 2 billion in 1927, 3 billion in 1960, 4 billion in 1974, 5 billion in 1987, and 6 billion in 1999. Forecasts suggest 7 billion by 2013, 8 billion by 2028, and 9 billion by 2054.

There are two main explanations of this dramatic rise. One is the impact of improvements in agriculture, so alleviating the constraining effect of food supply on the RESOURCE CAPACITY in at least some parts of the world; a second is the provision of better HEALTH CARE, another result of increased prosperity (Figure 11.7 overleaf).

Improvements in HEALTH CARE have been achieved by better diet and nutrition; by public health initiatives, such as clean water supplies and sanitation; by the development of better clinical techniques; and, over the last 60 years, by the use of antibiotics. The result of all this has been not only to reduce the DEATH RATE—by reducing infant mortality, by extending the average life span, and by combating disease—but also, and simultaneously, to

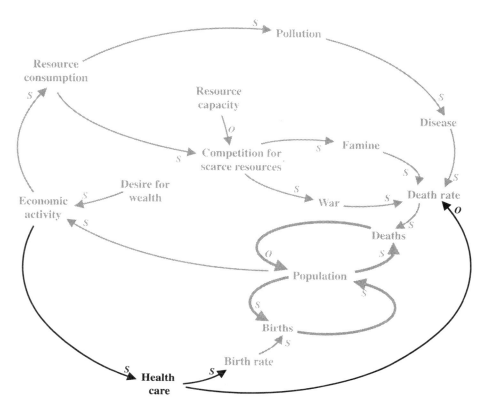

Figure 11.7

increase the BIRTH RATE, by virtue of the improved health of child-bearing women.

This widening of the difference between the birth rate and the death rate has a dramatic effect. Suppose that the birth rate is 15 births per 1,000 population, and the death rate 12 deaths per 1,000 population. The key driver of population growth overall is the net difference, 3 per 1,000. Suppose now that the death rate reduces from 12 to 10 per 1,000, while the birth rate increases by just one from 15 to 16 per 1,000. The net rate is now 6 per 1,000: *double* the previous rate. Small changes in the birth rate and death rate create a much bigger change in the net rate, and once the exponential growth engine starts spinning fast it spins progressively faster...

One policy that can be adopted to slow population growth is to reduce the birth rate, for example by advocating contraception and family planning. Experience over the last 30–40 years, however, suggests that encouraging contraception is a quick fix that has only limited impact, especially where it is most needed, in the developing countries. A far wiser policy is the EDUCATION OF WOMEN, although it takes a long time for societies to become willing to do this (Figure 11.8).

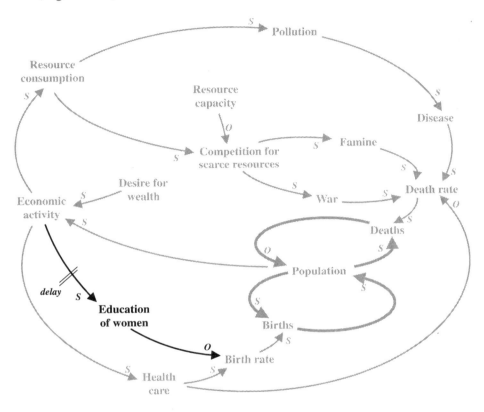

Figure 11.8

This is the picture that represents my mental model of the way things have been over the last 50 years or so. But not quite: In the last 20 years something else has been happening, and to explore this we need to take a trip to Mars.

Gaia

If you were to go to Mars, you would immediately notice some major differences between it and the Earth. Mars, for example, is very cold: Its surface temperature is around –53°C, as compared to the Earth's average surface temperature of about 14°C, but you might rationalize this by virtue of the fact that Mars is much further from the sun than the Earth. Another major difference concerns the atmosphere. Like Earth, Mars has an atmosphere (albeit a rather thin one) composed of the familiar gases oxygen, nitrogen, and carbon dioxide. But although the gases that make up the atmospheres on Mars and the Earth are chemically similar, the overall compositions of the two atmospheres are significantly different. The Earth's atmosphere is 21 percent oxygen, 78 percent nitrogen, and 0.03 percent carbon dioxide, with most of the rest being argon; the atmosphere on Mars by contrast is only 0.13 percent oxygen, 2.7 percent nitrogen, and a whopping 95 percent carbon dioxide, with the balance, once again, being largely argon.

There is a third difference too: The Earth teems with life, but Mars is literally stone dead.

The differences between the Earth's atmosphere and that of Mars intrigued a young British scientist, James Lovelock, who was working in the United States in the 1960s on the space program. Lovelock's project was to devise methods by which life could be detected on distant planets, using observations from Earth or from spacecraft. He soon realized that one of the most observable features of any planet from a distance was its atmosphere and so he asked: "Is there any characteristic of a planetary atmosphere that might indicate the presence of life?" Here he had some data. The Earth has life and an atmosphere rich in nitrogen and oxygen, but with little carbon dioxide; Mars is dead and has an atmosphere rich in carbon dioxide, but with little oxygen and nitrogen. Is this correlation accidental, or does this itself contain a clue?

James Lovelock

James Lovelock is one of today's most outstanding and influential scientist-philosophers and original thinkers. His academic background is impressive and multidisciplinary. His first degree is in chemistry, his PhD in medicine, and his DSc in biophysics — just the background you would expect for someone who takes a holistic, systems, boundary-breaking view. In 1954 he left the UK for a four-year visit to Harvard Medical School, followed by Yale, then taking up a post as Professor of Chemistry at Baylor University College of Medicine in Houston, Texas, in 1961. Since 1964, he has been an independent scientist and over the years has been showered with prizes and awards.

A landmark event was his development, in 1957, of the "electron capture detector," a device that can detect the minutest presence of various chemicals. Using this instrument, he showed that residues of pesticides were to be found in places as diverse as the bodies of penguins and mothers' milk, so providing important hard data to support Rachel Carson's influential environmental work *Silent Spring* (see page 23). In the 1970s, Lovelock's detector was also instrumental in proving the build-up in the atmosphere of chloro-fluoro-carbons (CFCs), manmade chemicals used in aerosols and refrigerants, and in identifying them as a major cause of the depletion of the atmosphere's ozone layer; the other being methane, produced as a by-product of farming and forestry. Since the ozone layer acts as a shield, preventing harmful, cancer-inducing, ultra-violet radiation from reaching the surface of the earth, our collective action in punching a hole in it—as is happening over Antarctica as you read this—doesn't seem like a good idea to me.

Lovelock currently lives in Cornwall, UK, and is a visiting fellow, appropriately enough, of Green College, Oxford.

Lovelock's knowledge of chemistry caused him to spot an important characteristic of the atmosphere of Mars. The mixture of gases in the Martian atmosphere is in what chemists call "chemical equilibrium," a scientific term meaning that the gases will not react with one another, however long they are left together as a mixture. He also recognized that the mixture of gases in the Earth's atmosphere is very far from chemical equilibrium. In fact, his calculations indicated that the equilibrium composition of the Earth's atmosphere would have no oxygen at all, 1.9 percent nitrogen, 98 percent carbon dioxide, and 0.1 percent argon, all at a temperature of around 240°C. This composition is very much like the atmosphere of Mars, and the higher temperature is consistent with the Earth's closer proximity to the sun.

Lovelock also knew, from geological and fossil evidence, that the composition of the Earth's atmosphere has been maintained at, or close to, the state we experience today for hundreds of millions of years—far, far longer than would be required for chemical equilibrium to be achieved. How is it that the Earth's atmosphere has been maintained stable, but so far from chemical equilibrium, for so long?

The answer to this question is best appreciated by reference to an example of a strange, stable, non-equilibrium state that we have already seen. In Chapter 1, we looked at the system composed of a bicycle and its rider (see pages 15 and 17) and saw that the natural equilibrium state of this system is for the bicycle, and the rider, to be spread-eagled on the ground. It is only when the system behaves as an open system, with energy continuously pumping through it, as achieved by the action of the rider's legs (an activity itself fueled by the rider's breathing), that the system of bicycle-plus-rider shows the emergent property of dynamic equilibrium: a highly ordered, self-organized state in which the system of the bicycle-plus-rider remains upright—rather than at any arbitrary angle or violently wobbling—while moving forward.

Lovelock's great insight was to recognize that the chemical composition of the Earth is an exactly similar situation. The Earth as a whole is an open system, with energy pumping through it from the sun, and comprised of all manner of global-scale feedback loops. As a consequence, the Earth as a whole has achieved a self-organized, highly ordered state of dynamic equilibrium, in which the composition of the atmosphere, the Earth's surface temperature, and life are as we experience them.

The system of the Earth as a whole, however, is of course vastly more complex than that of the bicycle-plus-rider. And the system of the Earth as a whole is just that, a single system comprising everything on Earth: the rocks, the oceans, the atmosphere, the weather, and all life. All of these are joined by a network of interconnected, global-scale feedback loops.

We are familiar with many of the dynamic properties of the Earth and the existence of global-scale feedback loops. For example, water in the oceans evaporates, so forming clouds, which eventually give rise to rain, returning the water to the oceans directly or by means of rivers. Oxygen is also cycled around: Atmospheric oxygen is consumed by animals in respiration, but released into the atmosphere by green plants during photosynthesis. These individual processes, however, have tended to be studied by geologists, biologists, meteorologists, this-ologists, and that-ologists, all of whom have seen "their" process in isolation, only in terms of their own discipline. Lovelock, in contrast, proposed that the whole Earth is a *single* highly ordered, self-organized system, in which everything is connected to everything else.

Lovelock calls this unity Gaia, after the Earth-mother goddess of the Ancient Greeks, a name suggested in 1967 by Lovelock's friend and neighbor William Golding, the author of *Lord of the Flies* and winner of the 1983 Nobel Prize for Literature. Lovelock first conceived the concept of Gaia in the late 1960s, gave his first public talk on the subject in 1971, had his first Gaia article published in 1973, and has continued to develop the theory ever since. He has written innumerable articles and four books, of which my favorite is *Gaia: The Practical Science of Planetary Medicine* (1991). Needless to say, Lovelock's ideas have generated much controversy over the years, especially among those scientists who persist in taking a parochial view. Nevertheless, in the *Amsterdam Declaration on Global Change*, drawn up by the world's leading earth scientists in July 2001, the Gaia theory was fully endorsed. Here is a quotation from the Declaration's first article: "The Earth System behaves as a single, self-regulating system comprised of physical, chemical, biological and human components. The interactions and feedbacks between the component parts are complex."

If the entire Earth is a single system then, according to systems theory, when you push "here," something is going to happen "there." And on a global scale, that could have significant consequences.

Global warming

One of the most important properties of the Earth is its surface temperature, currently around 14°C. This is the temperature at which life as we know it thrives and it is also a temperature that has been maintained, within a degree or two, for many millions if not hundreds of millions of years, even right through what we know as the Ice Ages, when the average temperature dropped, for a while, to about 11°C.

What determines the temperature of the Earth?

The surface temperature of the Earth is a result of a dynamic equilibrium between the rate at which heat is received from the sun, and the rate at which the Earth itself re-radiates its own heat back into space. If the sun gets hotter, for example, the rate at which heat is received will increase and, if all else stays the same, the Earth's surface temperature will rise; by the same token, if anything happens to increase the rate at which the Earth re-radiates heat back into space, the temperature will fall accordingly.

There are a number of characteristics of the Earth that influence the rate at which heat is re-radiated back into space. One is the overall coverage of the Earth by snow and ice, in contrast to open sea and forest. Since snow and ice are white, this causes heat to be reflected back into space, whereas the darker colours of open sea and forest absorb heat. If, for example, polar ice melts, then the relative proportion of snow and ice on the planet decreases, causing the Earth to reflect less heat back into space, driving the temperature

---

up, so melting yet more snow and ice — a reinforcing loop known as the *albedo effect*.

Another influence results from a special property of carbon dioxide molecules. Because the surface temperature of the sun is high, about 5,500°C, the heat radiation from the sun is formed of waves of very short wavelength. In contrast, the heat waves emitted by the Earth, whose surface temperature is about 14°C, are of much longer wavelength. Just as a blue-colored glass is transparent to blue light, which has a short wavelength, but is relatively opaque to red light, which has a long wavelength (it is this property that gives the glass its blue color), so carbon dioxide is transparent to "sun-heat" (short wavelength) but relatively opaque to "earth-heat" (long wavelength).

The result of this is that atmospheric carbon dioxide lets the sun's heat in unimpeded, but slows down the rate at which the Earth re-radiates its own heat back to space, so acting rather like a one-way blanket. The greater the amount of atmospheric carbon dioxide, the thicker the "blanket" and so the warmer the Earth; conversely, the lower the amount, the thinner the "blanket" and so the cooler the Earth. This is the *greenhouse effect*, and carbon dioxide and some other naturally occurring gases such as methane are known as *greenhouse gases*.

Over hundreds of millions of years the Earth's temperature has remained more or less constant, but three other things have also been happening. The sun, in fact, has been getting steadily hotter; that's what stars do as they become older. Simultaneously, the level of carbon dioxide in the atmosphere has been steadily reducing, from an estimate of about 0.1 percent one billion (or so!) years ago to 0.03 percent now — even though carbon dioxide is pushed into the atmosphere as a result of volcanic eruptions. Overall, however, these effects have balanced each other out. As the sun has become progressively hotter, our global "blanket" has become progressively thinner despite the effect of volcanoes, and all the while the Earth's surface temperature has stayed more or less the same. There is no evidence that, at any time over this very long period, the Earth has become overly hot or freezing cold.

What is going on? Is there some global thermostat, set by a mysterious someone, just as we set the temperature of our domestic heating and air conditioning systems so that the temperature in our homes stays constant, throughout both a cold winter and a hot summer?

Does the Earth have a thermostat?

As we have seen, the Earth's surface temperature has remained stable at around 14°C for many millions of years. By the same token, but on a much smaller scale, your body has a constant temperature of about 36.9°C. How come the temperatures of the Earth and of all human beings are stable in general, and stable at these specific temperatures in particular?

The answer is: "That's what emergence is all about." Systems at increasing levels of complexity show increasingly more startling emergent properties—properties that emerge at the level of the system and are not identifiable from the study of the component parts (see page 14). Just as the very simple bike-and-rider system stabilizes the property "position" at the value "vertical", the vastly more complex Earth system stabilizes the property "temperature" at the value "14°C," and the human body system stabilizes its temperature at the value 36.9°C.

The Earth and the human being are two examples of hugely complex systems, composed of a countless number of interconnected feedback loops—much, much more complex than anything in this book. When so many feedback loops operate in harmony together, as computer simulations show, all manner of emergent properties develop, of which, in the cases of the Earth and ourselves, temperature is just one. As we understand these complex systems more fully, we will gain greater insight into why these temperatures are the numbers they are, but for the moment the only explanation is "emergence."

The long-term maintenance of the Earth's surface temperature at about 14°C, even as the sun has been getting hotter, is a spectacular example of a concept I introduced in Chapter 1: the ability of self-organizing systems to self-correct (see page 17). Just as a bicycle rider can correct a wobble, the interactions of the multiple feedback loops within a more complex self-organizing system act to cushion the system against external shocks, at least to a certain extent. If the wobble on the bicycle is too severe, the rider falls off and the self-organized state of stable dynamic equilibrium suddenly disorders to a state of chaos, finally reaching a state of static equilibrium, with the rider and the bicycle flat and stationary on the ground. Many self-organizing systems have emergent self-correcting mechanisms that maintain self-organization as far as they can, but there is always some limit beyond which these mechanisms break.

In accordance with the principles of self-organization and self-correction, the Earth will seek to maintain its "natural" temperature and invoke feedback mechanisms to stabilize it whenever there is a disturbance. This can be represented as a causal loop diagram in terms of a balancing loop (Figure 11.9).

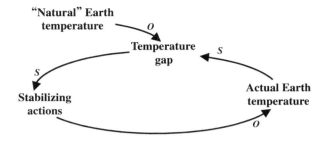

Figure 11.9

In this diagram the Ss and the Os have been determined on the basis that the TEMPERATURE GAP is defined as the ACTUAL EARTH TEMPERATURE minus the "NATURAL" EARTH TEMPERATURE, and so is positive when the earth is too warm. This triggers whatever STABILIZING ACTIONS are required to reduce the ACTUAL EARTH TEMPERATURE back down to the "NATURAL" EARTH TEMPERATURE.

For many millions of years the gradual increase in the temperature of the sun has tended to push the ACTUAL EARTH TEMPERATURE up, making the TEM- PERATURE GAP positive, so triggering an appropriate STABILIZING ACTION to bring the ACTUAL EARTH TEMPERATURE back down. And for many millions of years that STABILIZING ACTION has been to reduce the level of carbon dioxide in the atmosphere, so making our global "blanket" ever thinner.

One mechanism for this is driven by photosynthesis, the process whereby in sunlight green plants, such as grass and trees on land and marine algae liv- ing in the seas and oceans, extract carbon dioxide from the atmosphere to form sugars. This is the predominant source of all the carbon trapped in all living things—the so-called *biomass*—and the current policy of encouraging the creation of new coniferous forests to reduce atmospheric carbon dioxide is seeking to exploit this effect. The trapping of carbon in the biomass is rela- tively short term, however. Over a period of time, most of this carbon is returned to the atmosphere as carbon dioxide, either as a result of respiration whereby, primarily in animals, plant sugars consumed as food react with oxy- gen, or when a plant or animal dies and decays. It is only when dead plants and animals do not decay fully and become transformed into fossil fuels such as peat, coal, oil, and gas that the carbon dioxide extracted from the atmos- phere is much more permanently trapped.

A second, and much more powerful, long-term way of removing carbon dioxide from the atmosphere is achieved by a mechanism that pumps gaseous carbon dioxide out of the atmosphere and, quite literally, buries it as rock. The operation of this pump involves the weather, the oceans, geology, physics, chemistry, and—most importantly—life itself. Lovelock describes how the pump works most vividly in *Gaia: The Practical Science of Scientific Medicine*. Below is my brief summary.

The living pump

As raindrops fall through the atmosphere, carbon dioxide dissolves in the water to form carbonic acid. When this weakly acidic rain falls on to rocks containing calcium silicate (as many rocks do), then a chemical reaction can take place to form calcium bicarbonate and silicic acid. This is a natural chemical process called the weathering of rocks, which, in the absence of any life, takes place very slowly.

However, in the presence of land-based living organisms such as plants, trees, and soil bacteria, this process speeds up by a factor of about 1,000. A tree, for example, takes carbon dioxide from the atmosphere through its leaves and some of this is pumped down to the roots. The local concentration of carbon dioxide is therefore much higher around the roots than it would otherwise be, and since the roots are in contact with the rocks, the rate of weathering is much increased.

The calcium bicarbonate produced by weathering dissolves in water and so can be taken by ground water into rivers and then into the seas and oceans. In the oceans, there are vast numbers of photosynthesizing micro-organisms, known as coccolithophores, which absorb this dissolved calcium bicarbonate, transforming it into the insoluble solid, calcium carbonate, used for their shells and skeletons. And when these micro-organisms die, their shells and skeletons fall to the seabed as sediments, eventually to be compressed into the rocks we call chalk and limestone.

As a result, carbon dioxide originally in the atmosphere is transformed into chalk and limestone, pumped there by the weathering of rocks, mediated by the actions of land-based life and marine micro-organisms. The carbon dioxide trapped in rock stays there for many millions of years, but some of it, eventually, is churned from the depths of the Earth into a volcano and at last, in a stupendous eruption, it escapes into the atmosphere once more. The wheel has come full circle: Everything truly is connected to everything else.

Figure 11.10 overleaf is a causal loop diagram showing the action of the living pump, in the context of solar intensity and the activity of volcanoes.

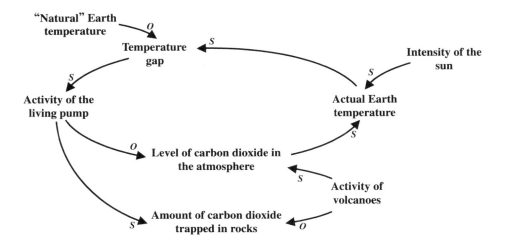

Figure 11.10

This is a single balancing loop with four dangles: the target dangle, "NATU-RAL" EARTH TEMPERATURE; two input driver dangles, the INTENSITY OF THE SUN and the ACTIVITY OF VOLCANOES; and an output dangle, the AMOUNT OF CAR-BON DIOXIDE TRAPPED IN ROCKS. This balancing loop acts to keep the ACTUAL EARTH TEMPERATURE in line with the "NATURAL" EARTH TEMPERATURE, as achieved by the ACTIVITY OF THE LIVING PUMP in reducing the LEVEL OF CAR-BON DIOXIDE IN THE ATMOSPHERE while, simultaneously, increasing the AMOUNT OF CARBON DIOXIDE TRAPPED IN ROCKS. And the ACTIVITY OF THE LIV-ING PUMP itself is determined by the population, during any year, of marine micro-organisms, which in turn is controlled by Gaia's self-organization.

Linking the loops together

For countless millions of years, this mechanism has acted to keep the Earth's temperature constant. Meanwhile, in the last few hundred years humans have been going about their business, and so Gaia's balancing loop has been acting in parallel with humans' constrained reinforcing loop of economic growth. For the most part these two loops have operated independently, since humans have been doing nothing of sufficient magnitude to disturb Gaia. We can represent these two non-interacting loops by Figure 11.11, in which, for simplicity, I have omitted the intensity of the sun and the activity of volcanoes and, for reasons we shall see shortly, altered the geometry of the balancing loop.

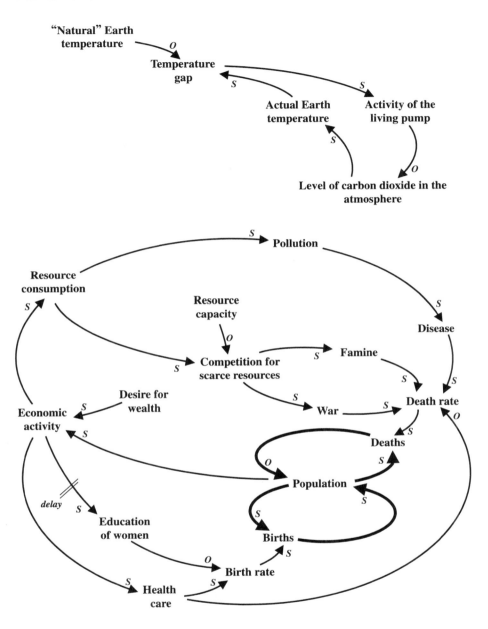

Figure 11.11

Everything is linked to everything else and so these loops are not independent. One of the most significant linkages is that between the POLLUTION attributable to economic activity and the level of carbon dioxide in the atmosphere. As we have already seen (see page 254), one of Gaia's ways of removing carbon dioxide from the atmosphere is by photosynthesis, trapping it as carbon in the biomass. We also saw that this carbon dioxide is released back into the atmosphere when a plant or an animal dies or decays, unless this decay is incomplete, resulting in the formation of peat, coal, oil, and gas. But when wood, peat, coal, oil, or gas is burnt, that carbon dioxide is returned to the atmosphere. This can happen naturally, as a result, for example, of forest fires caused by lightning. But it can also happen as a result of human activity: As soon as fire was discovered, burning a tree, or some peat, coal, oil, or gas, pumped that once-trapped carbon dioxide back into the atmosphere, progressively thickening the "blanket" (Figure 11.12).

For most of human history, the amount of carbon dioxide released by the burning of wood, peat, coal, oil, and gas has been well within Gaia's capacity to re-absorb it by means of the living pump, with the result that the Earth's temperature has remained sensibly constant. However, in the last two decades this has changed. The rates at which forests have been burnt for clearance and fossil fuels for energy have outstripped the living pump's ability to bury atmospheric carbon dioxide as rock, with the result that the LEVEL OF CARBON DIOXIDE IN THE ATMOSPHERE has been steadily increasing, driving the ACTUAL EARTH TEMPERATURE steadily upward. This is what global warming is all about.

Gaia's natural self-correcting mechanism, using the living pump, can no longer cope. So what happens? When the bicycle-plus-rider system goes over a bump that the rider cannot self-correct the system breaks, so maybe one answer is that we are witnessing an imminent catastrophe in which Gaia breaks down, so extinguishing all life as a consequence.

However, Gaia is much more complex than the system of the bicycle-plus-rider and has many more feedback loops. Another way of handling the situation in which one feedback system is unable to cope is to invoke, activate, or enhance a second one. Indeed, this happens when you get too warm. The human body has five known mechanisms to control body temperature and if you get too hot, one causes you to sweat and another increases the blood supply to the skin. Both these mechanisms operate together to help bring your temperature back down.

So before Gaia breaks, other mechanisms are invoked. What might these be?

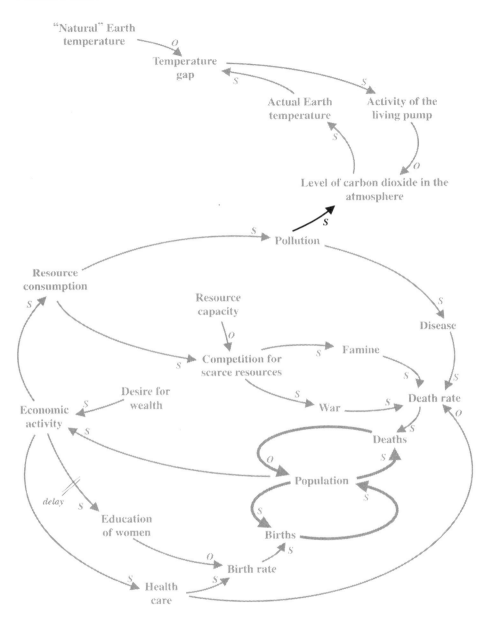

Figure 11.12

My view is that one is the action of storms. Storms dissipate energy and heat, as every bolt of lightning, every clap of thunder, and every hurricane demonstrates most dramatically. Storms are another of Gaia's ways of reducing the Earth's temperature (Figure 11.13 overleaf).

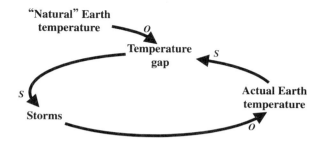

Figure 11.13

This is another balancing loop, also acting to maintain the "NATURAL" EARTH TEMPERATURE. The greater the TEMPERATURE GAP the more vigorous the STORMS; and the more vigorous the STORMS the greater the corresponding reduction in the ACTUAL EARTH TEMPERATURE. This balancing loop acts alongside the much slower living pump loop, so that both contribute to controlling the ACTUAL EARTH TEMPERATURE.

Figure 11.14 shows both loops operating together, in which I have used a dotted line for the living pump loop to indicate that it is operating much more slowly than the storms loop.

The impact of storms

Storms act directly to dissipate heat, so reducing the temperature locally. But is that the only effect? Are there any other links between humankind's constrained reinforcing loop fueling economic growth, and Gaia's balancing loop seeking to maintain a stable temperature?

Indeed there are. The first goes from ACTUAL EARTH TEMPERATURE through FLOODING to RESOURCE CAPACITY and RESOURCE CONSUMPTION, and captures two important consequences of a steady rise in the ACTUAL EARTH TEMPERATURE: the warming of the oceans, causing a vast volume of water to expand, and the melting of snow and ice. Both of these raise the level of the seas, flooding rich coastal agricultural land, devastating settlements, and causing the consumption of all sorts of resources to prevent flooding in the first place and to clear up the mess afterward. And two more are the links from STORMS through FLOODING and RESOURCE CONSUMPTION, representing the fact that the storms themselves cause flooding and destroy crops, forests, and property (Figure 11.15 on page 262).

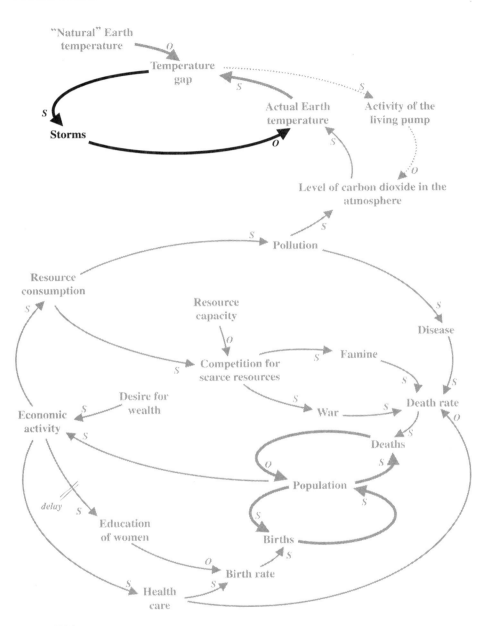

Figure 11.14

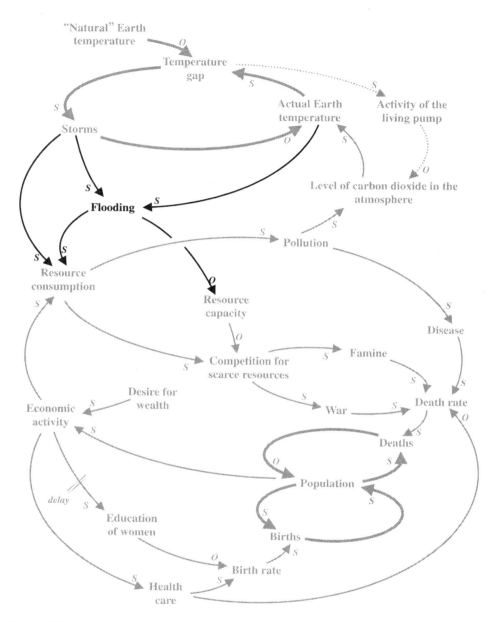

Figure 11.15

The result of all this is to increase the COMPETITION FOR SCARCE RESOURCES, and the consequences of that are FAMINE and WAR.

The four horsemen ride again

The overall effect of Gaia's mechanisms to maintain the "NATURAL" EARTH TEMPERATURE is to stir the four horsemen, driving a reduction in POPULATION until such time as the level of ECONOMIC ACTIVITY no longer disturbs the ACTUAL EARTH TEMPERATURE.

The action of storms is therefore not merely to reduce the temperature locally: A change in climate toward much stormier weather has a much deeper effect. The ultimate reason for the rise in the Earth's temperature is a disturbance in Gaia's global balance caused by humans. Humankind is an irritant, causing a "global disease." Just as we use antibiotics, pesticides, and fly-sprays to rid ourselves of those pests that we find irritating, maybe Gaia's self-correcting mechanisms are doing exactly the same thing—removing the irritant causing the temperature disturbance in the first place. And that irritant is us.

This is shown by all the balancing loops with the "NATURAL" EARTH TEMPERATURE as the dangle, such as the balancing loop that follows this path: ACTUAL EARTH TEMPERATURE, TEMPERATURE GAP, STORMS, FLOODING, RESOURCE CAPACITY, COMPETITION FOR SCARCE RESOURCES, FAMINE, DEATH RATE, DEATHS, POPULATION, ECONOMIC ACTIVITY, RESOURCE CONSUMPTION, POLLUTION, LEVEL OF CARBON DIOXIDE IN THE ATMOSPHERE and back to ACTUAL EARTH TEMPERATURE. This loop has three Os and so is, as expected, a balancing loop, seeking the "NATURAL" EARTH TEMPERATURE as its goal. There are many other balancing loops too; I counted ten driven directly by the ACTUAL EARTH TEMPERATURE and by STORMS, and there are many more convoluted ones as well.

This goes way beyond global warming

This case study on global warming is just one example of the ways in which Gaia's self-correcting mechanisms operate to maintain stability, and temperature is just one of many of Gaia's attributes. Figure 11.15 is therefore merely one instance—albeit an extremely important one—of what happens when humankind's desire to drive a reinforcing loop starts having an effect on one of Gaia's natural balancing loops. The most important inference from this diagram is the fact that it is fundamentally driven by just two dangles: humankind's DESIRE FOR WEALTH and the "NATURAL" EARTH TEMPERATURE, two dangles that are now pushing against one another. For the first time in human history, humankind is pushing against Gaia—and Gaia is pushing back harder.

It is of course possible to draw *exactly* analogous diagrams to correspond to humankind's impact on all the other major Gaia attributes too, diagrams dealing with, for example, the depletion of the ozone layer (which causes cancer), deforestation (which ultimately leads to soil erosion and the transformation of once fertile land into deserts), or the long-term destruction of biodiversity (who knows where that will lead). Each diagram has just two dangles: the HUMAN DESIRE FOR GROWTH and the "NATURAL" VALUE OF [WHATEVER] GAIA ATTRIBUTE, dangles that are pushing against one another in mutual conflict.

There are in fact two such generic diagrams, depending on whether the result of human activity is to increase the actual value of a particular Gaia attribute, as in the case of global warming, or decrease it, as in the depletion of the ozone layer. In the first case, in which HUMAN ACTIVITY increases the value of a particular attribute, the diagram is a generalization of the one we have already seen (Figure 11.16).

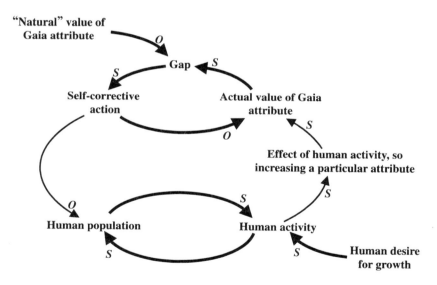

Figure 11.16

However, if the effect of human activity is to reduce the actual value of an attribute, as is the case with the depletion of the ozone layer, deforestation, and the reduction in biodiversity, Figure 11.17, which is very similar to the previous one, is more appropriate.

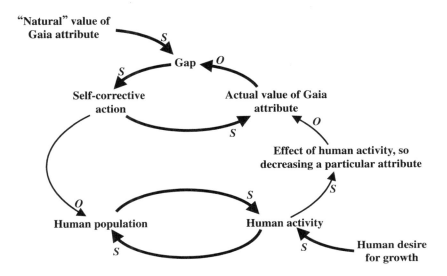

Figure 11.17

The only differences between these two diagrams are changes to four of the Ss and the Os, changes I have introduced to make the second diagram more obviously intelligible. In this second case, an increasing impact of HUMAN ACTIVITY generally results in a decrease in the ACTUAL VALUE OF a particular GAIA ATTRIBUTE, implying an O on that link. Furthermore, since most people find it easier to think about a positive GAP than a negative one, it makes more sense to define the GAP as the "NATURAL" VALUE minus the ACTUAL VALUE, so flipping the S and the O defining the GAP. An increasing GAP triggers whatever SELF-CORRECTIVE ACTION is required, with the effect of increasing the ACTUAL VALUE back toward the "NATURAL" VALUE, thereby maintaining stability—hence the last S.

In practice, of course, these two diagrams behave in exactly the same way. Once the impact of HUMAN ACTIVITY on Gaia is of sufficient magnitude, sooner or later Gaia's SELF-CORRECTIVE ACTION has the effect of reducing the level of HUMAN ACTIVITY. And if that means a reduction in the HUMAN POPU-LATION, then that is just too bad for humans. Gaia has been sustaining life on this planet for 3.6 *billion* years. The earliest hominids evolved about 3 million years ago; modern humans, *Homo sapiens*, have been around for only the last 350,000 years or so. Gaia does not need humans—but humans sure need Gaia.

What should we do?

Global warming is real. Figure 11.18 is a graph showing the average temperature of the earth since 1870.

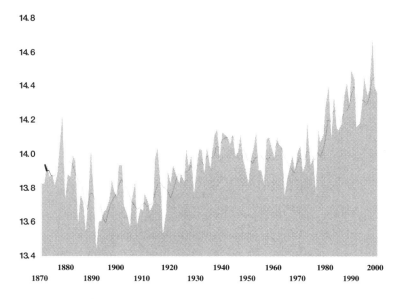

The boundary of the shaded area shows the average annual temperature; the line shows the value at the end of any one year of the average over the most recent five years.

Figure 11.18

As the population has grown, humankind's impact on Gaia has been getting steadily greater and, as the graph shows, there has been a steady rise in the average global temperature, particularly over the last 20 years. The magnitude of the change — measured in fractions of a degree — might be regarded as small, but this is merely an artefact of the measuring system. The trend upward is clear and the impact devastating. Are the increasingly more violent weather patterns all around the world, from the destruction caused by El Niño to the desperately cold temperatures in Siberia and Mongolia, to the floods in Britain, Mozambique, and Australia, just statistical fluctuations? Or might they be a result of Gaia's self-correcting mechanisms acting to maintain the temperature of the Earth constant? And if Gaia can't achieve this by losing heat fast enough back into space because of the blocking effect of greenhouse gases, maybe another way is to get rid of the cause—humans. The ultimate effect of storms and floods is to decrease the human population.

So what should we do? One approach is to deny that any of this is going on and plod on regardless. Remember the story of the frogs? And how small the signal was ten days before they were overwhelmed (see page 84)?

We don't know with certainty that we are about to be overwhelmed or whether or not it is too late. However, there are a range of policies that can be used to stop this system from destroying us before we destroy Gaia, policies that make sense in their own right even if it were to turn out that Gaia is not in fact in crisis. Two of them are shown on Figure 11.19 overleaf.

The development of RENEWABLE RESOURCES is potentially powerful, since this reduces overall RESOURCE CONSUMPTION and the COMPETITION FOR SCARCE RESOURCES; POLLUTION is also reduced, while the RESOURCE CAPACITY is increased. So maybe we should divert some of our ECONOMIC ACTIVITY into the search for RENEWABLE RESOURCES. Likewise, EVEN MORE EDUCATION, especially the EDUCATION OF WOMEN in the developing world, will, over time, be very beneficial. But not only women need to be educated—all of us do. Much of this book has been about how to manage growth and, on a local scale, this is generally regarded as a good thing. However, on a global scale perhaps it isn't, and maybe we have to regulate the overall level of economic activity so that we don't end up like the frogs—or indeed the Easter Islanders.

Easter Island

On the morning of 14 March 1774, while on his second great voyage of discovery, Captain James Cook stepped ashore on the remote Pacific Island we now know as Easter Island. Cook's was not the first European vessel to arrive there: The Dutch explorer Jacob Roggeveen had landed some 50 years earlier on Easter Day 1722, and the Spaniard Don Felipe González y Haedo visited in 1770. Here are some of Cook's own words describing the island: "The country appeared barren and without wood … being a dry hard clay and everywhere covered with stones."

Stones, indeed, were a major feature of the landscape: "On the east side, near the sea [were] three platforms of stonework, or rather the ruins of them. On each had stood four large statues, but they were all fallen down … We could hardly conceive how these islanders, wholly unacquainted with any mechanical power, could raise such stupendous figures."

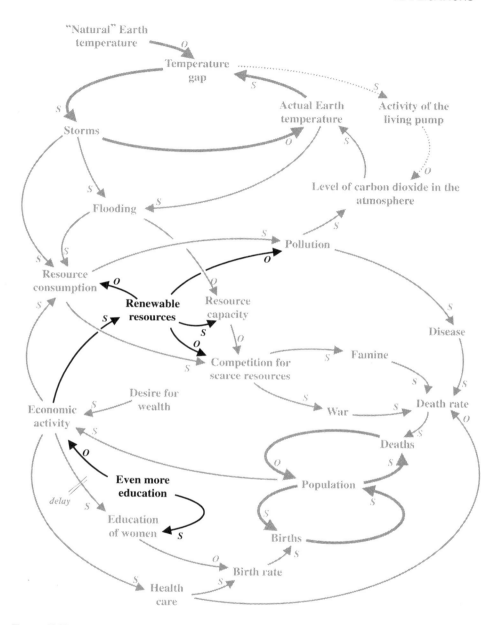

Figure 11.19

www.arttoday.com

The origin of these haunting statues, and the manner of their construction, remained a mystery for many years. There have been many fanciful explanations, including the influence of extra-terrestrial beings, but recent research has uncovered a more prosaic story.

When Cook arrived, the population on the island was around 2,000. Their existence was meager; this was no Polynesian paradise. Some 500 years earlier, however, around 1200, the story was very different: The population has been estimated as high as about 20,000 and the landscape was not "barren and without wood;" rather, it was forested and the islanders had a diet of vegetables, fish, and birds. Palm trees were the source of wood for canoes, allowing the islanders to fish; the toromiro tree was the source of wood for fire; the hauhau tree provided the materials for making rope. This combination of resources, together with the use of stone chisels, is sufficient to explain the quarrying, transport, and erection of the mysterious statues.

However, the islanders were consuming these resources faster than nature could regenerate them. Between about 1400 and 1500 the palm trees disappeared and so it was no longer possible to make canoes and catch fish; the hauhau trees vanished too, so the islanders could no longer build and transport the statues. The destruction of the natural habitat drove the extinction of the land bird population and sea birds no longer visited to eat and roost. Food became scarce and there was only one abundant food source left — each other. The resulting warfare caused the destruction of the statues, as rival clans vandalized each other's monuments.

So by the time Cook landed, the population had diminished from its peak of about 20,000 to around 2,000, all living an impoverished life. And after the introduction of European diseases and the abduction of islanders for slavery, the population fell to just 111 souls by 1877.

One last thought. Take a look at the causal loop diagram for global warming on page 262 and compare it to the business strategy diagram on page 222. Do you see the amazing similarities?

Both diagrams are about how a balancing loop interacts with a constrained reinforcing loop. In the business strategy case there are many balancing loops, representing each policy lever, and the objective is for the settings of the target policy levers to drive the growth of the constrained reinforcing loop.

In the global warming example there is also a constrained reinforcing loop, that of population growth, constrained by the four horsemen of famine, pestilence, war, and death. This diagram also shows two balancing loops—one representing the living pump and the other the effect of storms—both relating to global warming, but in reality Gaia has much more than the Earth's temperature to maintain, so there are also balancing loops for carbon dioxide and many other factors.

The big difference between the two diagrams is the direction of the links. In the business strategy diagram the overall direction of intent is from the balancing loops into the constrained reinforcing loop, as managers push and pull the various policy levers to drive their businesses. But in the global warming diagram, the runaway growth of the no longer adequately constrained reinforcing loop is pushing against the "NATURAL" EARTH TEMPERATURE, a "policy lever" that Gaia's self-correcting mechanisms seek to hold in the same position.

Who is going to "win"? Gaia or humankind?

Part IV
How to build a "laboratory of the future"

In which we turn our attention from systems thinking and causal loop diagrams to system dynamics modeling and plumbing diagrams.

Chapter 12 presents the key principles of system dynamics modeling and shows how a system dynamics model, as represented by a plumbing diagram, relates to the corresponding systems thinking description and the associated causal loop diagram.

As an example of how system dynamics models may be used in practice, Chapter 13 takes one of the causal loop diagrams of business growth shown in Chapter 8 and uses this as a framework for modeling. The context is how to grow a local motor dealership and the key decisions involved are very real and faced by every business. How much should we spend on marketing? And how do we best allocate the funds between advertising and promotions?

12
Turbo-charging your systems thinking

The emphasis of this book so far has been on the use of systems thinking in enhancing our understanding of complex systems, to help us feel confident in taking a holistic rather than a narrow view; to assist in building teams by encouraging the articulation, sharing, and mutual appreciation of one another's mental models; and to gain insight into the formulation of wise policies that stand the test of time and are not jeopardized by unforeseen circumstances. We have also seen how systems thinking can be beneficially used at all scales, from the specifics of particular business situations (such as the back office and television examples), to providing support to business strategy (the scenario planning example), to the determination of policy on matters of fundamental public importance (global warming).

The primary tool has been the drawing of causal loop diagrams, in which the interconnections of cause-and-effect relationships can be expressed as a network of interlinked reinforcing loops, which drive either exponential growth or decline, and balancing loops, which act to arrest the spinning of the reinforcing loops, sometimes steering the system toward particular targets or goals, expressed on a diagram as input policy dangles.

As we have seen many times now, even quite simple causal loop diagrams can result in very complex dynamic behaviors, which are hard to understand in retrospect and largely impossible to predict with any certainty.

The job of management, however, is to understand the past, to take decisions now, in order to influence the future as much as we possibly can to meet our overall goals and objectives. Managing the dynamic behavior of our business and organizational systems is our primary objective. Although causal loop diagrams are enormously helpful in understanding the underlying cause-and-effect relationships, very few of us can envisage how the dynamic behaviors of key variables—the customer base and market share, staff morale and the staff loss rate, shareholder value and reputation—are likely to evolve over time, in a highly complex environment of competitors, governments, and demanding consumers.

This is where computer-based simulation modeling can really add value, turbo-charging your thinking, because the computer model can act as your "laboratory of the future," enabling you to test the consequences of different policies and decisions before you have to commit.

There are a number of specialized software packages that enable you to draw causal loop diagrams, or take existing diagrams, and transform them into computer models enabling the time behavior of the system to be simulated. The result of the simulation is a set of graphs, with time as the horizontal axis and the variable of interest—customers, profits, reputation, or whatever—as the vertical axis, so that you can see how these variables are likely to evolve over time according to the logic implied by the causal loop diagrams. If you change any of the underlying parameters—such as the annual spend on advertising, which, with a time lag, will attract new customers, so increasing profits—the model will simulate the consequences and show you that, after a nice and expected rise in new customers and sales, a short while later sales fall again because customers become disaffected as a result of poor service, driven by the failure to recruit and train enough good staff to cope with the increase in demand caused by the advertising.

The purpose of this chapter is therefore to show how computer simulation models can be built from causal loop diagrams. The software product that I will be illustrating is called *ithink*, but this is not the only one available; two others are *Powersim* and *Vensim*. As with all software tools, the effective use of ithink, Powersim, and Vensim requires knowledge of a lot of detail. My intention here, however, is not to write a programming manual (the manuals for ithink are exceptionally good), but rather to give you an insight into how these products can be used.

System dynamics

The use of computer models to support systems thinking has its own name, *system dynamics*. Like systems thinking, system dynamics has a long and distinguished history, and the first specialized system dynamics programming languages, such as Dynamo, date back to the 1950s and 1960s. A key figure in the development of system dynamics is Jay Forrester (see page 180), whose original training was in electrical engineering, a subject very much concerned with the concepts of positive and negative feedback. This background, combined with Forrester's involvement in the early major uses of computers as well as his grappling with the complexities of huge defense systems, formed the ideal mix of skills to create system dynamics, the key features of which are summarized here.

System dynamics in one box

System dynamics is a computer modeling technique that enables the behavior of real systems to be simulated over time. System dynamics therefore offers the opportunity of transforming the necessarily static view of a causal loop diagram into a dynamic "laboratory of the future."

Like systems thinking, system dynamics offers many important insights, such as the fact that all variables can be classified as either stocks or flows:

➤ **Stocks** accumulate over time and can be measured at an instant in time.
➤ **Flows** increase or decrease stocks and can be measured only over a period of time.

System dynamics therefore incorporates all financial accounting, since all balance sheet items are stocks and all profit-and-loss account items are flows. The scope of system dynamics, however, is very much broader than conventional financial analysis and financial modeling, because there are many variables that can readily be incorporated within a system dynamics model but are hardly ever included in a financial model. Variables such as KNOWLEDGE, STAFF MORALE, and CUSTOMER SATISFACTION are important drivers of many businesses, but rarely appear in a published annual report or are to be seen within the accountants' spreadsheets.

The interactions between the stocks and flows for a particular system can be captured in a **plumbing diagram** or **stock-and-flow diagram**. Plumbing diagrams can always be mapped on to the corresponding causal loop diagrams, but plumbing diagrams usually contain more variables and more precise language.

Plumbing diagrams can be used as the basis for computer simulations, which show how the system evolves over time.

System dynamics and spreadsheets

Computer modeling is the stock-in-trade of almost every business manager, using spreadsheet products such as Excel. Given the ubiquity of spreadsheets, a natural question is: "Why should I bother with a different modeling technique? Can't I do all I need to in Excel?" It is of course true that, at the end of the day, both Excel (and the other spreadsheets) and ithink (and the other system dynamics products) are programming languages and, with sufficient ingenuity, both can be made to jump through all sorts of hoops. By the same token, with some ingenuity you might be able to use a hammer to perform a job that a screwdriver might do more easily. Tools tend to be designed with particular purposes in mind, and what is true for hand tools holds for software packages too. So let me spend a few moments explaining how system dynamics models differ from spreadsheets.

First, there is the issue of scope. Spreadsheets tend to be used for data-intensive, inward-looking number crunching, from analyses of sales by product, market, and channel, to the preparation of next year's budget by general ledger account. Spreadsheets look "down" into ever-increasing detail and "in" to the very corners of our organization. System dynamics models, in contrast, look "up" and "out": upward to broader concepts, breaking down boundaries, taking a holistic view; outward beyond our organization, into the market, into the overall context in which our business operates. System dynamics models can compute balance sheets and profit-and-loss accounts — but they can also do vastly more. Each of the causal loop diagrams in this book, for example, could act as the specification of a system dynamics model and give great insight into the dynamic behavior of the corresponding system. How many of these diagrams do you think would form the specification for a spreadsheet?

Secondly, there is the issue of structure. Although it is possible to capture feedback loops in spreadsheets, this is rarely — and usually not easily — done. System dynamics models, however, are designed explicitly to do just this and so can immediately and readily capture the essence of your business's engine of growth, simulating the driving force of the fundamental reinforcing loops, as well as the braking effects of any balancing loops. To see how this happens, let's refresh our memories of how most spreadsheet models are constructed and how they actually work.

Excel, which has as its antecedents products such as Lotus 1-2-3, Supercalc, and Visicalc, is the most familiar spreadsheet, an electronic form of the accountant's analysis paper structured as a grid of rows and columns. Usually the columns represent time slots (week by week, month by month, or whatever), and the rows items of interest such as "customers," "sales volume," "unit production costs," "net profits," "tax rate," and the rest. Each cell in the spreadsheet—the intersection of any row with any column—contains either a number that you have entered as input data or the specification of an arithmetical computation, such as "multiply the sales volume, which is found in row 7 of this column, by the unit price, in row 8 of this column, and put the result, the sales revenue, in this cell." The software does not require you to be as wordy as this: All you would put in cell D9 (for column D, "February," row 9, "sales revenue") is =D7*D8.

Spreadsheets have all sorts of features, such as the ability to replicate the rules of any one column across a range of other columns. The calculation rules for February (column D), for example, are very likely to be the same as for March (column E), and likewise for all the other months of the year. So having specified the row-by-row logic in the first column, it is very easy to copy the logic across the spreadsheet into the other columns.

For the most part, spreadsheets operate by going down the first column to calculate all the rows, then down the next column, and so on, for as long as you have written the program. This column-by-column method of operation, tracking through January, then February, then March, then April, is known as *time slice simulation*. The model simulates the behavior of the system, as defined by the rules in the spreadsheet, by "slicing" time according to predefined intervals, in this case months.

In most spreadsheets, the majority of the calculation rules operate on *different rows* within the *same column* ("sales revenue" = "sales volume" * "unit price," all for March), specifying all the calculations that take place within any time slice. However, in addition there is always a (usually much smaller) number of rules linking one column to the next, so defining how the model operates over time. These rules are generally of two types: first, the transfer of all closing balances (debtors, creditors, assets, and so on) of one column to the corresponding opening balances of the next; and secondly, all the rules that concern forecasts, for example rules stating that "sales volume grows by 1.5 percent per month," "overhead increases month by month in line with inflation," or whatever. Within the spreadsheet itself, rules of this second type are represented by references between *succeeding columns* for the *same row*. So using the example of sales growth, we might have in row 7 ("sales volume") of column E ("March") a rule referring to the preceding column D ("February") such as:

$$E7 = D7 * (1 + 0.015)$$

The growth rate (in this case, 1.5 percent per month) is usually an input, which might come from market research, judgment, or indeed hope.

Structurally, then, most spreadsheets have two principal sets of logic: one set going down the columns, and a second set connecting certain of the rows horizontally across the spreadsheet, as represented by Figure 12.1.

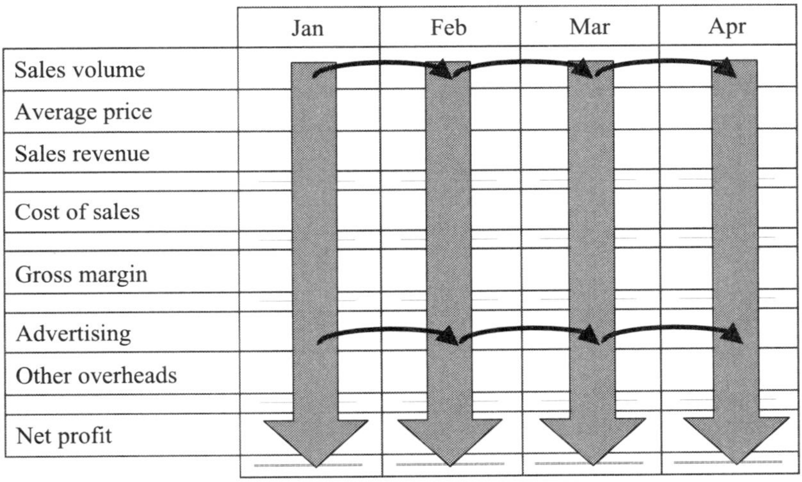

Figure 12.1

System dynamics models also use time slice simulation, but in a very different way. Rather than calculating (say) the sales volume in March by applying a percentage growth factor to the sales volume in February, a typical system dynamics model will calculate it from, for example, the advertising spend in February (or maybe earlier) by applying a fuzzy variable such as the EFFECT OF ADVERTISING ON ATTRACTING CUSTOMERS. In this way, system dynamics models capture the feedback loops that truly drive the business (Figure 12.2 overleaf).

Compared to spreadsheets, system dynamics models are therefore very different structurally and, as already mentioned, they tend to be of much broader scope, incorporating concepts and variables that you would never usually see in a spreadsheet. So to get the most out of this chapter and the next, you will need to forget almost everything you ever learnt about spreadsheets.

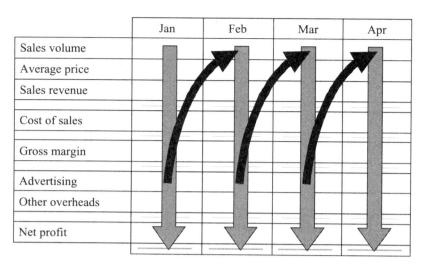

Figure 12.2

Forget spreadsheets

Forget all about rows, columns, and cells.

Forget all about formulae like D9=D7*D8.

Instead, think "stocks" and "flows."

Stocks and flows

The fundamental concepts in systems thinking are **stocks** and **flows**.

Stocks and flows

A stock is any variable that accumulates over time.

A flow is any variable that increases or decreases a stock.

Think about filling a bath with a leaky plug. To fill the bath you run the tap, but because of the leaky plug some water is also flowing out. But if the flow of water through the tap is faster than the flow out through the leaky plug, the water level in the bath will rise. If you stop the tap, the water will flow out and the level of water will drop. If, at a particular time when the level of the water is just right you adjust the tap "just so," you can arrange for the water level to stay constant, with the flow in from the tap just balancing the flow out through the leaky plug.

In terms of system dynamics modeling the two variables, the QUANTITY OF WATER IN THE BATH (as measured in cubic meters) and the LEVEL OF WATER IN THE BATH (as measured in centimeters of depth) at any time, are both stocks—they accumulate over time. And the two variables, the RATE OF INFLOW OF WATER THROUGH THE TAP (as measured in terms of cubic meters of water flowing per minute) and the RATE OF OUTFLOW OF WATER THROUGH THE LEAKY PLUG (measured similarly), are both flows—they act to increase or decrease the corresponding stocks, the QUANTITY OF WATER IN THE BATH and the LEVEL OF WATER IN THE BATH.

This system can be represented diagrammatically using some conventional symbols: a box for stocks and a pipe-and-tap for flows (Figure 12.3).

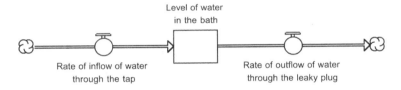

Figure 12.3

The "clouds" represent sources of inflows, or sinks for outflows, which are beyond the boundaries of the system of interest. The water flowing in through the taps does come from somewhere, and the water draining through the plug goes somewhere too, but, for the purposes of studying the system of the bath, these need not be taken into account—provided, of course, that the source can always provide plentiful water and the drain does not overflow!

What happens when time stops?

Imagine that time is suddenly frozen. What measurements would you have at that instant for:

➢ The QUANTITY OF WATER IN THE BATH?

➢ The LEVEL OF WATER IN THE BATH?

> ➤ The RATE OF INFLOW OF WATER THROUGH THE TAP?
> ➤ The RATE OF OUTFLOW OF WATER THROUGH THE LEAKY PLUG?

At the instant that time freezes, the two stocks—the QUANTITY OF WATER IN THE BATH and the LEVEL OF WATER IN THE BATH—have measurable values. The QUANTITY OF WATER IN THE BATH might be 0.25 cubic meters and the LEVEL OF WATER IN THE BATH 23 centimeters (or whatever). However, when time freezes the two flows cannot be measured—the flows have in essence stopped, since flows are intrinsically events that take place over time. When time stops, they have no value.

Another way of distinguishing stocks from flows
Stocks can be measured at an instant in time.
Flows can only be measured over time.

In general, any stock has at least one inflow and one outflow; there are many instances of stocks that have multiple inflows and outflows; and very occasionally, you come across a stock that, for a particular set of circumstances, has only an inflow or only an outflow.

Stocks, flows, baths, taps, drains, and humans
Here is an extract from *The Times*, 5 March 2001:

Lake Chad, once the fourth-largest body of water in Africa, has shrunk by almost 95% over the past 38 years. Climate change and increasing demands for water have drained the lake to such an extent that it will shortly be nothing more than a "puddle". The Lake Chad basin, a precious source of fresh water for at least 20 million people in Chad, Niger, Nigeria, Cameroon, Sudan and the Central African Republic, is a closed water system that depends on monsoon rains to replenish the water that drains from the lake. The lake is also shallow, meaning that its level responds rapidly to changes in rainfall and run-off. Since the early 1960s, the region has experienced a significant decline in rainfall, while the amount of water diverted to irrigate surrounding fields has risen steeply.

Stocks and flows in business

What are some stocks and flows in business?
How many stocks can you think of in business? And what are the corresponding flows?
You might like to note your thoughts in the table below.

Stock	Inflows	Outflows

The most obvious stock in business is stock itself, physical inventories of FIN-ISHED GOODS, WORK IN PROGRESS, or RAW MATERIALS. As every factory manager knows, when time stops, that stock is surely there and measurable. The inflows and outflows have various names depending on the context of the stock. If you are a retailer, for example, your stock is GOODS AVAILABLE FOR SALE and your outflows include MONTHLY SALES TO CUSTOMERS, MONTHLY STOCK PASSING ITS SELL-BY DATE, and MONTHLY THEFT; your inflows are MONTHLY RECEIPTS FROM SUPPLIERS, and maybe MONTHLY RETURNS FROM CUSTOMERS. Alternatively, in manufacturing, one stock is RAW MATERIALS, with inflows WEEKLY RECEIPTS FROM SUPPLIERS and WEEKLY RETURNS FROM THE SHOP FLOOR; and outflows WEEKLY ISSUES TO THE SHOP FLOOR, WEEKLY RETURNS TO SUPPLIERS, and WEEKLY RAW MATERIALS SCRAP. In each of these cases the stocks are all independent of time; the flows all explicitly refer to the time periods over which they apply.

Figure 12.4 overleaf is a diagram showing the main flows in and out of the stock RAW MATERIALS. The WEEKLY ISSUES TO THE SHOP FLOOR go into the stock WORK IN PROGRESS, which itself acts as the origin of the WEEKLY RETURNS FROM THE SHOP FLOOR. The two stocks of RAW MATERIALS and WORK IN PROGRESS are therefore linked; likewise, the WEEKLY RAW MATERIALS SCRAP and WEEKLY WORK IN PROGRESS SCRAP both contribute to the heap of SCRAP in the skip at the back of the factory, awaiting disposal. Also WORK IN PROGRESS feeds the stock of FIN-ISHED GOODS through the WEEKLY ISSUES TO FINISHED GOODS (Figure 12.5).

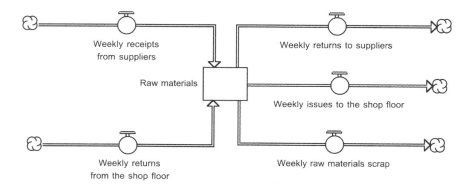

Figure 12.4

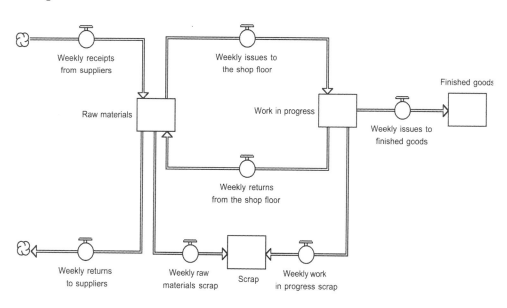

Figure 12.5

Diagrams of this type, capturing the interconnections between stocks and flows, are known as **stock-and-flow diagrams** or, more colloquially, **plumbing diagrams**. As we shall see shortly, plumbing diagrams are very closely related to causal loop diagrams.

A word on language. System dynamics modeling requires precision of thought and clarity of language. In everyday language, for example, the term "scrap" can be applied to both the stock of scrap—the pile at the back of the factory—and the flow—the amount of material scrapped each week. When drawing plumbing diagrams, however, it is important to distinguish between stocks and flows and to use the appropriate descriptions. This can on occasion be rather clumsy, especially in text, but the diagrams are usually clearer.

To help distinguish between stocks and flows, it is often helpful to think of how you would naturally measure the item in question. Scrap as a stock is naturally measured in terms of "quantity of stuff," "tonnes," or whatever; scrap as a flow in terms of "number of units disposed of per week." It is the "per week" that emphasizes the flow. There are many other business terms that can refer to both a stock and a flow and this can sometimes give rise to muddle, so do make sure that you know exactly what is meant in any given case.

Stocks, flows, and units of measure

As the example of physical inventory illustrates, the units of measure applied to stocks and flows are different. The stock of inventory at a wine merchant, for example, is measured in units of product, such as *12 cases of wine*; the flow of sales is measured in units of product per unit of time, say, *3 cases of wine per week*. Since flows take place over time, the measure used for the time period is important and the numerical value of the flow will change depending on the time period involved—3 cases of wine per week, for example, would correspond to 12 cases of wine per month, or about 150 cases of wine per year.

The numerical value of the stock, however, makes no reference to time at all. Throughout the year, at any time, the stock in the inventory at the end of each week, each month, each quarter, or at the year end will (assuming a perfect stock control system!) still be 12 cases of wine. This too is a diagnostic of whether or not an item is a stock or a flow: If the numerical value of the item in question varies with the length of the time period, it is a flow; if it doesn't, it is a stock.

Physical inventory is just one example of a stock in business. Table 12.1 overleaf is a list of some of the others, with some of their more common flows over any defined period, say each month.

Table 12.1

Stock	Typical inflows per month	Typical outflows per month
Inventory	Purchases, receipts	Sales, despatches
Staff	Hires, promotions in	Leavers, promotions out
Fixed assets	Purchases	Disposals
Fixed asset value	Purchases	Disposals, depreciation
Debtors	Sales	Cash receipts
Customer base	New customer acquisitions	Customer loss
Knowledge	Training and experience	"Human obsolescence"
Price	Price increase	Price decrease
Interest rate	Increase in interest rate	Decrease in interest rate
Tax rate	Increase in tax rate	Decrease in tax rate
Brand image	Increase in brand image	Decrease in brand image

Stocks, flows, and accounting
All balance sheet items are stocks.
All profit-and-loss account items are flows.

These statements are fundamental truths—and they are acknowledged in the language that accountants use when they refer to the balance sheet *as at* a particular date (freezing time), as opposed to the profit and loss *for the period ended* whenever (emphasizing the measurement over a period of time). All the formalism of accounting can therefore be incorporated within system dynamics, but as a glance at the table shows, system dynamics naturally encompasses far more than accounting. KNOWLEDGE, for example, is a vital stock in many businesses, but only a few formally recognize its value.

Knowledge is difficult to measure, but this is evidence of our poor ability to measure important things rather than an argument that knowledge is not a stock. If time freezes, KNOWLEDGE is still there and in principle measurable, if only we knew how, and the stock of knowledge can be enhanced by the flows of TRAINING AND EXPERIENCE. It also naturally erodes by virtue of "HUMAN OBSOLESCENCE," the tendency to lose touch with current thinking unless we actively read the professional press, go to conferences, and interact with colleagues.

Leif Edvinsson

Knowledge may be difficult to measure, but it isn't impossible. Some of the most impressive and innovative work in measuring the value of intellectual capital took place in Sweden during the 1990s, especially at the insurance company Skandia. Following some early internal developments initiated in 1991, in 1995 Skandia became the first organization in the world to publish two formal financial reports, the conventional one containing all the familiar management statements and accounting reports, and a second, supplementary report, entitled *Visualizing Intellectual Capital*, valuing the company's intellectual capital too. Skandia now publishes these two reports every six months.

The driving force behind this pioneering work was Skandia's vice-president and corporate director of intellectual capital, Leif Edvinsson. Now recognized as the world's leader in this fascinating field, Leif Edvinsson is currently Professor of Knowledge Economics at Lund University, a frequent speaker on the conference circuit, and co-author, with Michael Malone, of *Intellectual Capital: The Proven Way to Establish Your Company's Real Value by Measuring its Hidden Brainpower*.

For more information on Skandia try its website www.skandia.com, and for more on the measurement of intellectual capital log on to www.intellectualcapital.org.

STAFF MORALE is also a stock, as is COMPANY REPUTATION. In the realm of the more tangible, one of the most important stocks is PRICE. If time freezes prices are still there and measurable, but since we don't have specific names in the English language for the corresponding (monthly) flows, we have to resort to clumsy phrases such as INCREASE IN PRICE and DECREASE IN PRICE.

Another important stock is the INTEREST RATE. This sometimes causes confusion, since the use of the word "rate" seems to imply that this is a flow; a confusion enhanced by the fact that we frequently define interest rates in relation to time, such as "6 percent per annum." In fact the ANNUAL INTEREST RATE is a stock, because its role is to act as a price, the price of money, and the word "rate" implies not a rate over time, but a ratio with respect to the capital sum involved: The ANNUAL INTEREST RATE determines how much interest is paid each year for each £100 of capital.

If you are not convinced, try the test described on page 283, where I pointed out that the value of a flow varies with the length of the time period over which the flow takes place. Whether you invest some money at a fixed rate of 6 percent per annum over six months or over twelve, the ANNUAL INTEREST RATE is unchanged; it is 6 percent in both cases. What *does* change is the amount of interest received over any time period. For example, if you invest $100 at 6 percent per annum, compounded annually, over three months you will receive $1.50 in interest; over six, $3.00; over twelve, $6.00. In this example, the CAPITAL SUM INVESTED is a stock, and the INTEREST RECEIVED EACH YEAR is an inflow; the ANNUAL INTEREST RATE % is a second stock that acts as a rate dangle determining the value of the flow (Figure 12.6).

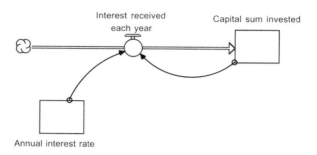

Figure 12.6

This plumbing diagram introduces a new feature, the **curly arrow** or **connector**, which indicates how the variables in the diagram are related. The curly arrows from ANNUAL INTEREST RATE and CAPITAL SUM INVESTED to INTEREST RECEIVED EACH YEAR imply that the value of the INTEREST RECEIVED EACH YEAR is determined by both the CAPITAL SUM INVESTED and the ANNUAL INTEREST RATE. The explicit nature of the relationship is not shown on the diagram, but is recorded "behind" the diagram on the "equations screen" of ithink as:

INTEREST RECEIVED EACH YEAR =
CAPITAL SUM INVESTED × ANNUAL INTEREST RATE / 100

Likewise, the TAX RATE is a stock not a flow, for once again the term "rate" does not imply a rate over time, but rather the computation of how much tax is payable for each $100 of taxable profit. So sometimes the term "rate" can be misleading: All flows are rates, but not all rates are flows!

Two more unifying concepts

Every variable can be classified as either a stock or a flow.

This is another of those startling unifying concepts of systems thinking, or in this case system dynamics: All variables are either stocks or flows, there are no other types. And here is another:

> **Stocks, flows, objectives, and actions**
> Most business objectives — and certainly all the most important ones — can be expressed as the optimization of a portfolio of stocks.
> The only actions that a manager can take are to readjust the flows.

That one needs some thinking about, but it is true. Most business objectives boil down to goals such as maximizing market share, maximizing shareholder value, keeping a high share price, having a high reputation, or keeping staff morale high. All of these are stocks. And since the optimization of any one (say, market share) might be in conflict with optimizing another (say, staff morale, the conflict being the choice between spending money on advertising as opposed to giving it to the staff as bonuses), the set of stocks needs to be managed as a portfolio and kept in overall balance.

In contrast, the only actions managers can take are those of hiring, firing, buying assets, disposing of companies, spending on advertising, and the like. All of these are flows. It is as if we are trying to manage a set of baths, interconnected in a complex way through a network of pipes, taps, and drains, so that as one bath empties another fills up. Our overall goal is to keep the water in each of the baths at particular levels simultaneously or, better still, for them to increase steadily and together. But the only actions we can take are to twiddle the taps and adjust the drains.

This water metaphor is of course the system dynamics version of the systems thinking discussion of levers and outcomes that we had in Chapter 10 (see page 208). Business outcomes are all stocks and the action levers are all flows.

Causal loop diagrams and plumbing diagrams

Take a look at the causal loop diagram in Figure 12.7 overleaf, which we saw in the last chapter. Which of these variables are stocks? And which are flows?

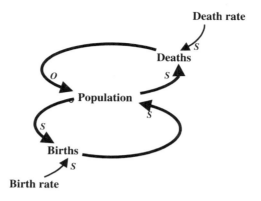

Figure 12.7

This diagram has three stocks and two flows. The stocks are POPULATION, the (ANNUAL) BIRTH RATE, and the (ANNUAL) DEATH RATE; the flows are the number of BIRTHS (PER YEAR) and the number of DEATHS (PER YEAR), which increase and decrease the stock of POPULATION respectively. As with the interest rate, despite the "rate" associated with the terms ANNUAL BIRTH RATE and ANNUAL DEATH RATE, these are stocks, not flows. In this case the word "rate" implies not a rate over time, but a ratio with respect to the total population — the ANNUAL BIRTH RATE is the number of births per 1,000 population per year, and likewise the ANNUAL DEATH RATE. These relationships can be expressed according to the equations:

BIRTHS PER YEAR = POPULATION × ANNUAL BIRTH RATE / 1,000
DEATHS PER YEAR = POPULATION × ANNUAL DEATH RATE / 1,000

Figure 12.8 is one way of representing this as a plumbing diagram.

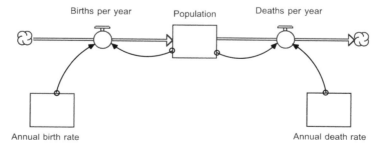

Figure 12.8

The curly arrows indicate quantitative relationships, so, for example, the curly arrows from ANNUAL BIRTH RATE and POPULATION into BIRTHS PER YEAR imply that the number of BIRTHS PER YEAR is determined by both the POPULATION and the ANNUAL BIRTH RATE as specified by the equation that we have just seen.

Compare the causal loop diagram and the plumbing diagram
Look at the two diagrams carefully and convince yourself that they are identical. Check in particular that there are two feedback loops and two dangles. How does the causal loop diagram capture the Ss, and in particular the O?

The two feedback loops in the causal loop diagram have been incorporated in the plumbing diagram as a combination of the flows and the curly arrows: from BIRTHS PER YEAR to POPULATION by the flow, and back by the curly arrow; and likewise for POPULATION and DEATHS PER YEAR. The two dangles, specifying the ANNUAL BIRTH RATE and ANNUAL DEATH RATE, are clear in both diagrams. The S in the causal loop diagram from BIRTHS PER YEAR to POPULATION, implying that as the number of BIRTHS PER YEAR increases the POPULATION increases, is shown by the fact that BIRTHS PER YEAR is an *inflow* into POPULATION. Likewise, the O from DEATHS PER YEAR to POPULATION, implying that as the number of DEATHS PER YEAR increases the POPULATION decreases, is captured in the plumbing diagram by the representation of DEATHS PER YEAR as an *outflow* from POPULATION. The Ss in the causal loop diagram from ANNUAL BIRTH RATE to BIRTHS PER YEAR and from ANNUAL DEATH RATE to DEATHS PER YEAR are not explicitly shown in the plumbing diagram, but are implied by the associated equations.

As a general rule, all inflows in a plumbing diagram will be associated with an S in the corresponding causal loop diagram; similarly, all outflows will be associated with an O. Other S or O relationships will not be explicitly shown on plumbing diagrams and need to be inferred from the context, or determined by reference to the underlying equations.

One-way links revisited
On pages 67 and 151 we saw two examples of some rather peculiar causal loop diagram

links. The first concerned the pouring of a cup of coffee and the relationship between the ACTION OF POURING OF COFFEE INTO THE CUP and the ACTUAL LEVEL OF COFFEE IN THE CUP; the other, the link between BIRTHS and the URBAN POPULATION. The peculiarity was that these links worked in only one direction. Taking the births example, as the number of BIRTHS increases the URBAN POPULATION increases, implying that this link is an S; but as the number of BIRTHS decreases the URBAN POPULATION does *not* decrease, as would be expected by the S; rather, it continues to increase, but somewhat more slowly.

I explained both of these anomalies in terms of the inherent unidirectionality of the corresponding real-world situation. Pouring coffee into a cup can only increase the amount of coffee in the cup, never decrease it; likewise, births can only increase a population, never decrease it. Since the real world can act in only one direction, the corresponding causal loop diagrams can also only act in one direction.

These anomalies can be explained much more concisely in terms of stock and flows. Both of these examples concern inflows to their corresponding stocks. The ACTION OF POURING OF COFFEE INTO THE CUP is an inflow to the stock of COFFEE IN THE CUP, and the number of BIRTHS per year is an inflow to the stock of URBAN POPULATION. Furthermore, these flows can act in only one direction—they are necessarily *uniflows*. As inflows, they must act to increase their respective stocks, hence in their causal loop diagrams they must be represented as Ss. But since these flows can act in only one direction, the causal loop diagrams only work in one direction as well.

The same applies to outflows that are necessarily uniflows, such as the number of DEATHS per year. In a causal loop diagram (see page 288), as the number of DEATHS increases the POPULATION decreases, and since these items are moving in opposite directions this link is shown as an O. If the number of DEATHS decreases, the population continues to decrease, but more slowly. This, of course, is a one-way O, and the explanation is the same: DEATHS can only decrease a population, never increase it. In a plumbing diagram, this is shown by representing the number of DEATHS PER YEAR as an outflow from the stock POPULATION, and in a causal loop diagram by the O designation of the link from DEATHS to POPULATION. Because the number of DEATHS PER YEAR is necessarily a uniflow, the causal loop diagram will work in only one direction.

The moral of the story is this. One-way Ss and Os arise in a causal loop diagram when a flow is linked to its corresponding stock, and when that flow is necessarily a uniflow. If the flow is an inflow the link is an S; if an outflow, an O. And because the flow is a uniflow, the causal loop diagram will only work in the "natural" direction of the flow. Not all flows, by the way, are uniflows; see, for example, page 324.

One aspect of the plumbing diagram in Figure 12.8 is that the stocks representing the ANNUAL BIRTH RATE and the ANNUAL DEATH RATE are not explicitly associated with their corresponding flows. By convention, another
representation is used in plumbing diagrams, symbolized by a circle and
called a **converter**, or an **auxiliary**, for variables that may be either stocks or
flows but do not need to be explicitly recognized as such (Figure 12.9).

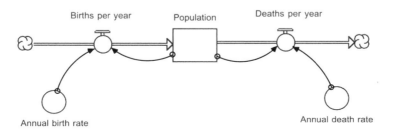

Figure 12.9

Although all variables are necessarily either stocks or flows, plumbing diagrams use three symbols: the box for stocks, the pipe-and-tap for flows, and the
circle for auxiliaries. When a stock or a flow is best represented explicitly and
when as an auxiliary is a matter of judgment, but in general it is good practice to
keep the number of stocks explicitly recognized as stocks to a minimum and
express the rest as auxiliaries. The flows to be explicitly represented as flows are
determined by the chosen stocks, any other flows taking the form of auxiliaries.

Plumbing diagrams are necessarily structurally equivalent to the corresponding causal loop diagrams and will show all the same feedback loops and
contain all the same variables. The two types of diagram, however, are visu-
ally different and have two other important differences.

First, as we shall see during the rest of this chapter, plumbing diagrams
usually contain more variables than the corresponding causal loop diagrams.
The reason for this is that, whereas causal loop diagrams focus on the cause-
and-effect relationships between the main variables, such as Figure 12.10:

Figure 12.10

plumbing diagrams are obliged to specify how each link actually operates, and so will include necessary additional variables, such as MARGIN (Figure 12.11):

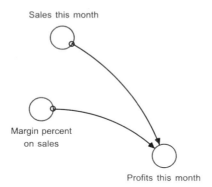

Figure 12.11

thereby indicating that PROFITS THIS MONTH are calculated from both the SALES THIS MONTH and the MARGIN PERCENT ON SALES.

Secondly, plumbing diagrams are much more specific as regards the names of the variables. For example, in the causal loop diagram for population growth we referred just to BIRTHS, whereas the plumbing diagram refers to BIRTHS PER YEAR, emphasizing the time-related nature of the flow. This too reflects the rigor required for modeling.

Modeling in ithink

The software product ithink has been designed specifically for system dynamics modeling and provides features to enable you to:

➤ Draw the plumbing diagram appropriate to your model.
➤ Specify the input values of the appropriate variables.
➤ Specify the relationships between appropriate variables.
➤ Derive outputs in the form of graphs and tables.

Once the plumbing diagram has been drawn and all the input variables and relationships specified, the model then simulates the behavior of the system over time, producing the required outputs.

The first—and most important—step in building an ithink model does not require the software, because it takes place independently of the computer. It is the process of problem analysis and the drawing of causal loop diagrams that capture the key elements of the system, as we have seen throughout this book. Computer modeling should start only after this has been very thoroughly done and the resulting causal loop diagrams validated by the appropriate team.

Causal loop diagrams therefore form the basic specification for an ithink model but, as already noted, the representation in ithink, which takes the form of a plumbing diagram, usually contains more variables.

The main ithink screen enables you to build plumbing diagrams very easily. The software provides you with all the main symbols—the box, the pipe-and-tap, the circle, and the curly arrow—that you can drag and drop on the screen as you wish. There are some other tools, notably the highly satisfying "stick of dynamite" that you can use to "blow up" symbols that are no longer required!

Once the diagram has been drawn, the next step is to specify the numerical values of some variables and all necessary relationships between the variables. The variables that require numerical values are:

➤ The initial values of all stocks.
➤ The values of all input dangles.

All other variables will be expressed in terms of algebraic relationships, as determined by the connections defined in the plumbing diagram. Since ithink "knows" what these connections are, it is in fact very easy to specify the required relationships.

Let me make this clear using the example of the very simple population growth model (Figure 12.12 overleaf).

The POPULATION is a stock and so requires an initial value, say, 10,000 in a particular location, as at the start of the year 2000. The ANNUAL BIRTH RATE is an input dangle, so let's assume 15 births per 1,000 population per year; likewise, the ANNUAL DEATH RATE is also an input dangle, so let's assume 12 deaths per 1,000 population per year. The number of BIRTHS PER YEAR and the number of DEATHS PER YEAR are calculated according to the following equations:

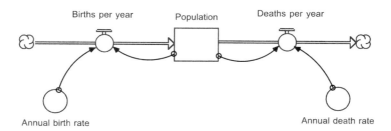

Figure 12.12

$$\text{BIRTHS PER YEAR} = \text{POPULATION} \times \text{ANNUAL BIRTH RATE} \,/\, 1{,}000$$
$$\text{DEATHS PER YEAR} = \text{POPULATION} \times \text{ANNUAL DEATH RATE} \,/\, 1{,}000$$

Within ithink, input data values and algebraic expressions are all brought together on the "equations screen," which is "behind" the plumbing diagram. For this population model, the equations screen looks like this:

Population (t) = Population (t - dt) + (Births - Deaths) * dt
INIT Population = 10000
INFLOWS:
⊸◯▷ Births = Population * Annual birth rate/1000
OUTFLOWS:
⊸◯▷ Deaths = Population * Annual death rate/1000
◯ Annual birth rate = 15
◯ Annual death rate = 12

The first line is the most arcane, but is in fact quite simple. It defines how the stock of POPULATION is calculated: The POPULATION at the end of the current time period (t) — say, the year 2005 — is equal to the POPULATION as at the end of the preceding period $(t - dt)$ — say, the year 2004, this value of course being the same as the POPULATION at the start of the current period 2005 — plus the difference between the inflow and the outflow (BIRTHS PER YEAR – DEATHS PER YEAR), as took place over the duration of the current period dt — say, the calendar year 2005.

Accountants will recognize this as the familiar recipe that the closing balance at the end of an accounting period equals the opening balance at the start of the period, plus the net movement over the period. Mathematicians will see it as a finite difference equation. Those of us who trust common sense will appreciate that the amount of water that will be in a bath in five minutes' time is the amount of water that is in the bath now, plus what flows in during the next five minutes, less what flows out.

The following line specifies the initial value of the POPULATION (10,000 as at the start of the year 2000), and the next two lines define how the numbers of BIRTHS PER YEAR and DEATHS PER YEAR are calculated. Finally, the last two lines specify the values for the ANNUAL BIRTH RATE (15 births per 1,000 population per year) and ANNUAL DEATH RATE (12 deaths per 1,000 population per year) that will apply throughout the model.

The model operates by following the algorithm specified by these equations for each year. Given the initial value of the POPULATION at the start of the year 2000, the model first calculates the flows over the calendar year 2000, a total of 150 BIRTHS and 120 DEATHS. Over the year 2000, the net increase in population (BIRTHS PER YEAR – DEATHS PER YEAR) is therefore 30, and so the POPULATION at the end of the year 2000 is calculated, in accordance with the equation specified in the first line, as $10,000 + (150 – 120) * 1 = 10,030$. This then becomes the initial value for the start of the next year 2001, and the same process is invoked for 2001, and so on for each year.

The good news is that this is all automatic. Once the input data items and the relevant equations are specified (this is usually quite easy), the operation of the model looks after itself and you need never look at any equations again. There is only one set of equations and there is no need to replicate formulae as is required in spreadsheets: The repetition over time is built into the program.

What we really want to know, of course, is the result of the model's operation, which, for this model over 50 years, looks like Figure 12.13 overleaf. Exponential growth masquerading as linear!

Suppose that you are an anthropologist studying the populations of some Pacific islands. Having built this model for one island, you would like to use it elsewhere, for different islands, with different initial populations, and different annual birth and death rates. Wouldn't it be convenient if there were an easy way to enter the base data?

In fact there is. It is a "control panel," which in this case looks like Figure 12.14 overleaf. This diagram is an image of the computer screen, which displays one knob and two sliding levers. The knob, labeled INITIAL POPULATION, can be used to specify the opening population level and is currently set at

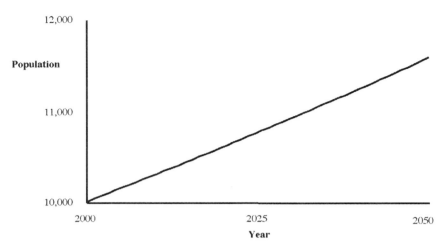

Figure 12.13

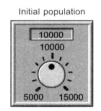

Figure 12.14

10,000; the two sliding levers refer to the ANNUAL BIRTH RATE and ANNUAL DEATH RATE respectively, and are current set at 15 births per 1,000 population per year, and 12 deaths per 1,000 population per year.

So if you are visiting a neighboring island and you want to run the model with different values, all you need do is use the cursor to turn the knob and slide the levers, for example, to those in Figure 12.15.

When you reset a knob or a lever a small U appears on the control panel, as a reminder that the current setting is different from the original. If you click on the appropriate U, the original settings are restored. This neighboring

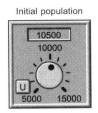

Figure 12.15

island has a somewhat larger INITIAL POPULATION (10,500) but a poorer diet. The ANNUAL BIRTH RATE is 13.5 per 1,000 per year, and the ANNUAL DEATH RATE 12.5 per 1,000 per year. If you run the model now, it will use the new knob and lever settings and show you a comparison of the population projections for the two islands (Figure 12.16).

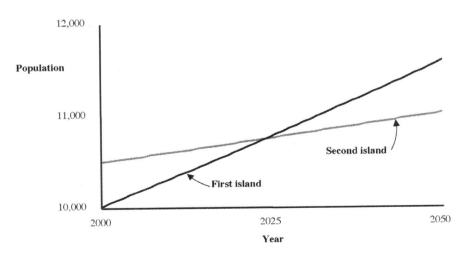

Figure 12.16

This graph indicates that, if the ANNUAL BIRTH RATES and ANNUAL DEATH RATES on the two islands remain constant at their initial values, then the POPULATION of the first island will overtake that of the second in about 25 years.

However, what if the ANNUAL BIRTH RATE and ANNUAL DEATH RATE do not remain constant over that time? Suppose that the second island is the beneficiary of an aid program to improve nutrition, which simultaneously increases the ANNUAL BIRTH RATE and reduces the ANNUAL DEATH RATE?

In this case, the ANNUAL BIRTH RATE and ANNUAL DEATH RATE for the second island are no longer constant but vary over time. This is catered for in ithink by allowing you to enter data graphically, directly on the screen, using the cursor to draw the shape of the graph you require. Suppose that your belief about the effectiveness of the nutrition program is to change the ANNUAL BIRTH RATE and ANNUAL DEATH RATE according to the patterns in Figures 12.17 and 12.18.

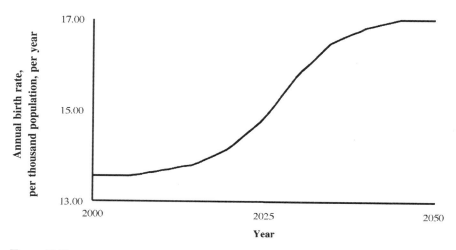

Figure 12.17

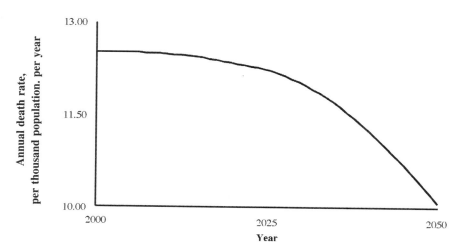

Figure 12.18

As the model runs, in each year it uses these graphs to determine the appropriate ANNUAL BIRTH RATE and ANNUAL DEATH RATE, and applies them accordingly. Figure 12.19 is the result.

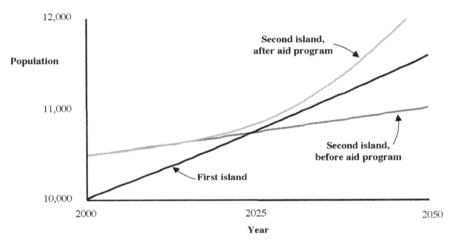

Figure 12.19

The control panel is also different, because the sliding levers for the ANNUAL BIRTH RATE and the ANNUAL DEATH RATE are replaced by the input graphs (Figure 12.20).

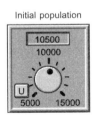

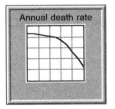

Figure 12.20

These input graphs represent a particular view of how the ANNUAL BIRTH RATE and ANNUAL DEATH RATE are likely to evolve over time. The only verifiable data points are the two known rates for the year 2000; all the others are conjecture. Different people, of course, will have different opinions, different mental models. Some might think that, as the quality of nutrition increases, young women will become healthier and so the ANNUAL BIRTH RATE will increase more quickly; others might think that the most immediate impact of the nutrition program will be to lower the ANNUAL DEATH RATE. In truth, nobody will have anything but the vaguest idea of what might happen in 25 years' time, let alone 50.

These opinions are not "right" or "wrong," but genuinely held, different beliefs. By being able to express input data in terms of a graph, which can easily be changed on the screen, ithink makes it very easy to alter the data to explore the effect of different assumptions, different views, different mental models. Perhaps some different opinions have only a modest impact on the output results; perhaps the impact is significant—the best way to gain an understanding of how the system behaves under different conditions is to try them out. System dynamics therefore provides a very powerful laboratory for testing policies before they are implemented. Just as pilots train in flight simulators and accountants make sure that every investment appraisal is supported by a dossier of spreadsheets showing a variety of sensitivity analyses, every wise manager should have a system dynamics model of their business as a whole.

Although this example is very simple and not immediately relevant to business, it does show all the main elements of system dynamics modeling. Real models are, of course, bigger and more complex, but they draw on the fundamentals that you have read and that are summarized in the box opposite.

System dynamics modeling in one box

All variables can be expressed either as **stocks**, which accumulate over time, or **flows**, which increase or decrease the corresponding stocks.

Real systems are complex, interconnected networks of stocks and flows, as represented on a **plumbing diagram**.

Plumbing diagrams are always consistent with the corresponding causal loop diagrams, but usually show more detail and use more specific language.

The ithink modeling software operates at three levels. The main one is the *diagram level*, which displays the plumbing diagram of the system of interest. "Behind" the diagram is the *equation level*, which specifies all the calculation rules required to run the model. "Above" the diagram is the *control panel*, which enables you to define and change the values of input variables by deploying easy-to-use features such as knobs and sliding levers.

A further very useful feature is the ability to define variables in terms of graphs, so allowing you to capture, for example, how you believe a particular input variable behaves over time. Most real problems involve a number of variables that do change over time, but you don't know the underlying algebraic equations. No matter. In your mind you have a feel about what the behavior might be — the variable goes up or it goes down; it rises steeply or slowly; it flattens out or continues to rise or fall. This pattern is a mental graph, a mental model, and your opinion of how such patterns behave underpins many of your decisions and actions. System dynamics modeling enables you to capture these "fuzzy variables" explicitly and to explore the consequences of alternative actions. This helps the process of determining wise policies and the agreement of wise actions.

13
Modeling business growth

Chapter 12 described the key features of system dynamics modeling. The purpose of this chapter is to show how this can be applied to modeling your business.

Clearly, your business might well be very different from that being run by another reader, so I can't present a model of your own business specifically. What I can do, however, is to draw on the material in Chapter 8, in which we examined business growth as limited by real-world constraints such as market saturation, and show how this can be used as a framework for a generic system dynamics model. Although the specifics may not correspond to your business precisely, I am sure that most of the general themes will.

A business example

The plumbing diagram of growth

Figure 13.1 is the causal loop diagram for the engine of business growth that we explored in Chapter 8.

Take a few moments to draw the corresponding plumbing diagram. Which variables are the stocks? And which the flows? Which of these do you wish to represent explicitly as stocks and flows and which as auxiliaries?

What additional variables do you need in the plumbing diagram that are not shown in the causal loop diagram to make the plumbing diagram complete?

This exercise has many possible valid answers; we all have different mental models. Also, the language used and the additional variables required in the plumbing diagram will vary according to the specifics of the business context; a service business will be different from a manufacturer or a retailer. So if your response is different from mine, no matter. More important than the specifics of any individual case is the clarity of the thinking.

To put my response into context, the business I have in mind is a motor dealer in a provincial town. The dealer has a franchise for a particular marque

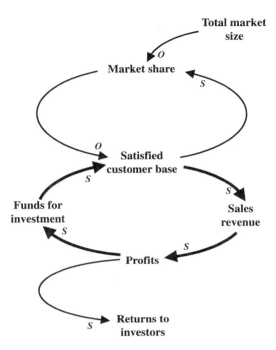

Figure 13.1

and is seeking to expand his business. The engine of growth results from selling cars to new customers and also existing customers who are trading in their old models. This SATISFIED CUSTOMER BASE generates the SALES REVENUE and PROFITS to provide the FUNDS FOR INVESTMENT, funds that are used for a variety of marketing activities designed to attract new customers and keep existing customers loyal to the marque.

As we all know the car market is highly competitive and, even though the marque is backed by a major manufacturer, it is not easy to increase local MARKET SHARE. Currently the SATISFIED CUSTOMER BASE, customers who have purchased a car from the dealership over the past five years, comprises 22,000 people and the business is currently selling around 1,540 vehicles a month, at an average price of £10,000 per car, in a local market of total volume 15,000 car sales a month. The ambition of the dealership is to grow the MARKET SHARE (measured in this case as the ratio of the dealership's monthly sales volume to the total local monthly sales) from its current level of just above 10 percent to about 12 percent, which is probably as high a market share as might be achievable.

Figure 13.2 overleaf is my plumbing diagram.

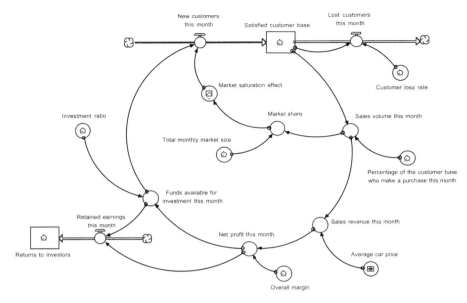

Figure 13.2

As compared to the causal loop diagram this shows all the expected features. The structures are the same, with both diagrams showing the reinforcing loop through the FUNDS AVAILABLE FOR INVESTMENT THIS MONTH, and the balancing loop through MARKET SHARE. The plumbing diagram, however, incorporates a number of additional variables to specify exactly how all the relationships work and the language is much more precise.

In addition, this plumbing diagram introduces a new feature. As you can see, some of the symbols contain imbedded representations:

    ♢   a knob

    ■   a sliding lever

    ▣   a graph

indicating that the corresponding variables appear in the appropriate form on the control panel shown in Figure 13.3.

These variables correspond, as expected, to the opening balances of the two stocks I have selected—the SATISFIED CUSTOMER BASE and the RETURNS TO INVESTORS—as well as to all the input dangles that specify the values of a variety of parameters that are needed to make the model work. There is also another item, which is neither a stock nor a dangle and is shown as a graph. I

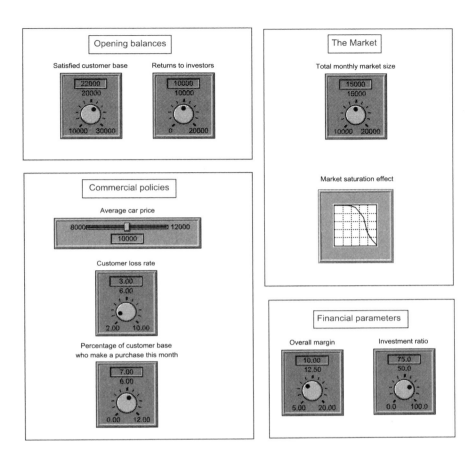

Figure 13.3

have termed this the MARKET SATURATION EFFECT, of which more shortly.

I chose to represent the SATISFIED CUSTOMER BASE as a stock since the way in which this builds over time is central to the growth of any business. This stock is associated with two flows, NEW CUSTOMERS THIS MONTH as an inflow and LOST CUSTOMERS THIS MONTH as an outflow. I am using the month as the length of the time period for simulation. This of course is something of an approximation, since not all calendar months are of equal length, but that should not make a material difference: I could easily use four-weekly periods if I wished.

The model operates by "time slice simulation," in which time is sliced into equal periods, in this case months. At the start of any month the SATISFIED CUSTOMER BASE has a particular value, an opening balance, and the first calculation is that of the SALES VOLUME THIS MONTH, computed by multiplying the current value of the opening balance of the SATISFIED CUSTOMER BASE by a quantity that I have termed the PERCENTAGE OF THE CUSTOMER BASE WHO MAKE A PURCHASE THIS MONTH. The concept here is that cars are purchased each month not only by new customers, but also by some of the people who have purchased cars through the dealership in the past and are returning for repeat purchases. The total monthly sales volume may therefore be expressed in terms of the PERCENTAGE OF THE CUSTOMER BASE WHO MAKE A PURCHASE THIS MONTH, this percentage being based on historical data and experience and incorporating both categories of purchase.

The SALES VOLUME THIS MONTH multiplied by the AVERAGE CAR PRICE gives the SALES REVENUE THIS MONTH, and if this is then multiplied by the OVERALL MARGIN, it determines the NET PROFIT THIS MONTH. The treatment of costs is, to say the least, broad brush, because all costs (except the marketing costs that will be accounted for in the FUNDS AVAILABLE FOR INVESTMENT THIS MONTH) are incorporated within the OVERALL MARGIN. It is of course possible to track various categories of cost if you wish, but too enthusiastic an approach in this direction runs the danger of transforming a system dynamics model into a spreadsheet.

Having determined the NET PROFIT THIS MONTH, the model calculates the FUNDS AVAILABLE FOR INVESTMENT THIS MONTH by multiplying the NET PROFIT THIS MONTH by the INVESTMENT RATIO, this being the percentage of the NET PROFIT THIS MONTH that is earmarked for investment. This implies that the investment decision is made on a month-by-month basis, in the light of the funds available. This is quite conservative and represents a business model in which there is an underlying budget, intended to be financed from the normal monthly cash flow and managed in conjunction with a monthly review, allowing for adjustments up or down as circumstances permit.

Another assumption is that any NET PROFIT THIS MONTH that is not earmarked for the FUNDS AVAILABLE FOR INVESTMENT THIS MONTH become RETAINED EARNINGS THIS MONTH and, as each month goes by, these sums accumulate into the stock of RETURNS TO INVESTORS. I have kept this as a stock with only a single inflow; I could have introduced an outflow, such as dividends or drawings.

In a car retailing business, many of the major marketing campaigns are organized by the manufacturer. Individual dealerships can stimulate the market by local advertising, mailshots, and the like, and so the FUNDS AVAILABLE

FOR INVESTMENT THIS MONTH are spent on activities of this sort. The objective of all this expenditure is to attract new customers. Let's suppose that the dealer's experience is that one new customer is attracted, on average, for every £1,250 spent. This suggests a relationship of the form:

NEW CUSTOMERS THIS MONTH
= FUNDS AVAILABLE FOR INVESTMENT THIS MONTH / 1,250

This relationship, however, implies that one new customer is acquired for every £1,250 spent, no matter how many customers there already are. This cannot be the whole story, since it becomes increasingly difficult to attract new customers as the MARKET SHARE increases. That is what the balancing loop in the causal loop diagram is all about.

This is captured by the variable that I have chosen to call the MARKET SATU-RATION EFFECT. The idea that I want to represent here is that, as the MARKET SHARE increases, the number of NEW CUSTOMERS THIS MONTH decreases. This is an archetypal fuzzy variable, something that I know exists but just don't know how to measure. As we have seen (see, for example, pages 65 and 225), systems thinking positively encourages the representation of such realities and system dynamics makes them very easy to handle. What we are looking for is some kind of number that depends on the MARKET SHARE and is big when the MARKET SHARE is relatively low, and small when the MARKET SHARE is relatively high.

How about something like Figure 13.4 overleaf? This graph shows how the MARKET SATURATION EFFECT changes with MARKET SHARE. When the MARKET SHARE is around 10 percent the MARKET SATURATION EFFECT is about 1.0, but as the MARKET SHARE increases beyond 11 percent the MARKET SATURATION EFFECT falls off steeply, approaching zero as the MARKET SHARE approaches 12 percent.

If we define the number of new customers this month as:

NEW CUSTOMERS THIS MONTH =
FUNDS AVAILABLE FOR INVESTMENT THIS MONTH / 1,250
× MARKET SATURATION EFFECT

then, when the MARKET SHARE is less than about 10 percent, the MARKET SAT-URATION EFFECT is close to 1 and the number of NEW CUSTOMERS THIS MONTH corresponds to one new customer for each £1,250 of the FUNDS AVAILABLE FOR

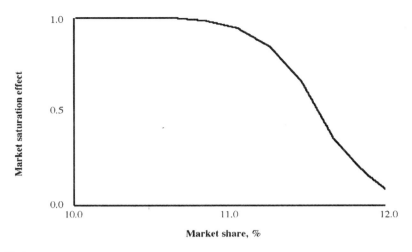

Figure 13.4

INVESTMENT THIS MONTH. However, as the MARKET SHARE increases through 11 percent and toward 12 percent, the MARKET SATURATION EFFECT rapidly decreases toward zero and so the number of NEW CUSTOMERS THIS MONTH becomes smaller and smaller, however large the FUNDS AVAILABLE FOR INVESTMENT THIS MONTH might be.

The action of the MARKET SATURATION EFFECT is therefore to slow down the rate of new customer acquisition as the MARKET SHARE approaches 12 percent. This, of course, is the effect of the balancing loop shown in the causal loop diagram.

The calculation of the number of NEW CUSTOMERS THIS MONTH from the FUNDS AVAILABLE FOR INVESTMENT THIS MONTH, as modified by the MARKET SATURATION EFFECT, completes the action of both the reinforcing and the balancing loops. This corresponds to one complete cycle of the model's operation, representing one "slice" of time, in this case one month. The last calculation is therefore that of the month-end closing balance of the satisfied customer base:

SATISFIED CUSTOMER BASE at period end =
SATISFIED CUSTOMER BASE at period start +
NEW CUSTOMERS THIS MONTH − LOST CUSTOMERS THIS MONTH

in which the outflow, the number of LOST CUSTOMERS THIS MONTH, recognizes that all businesses suffer this loss, calculated in this case as:

$$\text{LOST CUSTOMERS THIS MONTH} =$$
$$\text{CUSTOMER LOSS RATE} \times \text{SATISFIED CUSTOMER BASE} / 100$$

The closing balance of the SATISFIED CUSTOMER BASE at the end of this time period becomes the opening balance at the start of the next, and the cycle begins afresh. As a consequence, the net number of NEW CUSTOMERS THIS MONTH, as attracted by the marketing campaign financed by the FUNDS AVAILABLE FOR INVESTMENT THIS MONTH, less the number of LOST CUSTOMERS THIS MONTH, is incorporated into the SATISFIED CUSTOMER BASE to be used in the following month as the basis for the calculation of the next month's sales volumes, sale revenues, and profits. This month's marketing campaign therefore fuels next month's sales revenue and the engine of business growth spins away.

Life doesn't have to be complicated

Many people are startled when they come across the concept of fuzzy variables and their representation in system dynamics models. How can a concept as complex as the MARKET SATURATION EFFECT be represented simply by a number, between one and zero, that behaves like the graph we have just seen? The situation is surely far more complex than that.

Is it? I wonder. The reasons why the MARKET SATURATION EFFECT exists and behaves as it does are, I agree, highly complex — there are the market conditions, the activities of competitors, even the weather to take into account. But at the end of the day, the fundamental question you seek to answer is: "At a given level of MARKET SHARE, what is the most likely value of the number of NEW CUSTOMERS THIS MONTH that I will attract?" I would argue that the most direct — and most insightful — way of tackling this is exactly as I have suggested.

In Barry Richmond's excellent manual to the ithink software, there is a story about an economist and a systems thinker who are grappling with a very big problem about agricultural economics and the world food supply. They are discussing how best to model a particularly important variable, the total global annual production of milk. "This is really hard," says the economist, "we're going to need to know the total number of hectares of land under pasture, and how much of this is devoted to cows. Then we have to take into account the variation in milk-producing yield by different types of cow, and in different parts of the world. That requires understanding the different national GDPs, the amount of money spent on fertilizers, and we'll have to allow for global weather patterns too. It's a tough one. We'll have to build some very sophisticated econometric models."

The systems thinker rubbed his chin, thought for a moment, and then replied, "How about the total number of cows in the world, multiplied by an estimate of the average annual production of milk per cow?"

Life is indeed complicated, but there are often ways of taming the complexity without losing relevance.

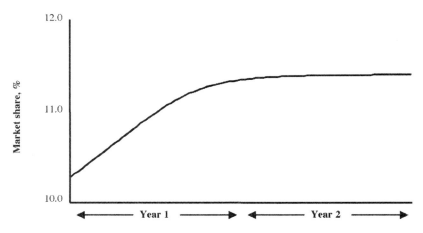

Figure 13.5

Some results of running this model over two years are shown in Figure 13.5.

The MARKET SHARE stabilizes at around 11.4 percent; to grow beyond this level is just not possible due to the very large sums required to "buy" incremental customers. The business overall, however, is sensibly profitable, generating a steady return of about £5,000,000 over each of the two years of the simulation (Figure 13.6).

Fuzzy variables

A central feature of this model—and a feature distinguishing system dynamics models from, say, spreadsheets—is the incorporation of the MARKET SATURATION EFFECT. As we have seen, the purpose of this variable is to capture the idea that, as the MARKET SHARE increases, it becomes progressively harder to attract new customers. This concept is familiar, but how many of our businesses measure it, or manage it? We all know that it is there, but few of our management information systems report on it. Given the importance of this concept—and many others like it—this is most perplexing. It is difficult to

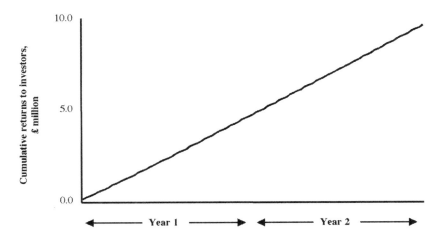

Figure 13.6

measure; but lots of the things that we do in business are difficult.

Despite the measurement problem, all of us, every day, take any number of decisions based on our personal assessments of such fuzzy variables. Where system dynamics can add real value is to make these fuzzy variables explicit, without the need for huge data-collection exercises or commissioning an extensive econometric study. All you need to do is draw some graphs of the ways in which you believe the world behaves. These graphs exist in your mind, but you have probably never drawn them, nor have you compared them with the graphs in the minds of your colleagues. Nevertheless, these graphs exist otherwise we wouldn't be able to take any decisions at all. We all have our mental models.

To capture a fuzzy variable, the first step is to define the two axes of the graph. In this case, we are interested in the way in which an increase in MAR-KET SHARE progressively chokes off the acquisition of new customers. So the horizontal axis is easy, MARKET SHARE. The vertical axis is more of a problem, because it is not obvious what it might be. So invent it—call it the MARKET SATURATION EFFECT and define it to be on a scale from zero to one.

The second step is to define the numbers along the horizontal axis. What is the range of MARKET SHARE over which this effect has impact? In this case, the range of interest is between 10 and 12 percent, a range derived from the judgment of informed people. This sets up the structure of the graph in Figure 13.7.

The third step is to draw the shape of the graph that you believe is true: How quickly does the graph dip down? Does it drop to zero? If so, at what point? Different people will have different views and both of the shapes in

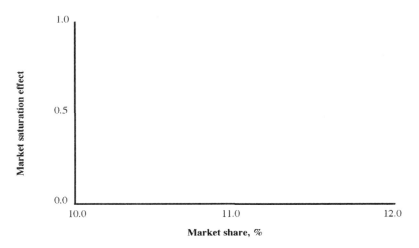

Figure 13.7

Figures 13.8 and 13.9 are plausible alternatives to the graph shown on page 308 as a representation of the saturation effect.

Which of the three graphs is "right"? It all depends on your mental models. In this case different mental models make a real difference: Figure 13.10 (page 314) shows the behavior of the SALES VOLUME THIS MONTH for each of the three MARKET SATURATION EFFECT graphs.

By allowing you to draw your graph on the screen, capturing your own personal mental model, a system dynamics model makes it extremely easy to explore the consequences of your beliefs and compare your views with those of your colleagues. Perhaps the difference in views has very little impact; perhaps it has a major impact—the system dynamics model can surely help. If the differences in view are material, then you can discuss why you see the world one way and someone else sees it a different way, and this may become an incentive to find out just what the data actually is. Good systems thinking diagrams and system dynamics models can be a powerful spur to measure the things that are truly important, rather than the things that can be easily measured.

Models for answers, models for learning

A second feature of this example was the almost cavalier disregard of the precise principles of accounting. I have used monthly time periods, which contain different numbers of days; I have aggregated all costs into a single overall margin; and I have totally ignored debtors, creditors, and the corresponding

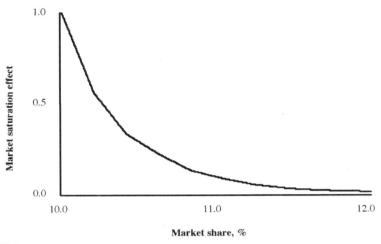

Figure 13.8

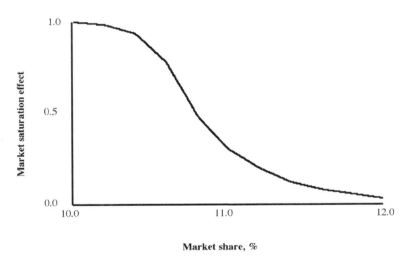

Figure 13.9

timing differences, making the implicit assumption that all transactions are in cash; nor is there is any reference to taxes, depreciation, or finance charges. No accountant, by the way, will be reading these words, for the book would have been thrown away in disgust, or any accountant would have had a heart attack, at around page 306!

There are three issues involved here. The first is clutter; the second is seeing the forest for the trees; and the third concerns what the model is actually being used for.

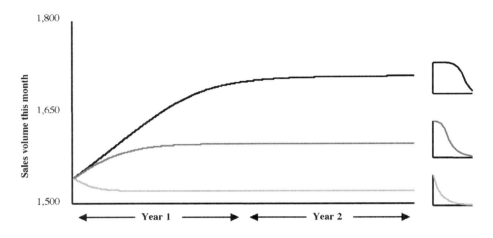

Figure 13.10

As we have already seen, all balance sheet items are stocks; all profit-and-loss account items (and all cash flow items) are flows. The full rigor of accounting can readily be incorporated into system dynamics modeling if you wish, but it sure clutters things up. System dynamics models look "up" and "out." They encourage a higher-level, rather than a lower-level, view; they espouse a holistic approach, broadening the boundaries of a problem, rather than a deeply analytical view, in which we dive to great levels of detail but on an increasingly narrow front. Spreadsheets are quite the reverse: They look "down" and "in," encouraging more analysis, burrowing ever deeper. If you want to analyze the general ledger, use a spreadsheet; if you want to understand the behavior of your business, use systems thinking and system dynamics.

This leads naturally to the issue of seeing the forest for the trees. What is really important and what isn't? Do you want to predict the day-by-day movements of cash in the bank account, tracking the receipts from every debtor and the payments to every creditor? Or do you want to understand more about how far you need to reset a management lever to grow the business?

Most importantly there is that fuzzy variable, the MARKET SATURATION EFFECT, which appears in the system dynamics model but is most unlikely ever to appear in a spreadsheet. I would argue that this variable is *the key variable* for this problem. It is, however, a variable that for most businesses is fuzzy indeed. Given this uncertainty, what purpose is there in going to great lengths to achieve great precision elsewhere?

One of the most pernicious aspects of spreadsheets is the apparent precision of the results. In a spreadsheet you can calculate any item you wish to umpteen decimal places and project forward, growing the sales revenue at 3 percent compound a year for 20 years. And after those 20 years' worth of calculations the spreadsheet will give you a number, arithmetically correct to umpteen figures. If you offer six weeks' credit, it will calculate the debtors too. But do these numbers actually mean anything?

System dynamics models do not promise such precision. Indeed, all the outputs I have shown have been graphs: graphs that go up or down, graphs that oscillate and maybe stabilize, graphs that grow or decline. You can print out tables of numbers if you wish, but the primary value of system dynamics models is the behavior as shown by the graphs. As you explore a model and change some of the parameters by twiddling the knobs and sliding the levers on the control panel, you soon get a good feel for whether the graphs change significantly or not. Does a virtuous circle become vicious? Does an oscillating system stabilize? Can the constraints on growth be alleviated? These are the insights that we require as managers, not a prediction of a specific number in seven years' time.

This leads to the third issue: What are we using a model for? In my view, models can be used for two main purposes—to get answers, or to gain understanding. A very good example of a model for answers is the kind of model that accountants use to optimize tax positions. Tax computations are lengthy and time consuming and there can often be a number of choices involved. As an example, I was once involved in a problem concerning capital gains tax rollover relief and a computer model was invaluable in carrying out a huge number of calculations (numerically accurately!) and in guiding the tax accountants to the most beneficial answer. In this case, the computations were extensive, the rules were well defined, and the data was "hard." The model saved a huge amount of time and gave us the numerical answer that we required.

Models for learning are very different. A flight simulator is such a model: The objective is not to discover the "best answer," such as the fastest possible way to land a plane; rather, it is to give trainee pilots a simulated experience, in safety, so as to equip them to fly the real plane with confidence. The experience is one of gaining an understanding of how to interpret all the information provided by the aeroplane's instruments, of how the complex machine responds to the various knobs, levers, and buttons that the pilot can turn, pull, or push in order to control and guide the plane's path through the air. In this case there is no answer—it is all about learning.

The same is true for system dynamics models. They give you, the wise manager, a simulated experience, in safety, so as to equip you to manage your business with even more confidence. The experience is one of gaining an understanding of how to interpret all the information provided by the outcome measures of your business, of how the complex business machine responds to the various knobs, levers, and buttons that you can turn, pull, or push in order to control and guide your business's path into the future. It is not about answers—it is all about learning.

So if you are open to learning, system dynamics and systems thinking are very powerful vehicles to help you do so. If all you want is "the answer," stick to spreadsheets.

Managing the marketing mix

Let me now enhance the model and make it rather more realistic.

One of the most important decisions that the car dealership management has to make is to determine the "marketing mix," the way in which the FUNDS AVAILABLE FOR INVESTMENT THIS MONTH should be allocated to activities such as advertising, sales promotions (for example extra items incorporated into the price of the car, like insurance, extras, or gifts), price discounts, and the like. These are some of the most important levers in the business.

Our model already incorporates the FUNDS AVAILABLE FOR INVESTMENT THIS MONTH, so let's add, for illustrative purposes, two components of the marketing mix, advertising and sales promotions.

Advertising and sales promotions
Are advertising and sales promotions stocks or flows? If they are stocks, what are the corresponding flows? If they are flows, what are the corresponding stocks? How would you draw a plumbing diagram capturing the essence of how advertising and sales promotions work in a business sense?

I think of advertising as a stock. As money is spent each month on advertising the stock grows, and the overall effect is to influence me to buy the product

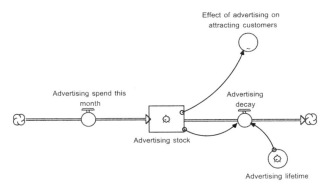

Figure 13.11

or use the service. When the advertising campaign stops I will remember the advertisements I liked, at least for a while. But over time I will forget and the impact of the advertising will steadily diminish. Figure 13.11 is a plumbing diagram that captures this.

Every month the ADVERTISING SPEND THIS MONTH progressively adds to the ADVERTISING STOCK. The knob indicates that the opening balance of this item, the value of this stock at the start of the model's simulation, is shown on the control panel. The depletion of the stock is shown by the flow ADVERTISING DECAY, which is controlled by the ADVERTISING LIFETIME, another variable appearing on the control panel. The idea here is that the ADVERTISING STOCK has a lifetime, beyond which the advertising no longer has any impact. This probably depends on the creativity and impact of the campaign and could be several months—say, six. What this means is that, in the absence of any inflows of ADVERTISING SPEND THIS MONTH, the ADVERTISING STOCK would drain away over a period of about six months, so about one-sixth of the ADVERTISING STOCK would be depleted in any one month. This suggests that a good, and simple, way of modeling the advertising decay is:

ADVERTISING DECAY = ADVERTISING STOCK / ADVERTISING LIFETIME

The commercial impact of the ADVERTISING STOCK at any time is represented by the EFFECT OF ADVERTISING ON ATTRACTING CUSTOMERS, a graph function representing the mental model of how the management team of the dealership believes advertising to work (Figure 13.12 overleaf).

This graph indicates that if the dealership spends nothing on advertising, it still expects to sell about 200 cars a month—sales attributable to the

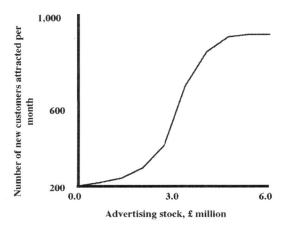

Figure 13.12

manufacturer's advertising, sales to customers who are attracted by the reputation of the marque, and sales to loyal existing customers who are making
repeat purchases. Advertising is expensive and the graph shows that the management team reckons it needs to have an ADVERTISING STOCK of around £3
million to attract significantly more than the base level of 200 new customers.
Increasing the stock from about £3 million to £4.5 million has a strong effect,
as shown by the steep rise of the graph, but as the stock rises toward £5 million diminishing returns set in and the effect of the advertising plateaus.

This graph, of course, is just one mental model and different people will
have different views. Many decisions concerning advertising are made on the
basis of mental models such as this, but without making the assumptions
explicit. As I have already pointed out, one of the great benefits of system
dynamics is the encouragement to do just this. The ease with which the
graphs can be drawn directly on the screen, run through the model, changed,
and run again, can allow great insight into the behavior of these important,
but often unmeasured, variables. As we saw in Chapter 10, variables of the
form the EFFECT OF [WHATEVER] IN ATTRACTING AND RETAINING CUSTOMERS
are critical in connecting the balancing loops defining the management
levers to the reinforcing loop driving business growth (see pages 216 and 225).
This graph is an example of what one of these variables might look like.

Another is associated with sales promotions. Figure 13.13 is the plumbing
diagram, which is structurally identical to that for advertising.

My mental model is that the impact of the PROMOTIONS STOCK is of much
shorter duration than the ADVERTISING STOCK, so the PROMOTIONS LIFETIME

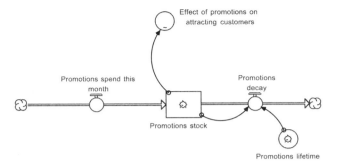

Figure 13.13

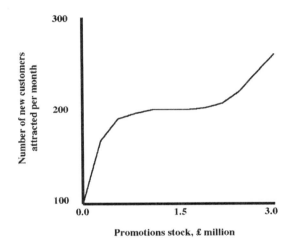

Figure 13.14

will be much shorter—say, a month or two. Also, the EFFECT OF PROMOTIONS ON ATTRACTING CUSTOMERS is different—say, a graph function such as Figure 13.14.

This captures the idea that about 100 new cars a month are sold on the basis of promotions financed by the manufacturer, but initially the curve rises quite steeply as customers are attracted by relatively inexpensive offers. There is then quite a broad plateau, where increasing the stock from around £0.8 million to £2.5 million has hardly any incremental effect. Above this level, however, the curve rises steeply once more, as customers are attracted by "big ticket" promotions such as holiday offers.

Once again, this is just one feasible mental model. There are many others. What is yours?

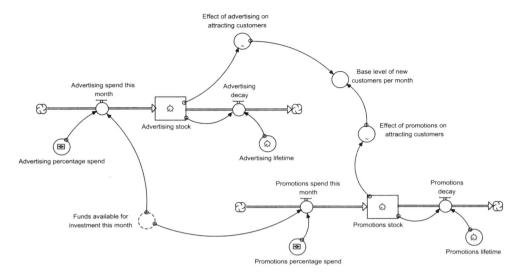

Figure 13.15

These two marketing mix variables can be brought together on a single diagram (Figure 13.15), which contains two additional concepts.

First, the BASE LEVEL OF NEW CUSTOMERS PER MONTH is simply the sum of the EFFECT OF ADVERTISING ON ATTRACTING CUSTOMERS and the EFFECT OF PROMOTIONS ON ATTRACTING CUSTOMERS. As the model clocks through each time period, at any instant the ADVERTISING STOCK and PROMOTIONS STOCK will have particular values, depending on the historical patterns of both the inflows of ADVERTISING SPEND THIS MONTH and PROMOTIONS SPEND THIS MONTH and the outflows of ADVERTISING DECAY and PROMOTIONS DECAY. At each instant, the model uses the two graph functions to transform the current values of the ADVERTISING STOCK and PROMOTIONS STOCK into a number of new customers by finding the appropriate points on the horizontal axes, going up to each graph, and then choosing the corresponding points on the vertical axes. The spend on each element of the marketing mix then becomes expressed in terms of a number of new customers, and these two numbers are added together to give the BASE LEVEL OF NEW CUSTOMERS PER MONTH. I have used the phrase "base level" because this is independent of the saturation effect of increasing market share that we discussed on page 307. The actual number of NEW CUSTOMERS THIS MONTH will be calculated from this BASE LEVEL OF NEW CUSTOMERS THIS MONTH by multiplying by the MARKET SATURATION EFFECT.

The second new concept introduced in Figure 13.15 is the marketing mix decision itself—the allocation of the expenditure between advertising and promotions.

One highly effective way of doing this is to specify two input parameters—the ADVERTISING PERCENTAGE SPEND and the PROMOTIONS PERCENTAGE SPEND—which define the policy for this allocation. These in fact represent the target expenditures we seek to achieve, expressing these targets in terms of an allocation rule rather than absolute amounts. The actual values of the ADVERTISING SPEND THIS MONTH and the PROMOTIONS SPEND THIS MONTH are then obtained by applying these two percentages to the FUNDS AVAILABLE FOR INVESTMENT THIS MONTH.

As input parameters these two percentages will appear on the control panel, in this case, as shown in Figure 13.16, in the form of sliding levers. These two percentages must, of course, add to 100 percent, and ithink offers the very useful facility of allowing you to couple together levers that must always add to 100 percent.

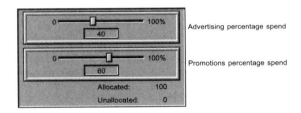

Figure 13.16

Figure 13.16 shows a 40:60 split in favor of promotions, with 100 percent of the funds allocated as required. These two levers are coupled, so that when you use the screen cursor to slide one lever the other slides automatically to ensure that the sum of the two lever settings can never exceed 100 percent. If the sum of the two settings is less than 100 percent, any residual is indicated by the number shown by "unallocated."

That completes my description of how the marketing mix is simulated. The additional plumbing diagram is of course part of a bigger picture, fitting alongside the diagram of the business growth engine that we have already studied. In fact, the marketing mix diagram fits alongside the business engine diagram very neatly: It takes as an input the FUNDS AVAILABLE FOR INVESTMENT THIS MONTH and produces an output, the BASE LEVEL OF NEW CUSTOMERS THIS

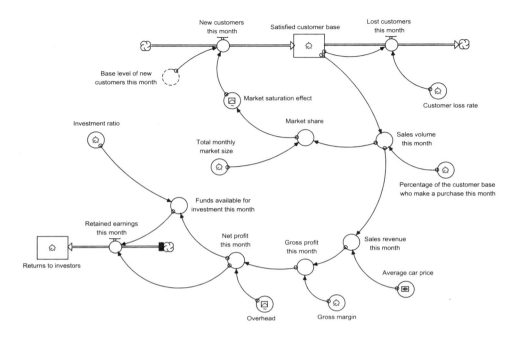

Figure 13.17

MONTH. The business engine diagram now looks like Figure 13.17.

This is very similar to the diagram on page 304, but there are a number of differences.

First, there is no link from FUNDS AVAILABLE FOR INVESTMENT THIS MONTH to NEW CUSTOMERS THIS MONTH. This link has been replaced by the marketing mix diagram, which is driven by this variable and computes the BASE LEVEL OF NEW CUSTOMERS THIS MONTH. This item has now also appeared on this diagram, feeding into NEW CUSTOMERS THIS MONTH, as modified by the MARKET SATURATION EFFECT. You will also notice that the circle associated with the BASE LEVEL OF NEW CUSTOMERS PER MONTH is shown as dotted, rather than solid; this indicates that this variable acts as a link between two different plumbing diagrams. The ability to link diagrams in this way enables highly complex systems to be depicted across several diagrams, so avoiding the need for just one highly cluttered — and hence unintelligible — diagram.

The link from the FUNDS AVAILABLE FOR INVESTMENT THIS MONTH, through the marketing mix diagram, and back to NEW CUSTOMERS THIS MONTH is the manifestation in the formalism of system dynamics of the link between the balancing loops of the management levers and the reinforcing loop of the business growth engine, which we explored in detail in Chapter 10. This example shows just two levers—advertising and promotions—with the targets implied by the allocation rule; any other levers can be linked in similarly.

There is one other new feature on this diagram. In Figure 13.2 there was a link directly between SALES REVENUE THIS MONTH and NET PROFIT THIS MONTH, as specified by an overall margin. Figure 13.17 introduces a new variable in the business growth engine loop, the GROSS PROFIT THIS MONTH, calculated from the SALES REVENUE THIS MONTH by applying a GROSS MARGIN. The NET PROFIT THIS MONTH is then calculated by deducting the OVERHEAD (excluding the spend on advertising and promotions) from the GROSS PROFIT THIS MONTH. The recognition of the OVERHEAD enables this monthly expenditure to be examined explicitly, as represented by the (somewhat spiky) graph in Figure 13.18.

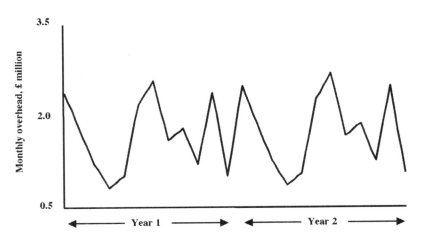

Figure 13.18

The calculation of the NET PROFIT THIS MONTH as:

NET PROFIT THIS MONTH = GROSS PROFIT THIS MONTH − OVERHEAD

raises a new possibility, that the NET PROFIT THIS MONTH might be negative if the OVERHEAD happens to be high.

This possibility has two implications: first, the impact on the FUNDS AVAILABLE FOR INVESTMENT THIS MONTH, and secondly, the impact on the RETAINED EARNINGS THIS MONTH. One way of catering for this eventuality is to limit the FUNDS AVAILABLE FOR INVESTMENT to a minimum of zero, using a conditional rule:

FUNDS AVAILABLE FOR INVESTMENT THIS MONTH =
    IF (NET PROFIT THIS MONTH > 0)
    THEN (NET PROFIT THIS MONTH × INVESTMENT RATIO / 100)
    ELSE (0).

This rule does exactly what it says: If the NET PROFIT THIS MONTH is a positive number, then the FUNDS AVAILABLE FOR INVESTMENT THIS MONTH are calculated by applying the INVESTMENT RATIO to the NET PROFIT THIS MONTH as usual; if the NET PROFIT THIS MONTH is zero or a negative number, then the FUNDS AVAILABLE FOR INVESTMENT THIS MONTH are set to zero. That makes sense, but a consequence is that the RETAINED EARNINGS THIS MONTH will be equal to the (negative) NET PROFIT THIS MONTH in its entirety, and so the RETAINED EARNINGS THIS MONTH will therefore *deplete* the RETURNS TO INVESTORS. Under these circumstances, the RETAINED EARNINGS THIS MONTH will act as an *outflow* to the RETURNS TO INVESTORS, rather than as an inflow.

Flows that may act as inflows or outflows depending on the circumstances are known as *biflows* (as opposed to uniflows; see page 290) and are represented by a double-headed pipe-and-tap (Figure 13.19).

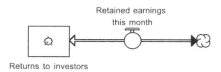

Retained earnings
this month

Returns to investors

Figure 13.19

The operation of a biflow is quite straightforward. In each time period, the model calculates the RETAINED EARNINGS THIS PERIOD and if this is positive, the RETURNS TO INVESTORS are increased; if it is negative, the RETURNS TO INVESTORS are depleted.

The control panel has also changed to incorporate all the new variables, and also to include a facility to view some of the key outputs directly (Figure 13.20).

So what are the results? Figure 13.21 on page 327 depicts some selected outputs for the settings as shown on the control panel, with two runs of the

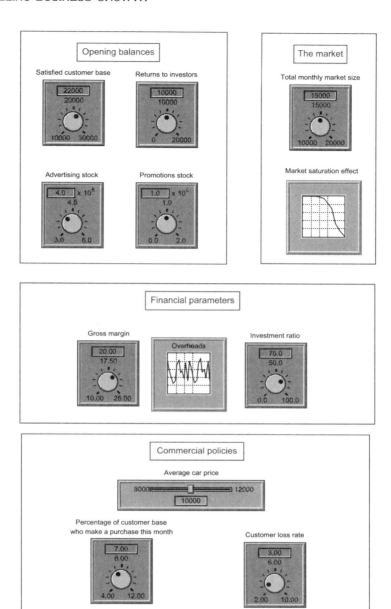

Figure 13.20 (continued overleaf)

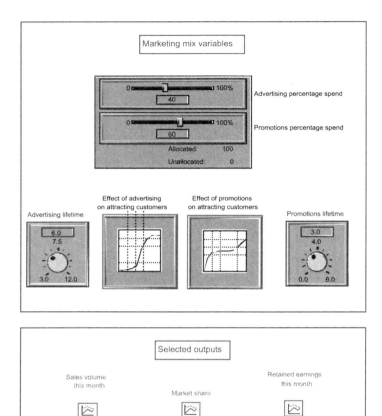

Figure 13.20 (cont.)

model, one with 20 percent of the FUNDS AVAILABLE FOR INVESTMENT THIS MONTH allocated to advertising and 80 percent to promotions; the other with a 40:60 split.

What policies would you invoke to optimize the business?

For a 20:80 split in favor of promotions, the SALES VOLUME THIS MONTH increases over the first quarter but then steadily falls away; increasing the relative allocation to advertising to give a 40:60 split stabilizes the SALES VOLUME THIS MONTH at around 1,650 cars per month. The RETAINED EARNINGS THIS MONTH—the inflow into the RETURNS TO INVESTORS and probably the most important diagnostic of the health of the business—is somewhat higher with relatively more advertising. In both cases, however, this figure bumps around

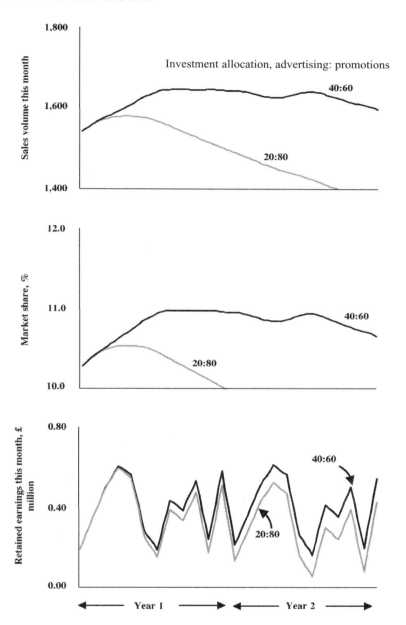

Figure 13.21

quite a bit, largely because of the month-by-month variation in overhead (see page 323).

Overall, the graphs seem to indicate that the effect of advertising is more powerful than that of promotions, so you might choose to shift the balance even more strongly toward advertising. Figure 13.22 shows what happens with an 80:20 split in favor of advertising.

The SALES VOLUME THIS MONTH has gone up to a steady 1,710 or so cars per month and we have removed that rather worrying wobble—if not decline—in the MARKET SHARE. The RETAINED EARNINGS THIS MONTH, however, haven't gone up that much. This is probably because the extra advertising is quite expensive and the incremental margin on the extra sales is only a little more than the additional spend on advertising. Also, the modeling assumption is rather cautious, in that we don't spend what we haven't got. The FUNDS AVAILABLE FOR INVESTMENT THIS MONTH are derived from the NET PROFIT THIS MONTH, so if the profits are a bit down then so are the FUNDS AVAILABLE FOR INVESTMENT THIS MONTH, and there is less money in total to allocate.

Is the 80:20 split the best deal?

The 80:20 split was an intelligent shot in the dark and it may be that it would be even more favorable to try 85:15 or even 100:0. Using the sliding levers on the control panel makes it very easy to try these out. As it happens, once the allocation to advertising has reached about 70 percent, any further increases in this percentage have very little effect—diminishing returns have set in.

But where? The graph of the EFFECT OF ADVERTISING ON ATTRACTING NEW CUSTOMERS is one example (see page 318), as shown by the flattening out at levels of the ADVERTISING STOCK above about £4.5 million. This is in contrast to the graph of the EFFECT OF PROMOTIONS ON ATTRACTING NEW CUSTOMERS (see page 319), which, after a plateau, rises.

However, there is another constraint, the market share limit, which acts independently of all the other variables. As the graph of the MARKET SATURATION EFFECT on page 308 shows, it is really tough to shift the MARKET SHARE through 11 percent and even harder to get beyond 11.5 percent. In fact, the graph on page 329 shows that an 80:20 split pushes the MARKET SHARE to a stable 11.4 percent, quite close to the maximum possible.

So there are two, independent constraints driving the diminishing returns: the effect of advertising, which plateaus at ADVERTISING STOCKS above about £4.5 million, and the MARKET SATURATION EFFECT, which makes it very hard to go beyond 11.5 percent MARKET SHARE.

But which constraint bites first? If the advertising constraint comes into effect first we would expect that the MARKET SHARE would plateau, but at a level

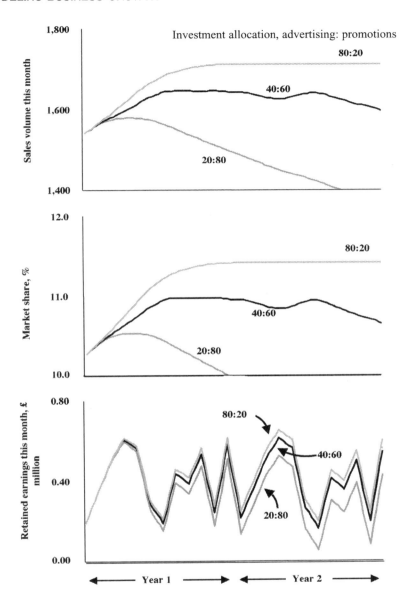

Figure 13.22

less than 11 percent or so. However, if the market share constraint bites first, then the MARKET SHARE will rise to a level around 11.5 percent and not budge from there, however much is spent on advertising and promotions.

Figure 13.22 shows that the MARKET SHARE is limiting at around 11.4 percent, very close to the market share constraint. This suggests that the market share constraint is biting first.

If it is, then this has a significant implication: Maybe we are spending too much on advertising and promotions, throwing money away on campaigns that just can't break through the market share constraint.

We can test this in the model. The important variable here is the INVEST-MENT RATIO, the percentage of the NET PROFIT THIS MONTH that determines how much is earmarked for the FUNDS AVAILABLE FOR INVESTMENT THIS MONTH, which in turn sources the ADVERTISING SPEND THIS MONTH and the PROMOTIONS SPEND THIS MONTH. If we reduce the INVESTMENT RATIO, less money is put into the FUNDS AVAILABLE FOR INVESTMENT THIS MONTH, but this may not matter too much. What does matter is that any money not earmarked for investment increases the RETAINED EARNINGS THIS MONTH, and hence the RETURNS TO INVESTORS.

So what happens when the INVESTMENT RATIO is 50 percent and there is an 80:20 split of the remaining FUNDS AVAILABLE FOR INVESTMENT between advertising and promotions?

Figure 13.23 is the result, superimposed on the last set of graphs with the INVESTMENT RATIO set at 75 percent.

This run of the model shows a slightly lower SALES VOLUME THIS MONTH and MARKET SHARE as compared to the results of the model with the INVEST-MENT RATIO set at 75 percent, as we would expect since there is significantly less money being invested. Nevertheless the reduction is small. When the INVESTMENT RATIO was 75 percent a large sum of money was being thrown away each month, vainly trying to fuel the reinforcing loop of the growth engine with advertising and promotions, when the balancing loop of market saturation was pushing back harder. Spending much less money has almost no measurable impact on sales, but look what it does to the RETAINED EARNINGS THIS MONTH! They have doubled every month. When the INVESTMENT RATIO was 75 percent, 25 percent of the NET PROFIT THIS MONTH was channeled into RETAINED EARNINGS THIS MONTH. Now, with the INVESTMENT RATIO set at 50 percent, the other 50 percent ends up in the RETURNS TO INVESTORS.

As we can see, in this much more realistic case the issue was not really about the allocation of funds between advertising and promotions—it was about being wise in deciding how much to spend in the first place.

As we saw in Chapter 8, it is very tempting to pedal increasingly more vig-orously to drive the growth engine. But when the reinforcing loop is being constrained, this can be a very exhausting—and impoverishing—thing to do.

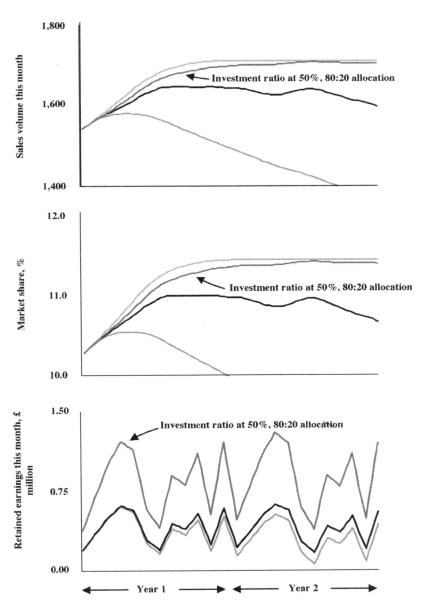

Figure 13.23

Epilogue: Complexity tamed

Well, that's it! I trust you enjoyed reading the book and that you are now totally convinced not only that complexity can indeed be tamed but also that you can do it.

The best way to prove that you can is to do just that—do it. Next time you're in a meeting, dealing with a really complex problem, see if you can sketch the cause-and-effect relationships, linking them together to form some meaningful loops. You might do it quite quickly; it might take several days and some considerable thought. No matter, try it. If you do, you will discover that, quite suddenly, you will compile a diagram that makes sense—real sense— truly seeing the forest for the trees. When that happens, take it to a meeting and say, "Can I just sketch how I see this problem? I'd appreciate your feedback. Do you all see things the same way?"

You will be amazed by what will happen. You will stimulate constructive discussion and debate, because you will be examining the problem at the right level—the level of the mental model. Sharing mental models in a business context makes sense. It underpins teamwork, it underpins decision making, and it underpins wisdom.

So if you have enjoyed this book, use it. Pick up a felt-tip pen, go to the flipchart, say, "I see the world this way. Do you see it this way too?" and see what happens.

The case studies I describe are all based on my experience working in this field for over 15 years and I emphasize that they all reflect my mental models rather than those of others. I therefore take full responsibility for them and if you feel that they reflect the world as it is, that's great. If not, I respect your view of the world and am very happy to engage in discussion, so please contact me at dennis@silverbulletmachine.com.

Let me know what happens, too. As I trust has come through on every page, I am an evangelist and an enthusiast. I love collecting stories about how real problems have been successfully tackled using systems thinking and system dynamics, so do contact me.

Wisdom, as an innate characteristic, is rare. But everyone can learn how to draw causal loop diagrams, to trace and understand causality, to explore the consequences of alternative actions or policies, to help make decisions that truly stand the test of time. We can indeed all become wiser.

Bibliography

Here is my personal selection of books on systems thinking and related topics. The page numbers refer to where these are mentioned in this book.

On systems thinking in general

Managing with Systems Thinking, Michael Ballé, McGraw-Hill, London, 1994. A highly readable introduction to systems thinking and its application to management.

The Heart of the Enterprise, Stafford Beer, John Wiley, Chichester, 1979 (page 24). Stafford Beer is the evangelist of management cybernetics and has written many books. This is the primary source for his Viable Systems Model.

The Viable System Model, Interpretations and Applications of Stafford Beer's VSM, Raul Espejo and Roger Harnden (eds), John Wiley, Chichester, 1989 (page 24). A compendium of papers on Stafford Beer's Viable Systems Model.

General System Theory: Foundations, Development, Applications, Ludwig von Bertalanffy, George Brazilier, New York, revised edn 1976 (page 23). The primary source for von Bertallanfy's General System Theory.

Systems Thinking, Systems Practice, Peter Checkland, John Wiley, Chichester, 2nd edn 1999 (page 23). The classic exposition of Checkland's soft systems methodology. This edition is a reprint of the original 1981 edition, with an additional, specially written 30-year retrospective.

Industrial Dynamics, Jay Forrester, MIT Press, Cambridge, MA, 1961 (pages 21, 23). The seminal text on system dynamics and systems thinking, which still reads freshly today.

Urban Dynamics, Jay Forrester, Pegasus Communications, Waltham, MA, 1969 (pages 21, 240). In this book Forrester looks at issues concerning urban development, including overcrowding and inner-city decay.

World Dynamics, Jay Forrester, Wright-Allen Press, Cambridge, MA, 2nd edn 1973 (pages 21, 240). Forrester's canvas is even broader here, in his investigation of global problems such as population growth and pollution.

334

SEEING THE FOREST FOR THE TREES

Systems Thinking: Managing Chaos and Complexity, Jamshid Gharajedaghi, Butterworth Heinemann, Oxford, 1999 (page 24). A very thought-provoking and up-to-date survey of the field.

Complexity: Life at the Edge of Chaos, Roger Lewin, Phoenix, London, 2nd edn 2001 (page 24). A lucid, intelligible, and non-mathematical survey of complexity theory, including a chapter on its application to business.

The Limits to Growth, Donella Meadows, Dennis Meadows, Jørgen Randers, & William Behrens, Universe Books, New York, 1972 (pages 22, 23). One of the most powerful demonstrations of how systems thinking can tame complexity on a global scale.

Beyond the Limits, Donella Meadows, Dennis Meadows, & Jørgen Randers, Earthscan, London, 1992, An update on *The Limits to Growth*, reviewing what has happened since the original study.

The Fifth Discipline, Peter Senge, Doubleday, New York, 1990 (pages 2, 13, 23, 182). A persuasive and articulate exposition of the role of systems thinking in management, alongside the four other key disciplines of personal mastery, mental models, shared vision, and team learning.

The Fifth Discipline Fieldbook: Strategies and Tools for Building a Learning Organization, Peter Senge, Charlotte Roberts, Richard Ross, Bryan Smith, & Art Kleiner, Nicholas Brealey, London, 1994. A companion to *The Fifth Discipline* packed full of examples, explanations, discussions, and anecdotes, and with a good description of the main systems thinking archetypes.

The Dance of Change: The Challenges of Sustaining Momentum in Learning Organizations, Peter Senge, Art Kleiner, Charlotte Roberts, Richard Ross, George Roth, & Bryan Smith, Nicholas Brealey, London, 1999. Very similar in style to the fieldbook and containing many additional examples.

Business Dynamics: Systems Thinking and Modeling for a Complex World, John Sterman, McGraw-Hill, 2000 (pages 23, 69). John Sterman is the current Director of the System Dynamics Group at MIT, and this thousand-pager, with an accompanying CD-ROM, is a comprehensive description of the current state of the art.

Cybernetics, or Control and Communication in the Animal and the Machine, Norbert Wiener, MIT Press, Cambridge, MA, 2nd edn 1961 (pages 21, 23). The current edition of Norbert Wiener's 1948 classic.

On creativity and innovation

The Art of Innovation: Lessons in Creativity from IDEO, America's Leading Design Firm, Tom Kelley with Jonathan Littman, HarperCollinsBusiness, London, 2001. An exhilarating, invigorating romp through the experiences of IDEO, who have designed everything from handheld computers to heart defibrillators.

Story: Substance, Structure, Style and the Principles of Screenwriting, Robert McKee, Methuen, London, 1999. An insider's guide to applying creativity systematically to the process of writing TV and film scripts. If you like *Casablanca* or *Chinatown*, McKee's descriptions of how the screenplays actually work on a word-by-word basis are riveting.

Smart Things to Know about Innovation and Creativity, Dennis Sherwood, Capstone, Oxford, 2001 (page 237). This book focuses on creativity and innovation, including how to use the *InnovAction!*™ process in scenario planning.

On strategy and scenario planning

The Living Company: Growth, Learning and Longevity in Business, Arie de Geus, Nicholas Brealey, London, 1997 (page 2). A powerful rallying call to those who believe in the importance of the human spirit in organizations, even large ones. The central metaphor is the organization as a living being.

Leading the Revolution, Gary Hamel, Harvard Business School Press, Cambridge, MA, 2000 (page 232). An upbeat, provocative, challenging, and often witty view on strategy, with innovation as the key theme throughout.

Scenarios: The Art of Strategic Conversation, Kees van der Heijden, John Wiley, Chichester, 1997. A well-written discussion of scenario planning by a leading member of the Shell scenario planning community.

Synchronicity: The Inner Path of Leadership, Joseph Jaworski, Berrett-Koehler, San Francisco, CA, 1996. Joseph Jaworski is an American lawyer who managed the Group Planning function in Shell. This largely biographical book is a fascinating story in its own right and also gives great insight into organizations and management.

Scenario Planning: Managing for the Future, Gill Ringland, John Wiley, Chichester, 1998. A comprehensive description of most of the different methods of scenario planning.

The Art of the Long View: Planning for the Future in an Uncertain World, Peter Schwartz, John Wiley, Chichester, 1996. Peter Schwartz was one of the originators of scenario planning, working first at Stanford Research Institute, then at Shell, and most recently with GBN, the Global Planning Network. Part biography, part history of scenario planning, this is indeed a good read.

On Gaia and related environmental matters

Silent Spring, Rachel Carson, Houghton Mifflin, Boston, MA, 1962 (pages 23 and 249). When first published this book created a fire-storm of controversy and attack. Today we see it as one of the truly seminal works that shook some of us out of our complacency as regards the environment. There are still some, however, who remain to be shaken.

"Easter's End," Jared Diamond, *Discovery*, August 1995. A lively magazine article on the Easter Island story.

The Day the World Took off: The Roots of the Industrial Revolution, Sally Dugan & David Dugan, Channel 4 Books, London, 2000. My source for the story about tea.

Gaia: The Practical Science of Planetary Medicine, James Lovelock, Gaia Books, London, 1991 (pages 251, 255). A beautifully produced book, explaining the Gaia hypothesis in well-illustrated, non-technical language. The lily pad story is here too.

The Ages of Gaia: A Biography of our Living Earth, James Lovelock, Oxford University Press, Oxford, 1995. A rather more technical account.

Homage to Gaia: The Life of an Independent Scientist, James Lovelock, Oxford University Press, Oxford, 2000. Lovelock's autobiography, representing a very rare breed, a professional scientist working as an independent, freelance thinker and researcher, rather than being on the payroll of a pharmaceutical company, a university, or the military.

A Green History of the World: The Environment and the Collapse of Great Civilisations, Clive Ponting, Penguin, Harmondsworth, 1993. An environmentalist's view of history (in contrast to a history of environmentalism), including a description of the Easter Island catastrophe.

Captain Cook's Voyages 1768–1779, Glyndwr Williams (ed.), Folio Society, London, 1997. A narrative of Cook's explorations, based on his original journals.

On intellectual capital

Intellectual Capital: The Proven Way to Establish Your Company's Real Value by Measuring its Hidden Brainpower, Leif Edvinsson & Michael S Malone, Piatkus, London, 1997 (page 285). The standard work, by the leader in the field.

On the Theory of Constraints

The Goal: Beating the Competition, Eliyahu M Goldratt & Jeff Cox, Gower, Basingstoke, 1993 (page 149). The original business novel, in which Goldratt disguises what is in fact a textbook as a story.

Goldratt's Theory of Constraints: A Systems Approach to Continuous Improvement, H William Dettmern, ASQ Quality Press, Milwaukee, WI, 1996. A description by an author who does not have the vested interests of Goldratt himself!

On philosophy

The Metaphysics, Aristotle, Hugh Lawson-Tancred (trans.), Penguin, Harmondsworth, 1998 (page 18). The words that we now paraphrase as "the whole is greater than the sum of its parts" are to be found in Book Eta, Part 6, on page 248 of this edition.

Websites

As you would expect, there are a huge number of websites on systems thinking and system dynamics, let alone on topics such as strategy and the environment. Here are just a few for systems thinkers.

http://sysdyn.mit.edu/
The site of the Systems Dynamics Group at MIT.

http://www.albany.edu/cpr/sds/
The site for the System Dynamics Society.

http://www.fieldbook.com
A site devoted to *The Fifth Discipline Fieldbook* and *The Dance of Change*.

http://gwis2.circ.gwu.edu/~stephenw/sdlinks.htm and
http://info.uni-klu.ac.at/users/gossimit/links/bookmksd.htm
Two sites providing systems thinking and system dynamics links.

http://www.pegasuscom.com
The site of Pegasus Communications Inc., where you will find a host of valuable resources, as well as the opportunity to subscribe to the informative newsletter *The Systems Thinker*.

Software

ithink

Developer
High Performance Systems, Inc.
45 Lyme Road, Suite 300
Hanover
NH 03755, USA
Tel: (+1) 603 643 9636
Fax: (+1) 603 643 9502
Website: www.hps-inc.com

UK distributor
Cognitus Ltd
1 Park View
Harrogate
North Yorkshire HG1 5LY, UK
Tel: (+44) (0)1423 562622
Fax: (+44) (0)1423 567916
Website: www.cognitus.co.uk

Powersim

Developer
Powersim
PO Box 3961 Dreggen
N-5835 Bergen
Norway
Tel: (+47) 5560 6500
Fax: (+47) 5560 6501
Website: www.powersim.com

UK distributor
Powersim
Fays Business Centre
Bedford Road
Guildford GU1 4SJ, UK
Tel: (+44) (0)1483 557290
Fax: (+44) (0)1483 557289
Website: www.powersim.com

Vensim

Developer
Ventana Systems, Inc.
60 Jacob Gates Road
Harvard
MA 01451, USA
Tel: (+1) 508 651 0432
Fax: (+1) 508 650 5422
Website: www.vensim.com

UK distributor
Ventana Systems UK Ltd.
Ventana House
41 Western Way
Salisbury, Wilts SP2 9DR, UK
Tel: (+44) (0)23 8090 9838
Fax: (+44) (0)709 2024 736
Website: www.ventanasystems.co.uk

Index

accounting 207, 225–6, 312, 314
    and stocks and flows 274, 275, 284, 314
"active" listening 186
actual, in a balancing loop 56–7, 103–27, 226–31
advertising 134, 181–2, 316–31
    as a stock 316–18
    effect of on sales 207–8
    mental models of 317–18
albedo effect 252
Amazon.com 92–3
allocation of investment 224–5, 320–1, 323
ambition, role of in strategy formulation 229–31, 232, 238
Amsterdam Declaration on Global Change 251
answers, models for 312–16
Apocalypse, Four Horsemen of 244, 263, 270
archetypes 143
Aristotle 18, 337
arrow, curly 27–8, 286, 289
auxiliaries 291
    circle symbol for 291

back office, systems thinking analysis of 25–39
balance sheet items
    and stocks 274, 284
    in system dynamics 274, 275
balancing loops 55–7, 70, 103–26, 138
    and levers 211–12
    and targets or goals 59, 104, 107
    and time delays 107–8, 117–21
    dynamic behavior of 104, 107
    goal-seeking behavior of 59, 103–8
    how to identify 60–1, 70
    in business 108–21
    in relation to asset policy 110
    in relation to budgeting 108–14, 121–5
    in relation to pricing 109–10
    in relation to staff 110–17
    interaction with reinforcing

loops 70, 97–102, 139, 142, 212–13, 214–21
    linkage of 114–21
    oscillatory behavior of 104–7, 117–21
    structure of 60–1, 70
    with three Os 112–13, 115
Bank of England's Monetary Policy Committee 120
Barham, First Lord of the Admiralty 184
BBC (British Broadcasting Corporation) 48, 165, 191
Beer, Stafford 22, 24, 333
beliefs, organizational 181, 233–4
Bertalanffy, Ludwig von 21, 23, 333
bicycle 15, 16
    as an example of a stable dynamic state 15, 16, 249–50, 253
biflows 324
Big Brother 48
biodiversity, destruction of 264
biological systems 17
biomass 254
birth rate 151, 153, 241, 288–300
boom and bust 73, 87–94
Boulton, Matthew 19
boundaries 57–9
    and dangles 58
    apparent conflict with holistic view 58
    of system 58, 127–8
braking, of reinforcing loop 97–8, 138, 142, 143, 146, 147, 162–3
budget 202, 227–8
    as distinguished from target 202
    in a balancing loop 108–14
budgeting system 228
building blocks, of systems thinking 8, 54–7, 62–3
Bush, President George W 240
business cycles 121
business growth 139–63 *see also* growth
business objectives, to optimize a portfolio of stocks 287
business strategy 202, 229
    and risk 239

and systems thinking 209–31, 238
    definition of 204
    role of ambition, vision, and imagination 229–31, 232–5
buyer, view of in contract negotiations 189–95, 197–200
buyer–contractor relationship systems thinking case study 188–201

capital, intellectual 285
carbon dioxide 248, 252, 254–8
Carson, Rachel 23, 249, 336
Caulerpa taxifolia, exponential growth of 85
causal loop diagrams 6, 22, 29, 126, 127–37
    after-the-event obvious nature of 37, 179
    and clutter 87, 129–31
    and computer simulation models 7, 225, 272–3, 275, 293, 302–4
    and consensus 197
    and making mental models explicit 47, 185, 197
    and plumbing diagrams 274, 287–92
    and reality 37, 133–4, 179, 180
    and time delays 33, 34, 39
    are never complete 136–7
    as a means of building high-performing teams 7, 185
    as a means of communication 7, 183, 185–6
    avoidance of "increase in" and "decrease in" 132–3
    behavior independent of language used 64
    best practice 127–37
    challenges to 178–9
    complex dynamic behavior of 7, 272
    cynical response to 179
    different people draw different diagrams 130–1, 175, 180–3, 197
    don't fall in love with 136
    how to draw 68–9, 127–37
    importance of reality in 37, 133–4, 135–6, 179
    importance of wastepaper basket 58, 131, 135

limitations of 7
"obvious" nature of with hindsight 37, 179
tenacity in drawing 134
12 golden rules of 137
use of nouns not verbs 131–2
when to add Ss and Os 134
where to start drawing 128–9
causality, chains of 5, 28, 51, 70
cause and effect, chains of 5, 28, 51, 70
cause-and-effect relationships 70, 126, 206, 207, 213
and time delays 33, 34
Chad, Lake 280
chains of causality 5, 28, 51, 70
change program, impact of, as represented in causal loop diagrams 217
chaos 17, 22, 253
Checkland, Peter 22, 23, 333
chess 235-6
circle, vicious or virtuous see reinforcing loop
clouds
in plumbing diagrams 279
Club of Rome 22, 23
clutter
in causal loop diagrams 87, 129–31
in system dynamics models 275, 313–14
communication 21
role of causal loops in helping 7, 71, 183, 185–6
competition for scarce resources
resolution of 96–102
systems thinking analysis of 95–102
competitors
as a constraint on growth 143, 145, 210
complex adaptive systems 22
complex systems 120
complexity 1, 4, 7, 70, 126
complexity theory 22
complexity
detail 120
dynamic 120, 126, 135
component parts 2, 13, 14, 52, 186, 201
compound interest, and exponential growth 80, 285–6
computer simulation models 7, 21, 22, 23, 225, 238, 273, 274–8

and causal loop diagrams 7, 225, 272–3, 275, 293, 302–4
conditional rules 324
conflict 96–102, 167–9, 172–3, 195–6, 201
conflict resolution, systems thinking analysis of 96–102, 188–201
connectedness 2, 3–5, 13, 39, 51, 186, 201
and ripple effect 5
between levers and outcomes 206–9, 213, 238–9
connections, how to build between people 186–7
consensus, in drawing causal loop diagrams 135–6
constraints
how to break through 146–9, 164
importance of in connection with ordered systems 16, 187
to growth 139–46, 147
two policies for breaking through 162–3
ultimate 156
context 234–5
contractor, view of in contract negotiations 195–200
contracts, systems thinking case study 188–201
control panel 225, 295–7, 299, 301, 304, 305, 315, 321, 324, 325–6
control, of inventory 118–19
Cook, Captain James 267–9
Coopers & Lybrand 187
cost control, systems thinking case study 34–8, 40–8
cost cutting 40
Coster, Malcolm 187
costs
representation in causal loop diagrams 34–8, 129–31, 214, 215, 223, 224
representation in ithink models 306, 312–14, 323
creativity 235–8
Ctesibius 20
curly arrow 27–8, 286, 289
cycles, business 121

dangles 57–9, 70–1, 80, 87, 126, 142, 226
and defining system boundaries 58, 70–1, 127–8
explicit 85–7
implicit 85–7
input 57, 129, 211, 220
output 57, 129

policy 211, 220
rate 80, 153, 241, 189
target 106, 153, 156, 241, 244
use of in drawing causal loop diagrams 127–9
death rate 153, 241–7, 288–300
decision making under uncertainty 232–3, 239
decisions 1, 202
and scenario planning 239
in business strategy planning 239
influence of mental models 180–2
investment allocation 224–5, 316, 320, 321
testing of 325–31
decisiveness 50
decline, exponential 81, 126
see also reinforcing loop
de Geus, Arie 2, 335
delays 33, 34, 39
between levers and outcomes 206–9
in balancing loops 107–8, 117–21
deregulation, impact on TV industry 165, 170
detail complexity 120
detail 1, 129–31
diagram level 301
difference between birth rate and death rate 154, 246, 293–300
dot-coms 92–4
double acting steam engine 19–20
Douglas, Michael 25
Dürer, Albrecht 244
dynamic behavior of complex systems 120, 142, 154, 272
when to leave alone 119
difficulty in predicting 119–20
dynamic complexity 120, 126, 142
dynamic equilibrium 251–2
dynamic systems 15
dysfunction, origins of in groups 183

Earth
as a single system 250–1
as an open system 250
atmosphere of 248–50
mechanisms to maintain stability 251–5, 258-9
temperature of 247–8, 251–63

Easter Island 267–9, 270
econometrics 207
economic activity 154–5,
    241–2
    consequences of 243
education of women, impor-
    tance of 247, 267, 268
Edvinsson, Leif 285, 337
El Niño 266
elephant 127
    what happens when you
    cut one in half 13, 51–2,
    58
emergence 14–16, 184, 186,
    201, 253
emergent properties, of com-
    plex systems 14–16, 184,
    186, 201, 253
emissions, of greenhouse gases
    240, 252, 266–7
energy flow, through systems
    15, 186, 188, 201, 250
engine, control of speed of 19
engine of growth, business 75,
    147
environment
    flow of energy from 15
    protection of 23
equation level 301
equations 286, 288, 294–5
equilibrium
    chemical 249
    dynamic 250, 251–2
    static 249–50, 253
Espejo, Raul 24, 333
Excel 274–8
explicit dangles 85–7
exponential decline 81, 126
    fundamental behavior of
    reinforcing loop 81, 126
exponential growth 78–80, 82,
    83–5, 126, 138, 210
    and compound interest 80
    and population growth 80
    characteristics of 78, 80,
    83–5
    does not go on for ever
    140
    fundamental behavior of
    reinforcing loop 80, 81,
    126

feedback 16–18, 20, 186, 201
    and information flow 16,
    20, 186
    and control of engine
    speeds 19
    in the sense of personal
    counseling 16
feedback loops 50–71, 126
    and grumpy feelings 53–4
    and language 63–4

are everywhere 53
    as captured in system
    dynamics models 288,
    289, 304
    can be only either reinforc-
    ing or balancing 62, 126
    definition of 51
    difficulty of capturing in
    spreadsheets 275
    identification of as reinforc-
    ing or balancing 61, 126
    interconnected 53, 126
    on a global scale 250, 253
    properties of 51–3
feedback, negative 57
    see also balancing loop
feedback, positive 55
    see also reinforcing loop
financial accounting
    and stocks and flows 274,
    284
    and system dynamics 274,
    312–16
flight simulator 300, 315
flock of birds 14, 15
flooding 260–3
flows 274, 278–87, 301
    and profit-and-loss items
    274, 284
    biflows 324
    definition of 274, 284
    examples in business 281–6
    must be measured over
    time 274
    not measurable when time
    stops 280
    pipe-and-tap symbol for
    279
    rates that are stocks not
    flows 285–6
    representation as auxiliaries
    291
    representation of 279, 291
    the only action a manager
    can take is to readjust 287
    uniflows 290
Forrester, Jay 21, 22, 23, 179,
    180, 240, 273, 333
Four Horsemen of the Apoca-
    lypse 244, 263, 270
frogs, story concerning expo-
    nential growth 83–5, 154,
    267
front office 25
fundamental building blocks in
    system dynamics modeling
    54–7
    there are only two, the
    reinforcing loop and the
    balancing loop 62–3
future, prediction of 232–5, 238
future worlds 234, 235, 238–9

fuzzy link 220
fuzzy variable 65–6, 71, 207,
    215–16, 220, 225
    how to represent 311–12
    in system dynamics models
    277, 301, 307, 308, 310–13,
    314, 317–19
    representation of in ithink
    307
    made explicit by system
    dynamics 307–8, 310–13
    measurement of 310–11

Gaia 247–70
gamblers 233
gas, greenhouse 240, 252,
    266–7
General System Theory 21,
    23, 333
George, Sir Edward 120
Gharajedaghi, Jamshid 24,
    334
global warming 138, 240
    systems thinking case study
    241–70
goal posts, changing of 118–19
goals 126, 127
    and balancing loops 126
    representation as dangles in
    causal loop diagrams
    57–9, 127
Golding, William 250
Goldratt, Eliyahu 149, 337
González y Haedo, Don Felipe
    267
graph functions 298, 299, 304,
    307, 308, 310–12, 313,
    317–18, 319, 325, 326
graphs
    in ithink control panel
    304, 305, 325, 326
    role of in system dynamics
    315
greenhouse gas 240, 252,
    266–7
growth 74–7
    drivers of 233–4
    exponential 78–80
    how to stimulate, despite
    constraints 146–9, 162–3
    ithink business model of
    302–31
    ithink population model of
    292–300
    limits to 77, 143
    linear 77–8
    of a business 74–7, 138,
    139–63, 210, 219
    patterns of 77–83
    ultimate constraint on 156
guides 233–4

half elephant trap 58, 128
Hamel, Gary 232, 335
Harnden, Roger 24, 333
Hatfield rail disaster 87–92, 189
health care, impact of on population growth 245–6
heap, in contrast to a system 2
heartbeat 15
helicopter view, importance of 18
high-performing teams 2, 7, 16, 71, 184
holistic view 1, 5–6
homoeostasis 17
"how might this be different?", importance of asking when generating new ideas 237
hurricanes 14, 15

IBM 92
ideas, how to generate 235–8
imagination
    how to encourage 232
    how to stimulate 235–9
    role of in strategy formulation 229–31
implicit dangles 85–7
industrial revolution 150, 160
inflation 120
influence diagram see causal loop diagrams
information flow within systems 16, 21, 186
InnovAction!™ 237
input dangles 57, 129, 211, 220
intellectual capital 285
interest rate
    setting of 120–1
    as a stock 285–6
inventory control 118–19
investment
    allocation and rationing of 224, 321–3
    impact of, as represented in causal loop diagrams 75, 147, 218–21, 222
    ithink modeling 304, 321
ithink 273, 275, 301, 339
    population growth example 292–300
    motor trade example 302–31

knob, in ithink control panel 295–7, 304, 305, 325, 326
knowledge, as a stock 284
Kyoto Protocol 240

laboratory of the future 273, 274

Lake Chad 280
Lancaster, University of 22
language
    and feedback loops 63, 114, 125
    and systems dynamic modeling 282–3
    in causal loop diagrams 131–3
Law, John 159
leadership 201
    and energy flow 16, 188, 201
    and injection of energy into teams 16, 188, 201
learning, models for 312–16
levers 202–39
    and balancing loops 211
    and strategy 204, 238–9
    as hierarchies 203–4
    in scenario planning 234
    in ithink control panel 225
    mapped onto organizational structures 203–4
    names 202
    not directly connected to outcomes 205–9, 210, 213, 287
    reverse engineering of 238–9
    settings 202, 237–8
Lewin, Roger 24, 334
Lewis, Michael 25
life
    and Gaia 247–70
    as open system 21
    presence detected by study of planetary atmosphere 248–9
    presence on Earth, absence on Mars 248
lily pads, exponential growth of 83–5, 154
limits to growth 143, 160
    of a business 146
    systems thinking archetype 98, 143
linear growth 78, 82, 83
links 27–30, 70
    always S or always O 64–5
    and arithmetic 141
    can only be S or O 59
    can they sometimes be S and sometimes O? 64–5
    fuzzy 65–6, 220; see also fuzzy variable
    identification of 68, 69, 141
    in causal loop diagrams 27–30
    O 28, 29, 69, 70
    S 28, 29, 69, 70

that work in one direction only 66–8, 151–2, 289–90
listening 133, 186
    "active" 186
    importance of in teamwork 186
    "passive" 186
living pump 255, 258
Lotus 1-2-3 275
Lovelock, James 248–9, 336

Malone, Michael 285, 337
management 37–9, 117, 135, 163, 181, 202, 206–8, 212, 316
    and adjusting flows 287
    and setting levers 204, 208–9
    and system dynamics models 316
    and time delays 118
    job of 208, 272
    of business growth 145–9
    of inventory 118–20
    of marketing mix 316–31
    of supply chain 118–20
    of talent in the TV industry 164–78
    of uncertainty 198
    use of control panel 117, 202
management cybernetics 22
market saturation 140–1
marketing mix, modeling 316–31
Mars 247
    absence of life on 248
    atmosphere of 248–50
    temperature of 248–50
Marshall, Steve 191
Martian Test, in scenario planning 235, 237
Massachusetts Institute of Technology (MIT) 21, 22, 23, 180, 182–3
Meadows, Dennis 23, 334
measure, units of, and stocks and flows 283
measurement, of fuzzy variables 310–11
measures, of performance 134, 225–6, 310–12
mechanical feedback 19–20
Meinesz, Alexandre 85
mental models 71, 135–6, 180–3, 186, 213
    and teamwork 41, 184, 186
    as captured by graphs of fuzzy variables 311, 317–19
    different people hold different mental models 44–5, 45–8, 130, 135–6, 300, 311–12, 318, 319

mental models (*cont.*)
  influence on decisions and
  behavior 185, 318
  made explicit by causal
  loop diagrams 135–6
MIT 21, 22, 23, 180, 182–3
mix, marketing, modeling of
  316–31
model, computer simulation
  7, 21, 22, 23, 225, 238,
  273, 274–8
  what is it being used for?
  315
models for answers, models for
  learning 312–16
motor dealer, system dynamics
  model of 302–31
myopia, organizational 1, 13,
  37–9

name
  of levers 202
  of outcomes 204
negative feedback 57
  see also balancing loop
Nelson, Vice-Admiral Horatio
  184, 185, 188, 201
non-equilibrium state 249

O link 28, 29, 69, 70, 126 *see
  also* Ss and Os
objectives
  representation as dangles in
  causal loop diagrams
  57–9, 106, 108–17
  to optimize a portfolio of
  stocks 287
one-way links 66–8, 151–2,
  289–90
open systems 15, 22, 250
  the Earth as 250
order 186
  creation of within a system
  15
organizational myopia 1, 13,
  37–9
oscillation, of systems 107,
  118–21, 126
outcomes 126, 127, 202–39
  and balancing loops 209
  and reinforcing loops
  209–10
  cannot be directly influenced by managers 206,
  208, 210
  how to discover "good"
  ones 238–9
  in scenario planning 234
  names 204
  not directly connected to
  levers 205–9, 213, 287
  settings 204

target settings of 204, 209,
  226–31
output dangles 57, 129
outsourcing 138
  systems thinking case study
  188–201

Paddington rail disaster 88, 89,
  92
partnering 198
  systems thinking case study
  188–201
parts, sum is greater than 5,
  14, 18
"passive" listening 186
performance measures 134,
  225–6, 310–12
personal counseling 16
personal mastery 183
physical capacity 153, 156,
  243, 244
plumbing diagrams 282, 301
  examples 279, 282, 286,
  288, 294, 304, 317, 319,
  320, 322
  and causal loop diagrams
  287–92, 302–4
  and computer simulations
  292, 302–4
policies
  systems thinking as an aid
  to setting 57, 71, 87, 120,
  127, 164, 169, 179, 183,
  197–200, 202, 204, 210,
  267, 301
  testing of 7
pollution 22, 243–7, 257–70
population, global 245
population growth 150–63,
  241–7
  exponential nature of 80
  system dynamics example
  in ithink 288–300
positive feedback 55
  see also reinforcing loop
power, in relationships 280
Powersim 273, 339
precision, and system dynamics
  models 315
prediction, of the future
  232–4, 238–9
professional firm, relationship
  innovation in 187
profit and loss account items
  and flows 274, 284
  and system dynamics 274–5
promotions
  as a stock 318–19
  modeling of 316–31
public policy
  and systems thinking
  241–70

pump, living 255, 258
public health 160, 245

quality 40–8, 42
quick fixes 7, 13, 71, 159, 164,
  166, 168–9, 198

rail disasters 88–92
Railtrack 88–92, 189–91
RAND Corporation 21
rate dangles 80, 153, 241
rate, birth 151, 153, 241
rate, death 153, 241
Ratner, Gerald 90–1
reality, importance of in causal
  loop diagrams 179, 180
regulation, as a constraint on
  growth 143, 144
regulator, whirling 19
reinforcing loops 31–2, 54–5,
  70, 72–102, 125–6, 138,
  220
  all show exponential
  growth or decline 59,
  76–94, 140
  and boom and bust 73,
  87–94
  and competition for scarce
  resources 95–102
  and outcomes 209–10
  as engine of business
  growth 74–7, 139–63, 210
  behavior as vicious and
  virtuous circles 55, 72–4,
  126
  flip from virtuous to vicious
  73, 90–4, 126, 146
  how to identify 60–1, 70
  interaction with balancing
  loops 70, 97–102, 139,
  142, 212–21
  linking of 94–102
  reinforcing loops,
  constrained 270
  and "pedaling harder"
  138, 162–4, 330–1
  "taking the brakes off"
  97–8, 138, 162–4, 330–1
resources
  competition for 95–102
  finite nature of 22, 243
reverse engineering, of lever settings 238–9
reversibility test, of the nature of
  a link as an S or an O
  28–9, 151–2
  dangers of relying on 68
Richmond, Barry 309
risk 198
  and business strategy
  planning 239
  and scenario planning 239

Roggeveen, Jacob 267

S link 28, 29, 69, 70, 126
Ss and Os 28, 29, 70, 121–6, 134
  all links are either S or O 59, 64–5
  and arithmetic 141
  how to distinguish between 28, 59, 66–9, 151–2, 289–90
  that work in one direction only 66–8, 151–2, 289–90
  ultimate test of 69
SAGE 180
sales, effect of advertising on 207–8, 134, 181–2, 316–31
Santa Fe Institute 22
saturation, of a market 140–1
scenario, definition of 238
scenario planning 232–9
  and risk 239
  benefits of 239
scientific method 12–13
self-correction 17, 253, 263
  what happens when it can't cope 17, 253, 256
self-inflicted wounds, as a constraint on growth 146
self-organization 14–16, 184, 186, 253
Senge, Peter 2, 13, 23, 182–3, 240, 333
settings
  of levers, actual 202
  of levers, target 202, 224–31
  of outcomes, actual 204
  of outcomes, target 204, 224–31
shared vision 183
shower, dynamic behavior of 107–8
silo mentality 1, 13, 37–9
simulation
  and plumbing diagrams 292, 302–4
  of the dynamic behavior of complex systems 6–7, 21, 23, 238, 272–4
  time slice 276–7, 305, 308
simulation models 7, 21, 22, 23, 225, 238, 273, 274–8
simulator, flight 300, 315
Skandia 285
Smith, Adam 158, 162
soft systems methodology (SSM) 22, 23
South Sea Bubble 94
Southall rail disaster 88, 89, 92
spreadsheets
  and system dynamics 274–8, 314–16

operation of 275–8
SSM 22, 23
stable non-equilibrium state 15, 17, 249–50
Standard and Poor's index, change in 121
stars, management of 48, 164–78
static equilibrium 249–50
steam engine, double-acting 19–20
Sterman, John 23, 334
stock-and-flow diagram 274, 282
  see also plumbing diagram
stocks 274, 278–87, 301
  and balance sheet items 274, 284
  and rates such as interest rates 285
  box symbol for 279
  business objectives and optimizing a portfolio 287
  can be measured at an instant in time 274, 280
  definition of 274, 278
  examples in business 284
  have value when time stops 279
  optimizing one might be in conflict with optimizing another 287
  representation as auxiliaries 291
  representation of 279
  that are rates 285–6
stocks and flows 278–87, 301
  all variables are either the one or the other 286
  and accounting 274, 275, 284, 314
  and units of measure 283
  how to distinguish between 278, 280
  in business 281–7
strategic planning, and decisions 202, 232-4, 239
strategic targets, setting of 229–34, 239
strategy 138, 202–39
  and risk 239
  and systems thinking 209–31, 238
  as a process of resetting levers 204, 238–9
  definition of 204
  different ways of formulating 232
  role of ambition, vision, and imagination 229–35
style, organizational 233–4
Supercalc 275

supply chain management 118–20, 145
system 12–13
  and connectedness 2, 3, 13, 51, 126, 201
  and dynamic complexity 120, 143
  behavior independent of the language we choose to describe it 63–4, 114, 125
  biological 17
  budgeting 57, 108–17, 228, 231
  chaotic behavior of 17, 22, 253
  complex adaptive 22
  definition of 2
  dynamic behavior of 15, 119, 143, 154
  emergent properties of 14–16, 184, 186, 201, 253
  energy flow through 15–16, 186, 201
  importance of constraints in maintaining order in 16, 187, 201
  importance of feedback in 16–18, 186, 201
  importance of information flow in maintaining order in 16, 186
  must be studied as a whole 3, 5–6, 13, 14, 18, 37–8
  nothing to do with IT 2
  order in 15–16, 186
  open 15, 22
  properties that are not properties of constituent parts 6, 14–16
  self-correction 17, 253
  self-organization 14–16, 253
  static equilibrium 253
  time dependent behavior of 6, 120
system boundaries 57–9, 70–1, 127–8
  and dangles 58, 127–8
  apparent conflict with holistic view 58
system drivers, representation as dangles in causal loop diagrams 57–9, 127–8
system dynamics 21, 273–7
system dynamics models 6, 7, 7, 225, 238, 301, 316
  and the avoidance of clutter 275, 313–14
  and control panels 295–7, 299, 301, 315, 321
  and encouragement of fuzzy variables 225, 277, 298, 301, 307–14, 318, 319

system dynamics models (cont.)
  and financial accounting
    274, 275
  and precision 314–15
  and spreadsheets 274–8
  and units of measure 283
  entry of data into 293,
    295–7, 298, 300, 301
  graphical entry of data
    298, 300, 301
  importance of graphical
    output 292, 297, 299, 310,
    315, 327, 329, 331
  importance of language
    282–3
  scope of 275, 277, 314–16
system outputs, representation
    as dangles in causal loop
    diagrams 57–9, 127–9
systems analysis 22
systems engineering 21
systems perspective 12–24,
    186–7, 201
systems thinking 1–3, 18–24
  and business strategy
    209–31, 238
  and encouragement of
    fuzzy variables 65–6,
    133–4, 225–6, 318
  and public policy 240
  archetypes 143
  as a big idea 1
  benefits of 7, 71
  case studies 3, 25–39,
    40–8, 150–61, 164–78,
    188–201, 241–70
  legitimization of taboo
    subjects 133–4
  origins of 18–24
  power of in business strat-
    egy planning 208–31, 238
  summary of 70–1

talent, management of 164–78
target dangles 106, 153, 156,
    241, 244
target settings of levers and
    outcomes 202
targets
  in balancing loops 56, 58,
    70
  representation as dangles in
    causal loop diagrams 58,
    87, 127
tax, use of models in 315
tax rate, as a stock 286
tea, influence of on population
    growth 150–63
team learning 183
teamwork 2, 6, 14, 16, 71,
    184–8, 200
  and listening 183, 186–7

and mental models 71,
    184
and the "telephone direc-
    tory test" 184, 185
technology, impact on TV
    industry 165, 170
telephone directory test, as a
    diagnostic of teamwork
    185
television industry, systems
    thinking case study
    164–78
temperature, human 17
  as an emergent property
    253
  five mechanisms of control
    17
temperature, of the Earth
    247–8, 249, 251–63
  as an emergent property
    253
  data for 266
  mechanisms of control
    251–6, 258–9
tendering of contracts, systems
    thinking case study
    188–201
test of time 1, 7, 39, 71
thermostat
  of the Earth 252, 253
  of human beings 253
time delays 33, 34, 39
  and balancing loops 108,
    117–21
  between levers and out-
    comes 206–9, 238-9
time slice simulation 276, 277,
    305, 308
time, test of 1, 7, 39, 71
today's world, in scenario plan-
    ning 234, 235, 238–9
trust 101–2
tulip mania 94
twelve rules, of drawing causal
    loop diagrams 137

uncertainty 138
  and decision making
    232–4, 233–4, 238–9
unforeseen circumstances 1
unidirectionality 68, 152, 290
uniflows 290, 324
United Nations 99
units of measure, and stocks
    and flows 283
urban populations, growth of
    150–62

variables, fuzzy see fuzzy vari-
    ables
variance, definition of 121–5
Vensim 273, 339

Viable Systems Model 22
vicious circle 31–2, 42–3
  has same structure as virtu-
    ous circle 55, 73–5; see
    also reinforcing loop
virtuous circle, has same struc-
    ture as vicious circle 54,
    73–5; see also reinforcing
    loop
Visicalc 275
vision, role of in strategy formu-
    lation 229–30, 232
vortex 14

Wall Street 25
war 96, 98, 243
warming, global 138
  systems thinking case study
    240–70
wastepaper basket, importance
    of in drawing causal loop
    diagrams 58, 131, 135
Watt, James 19–20
weathering of rocks 255
Whittington, Richard, Lord
    Mayor of London 154
whole is greater than the sum of
    its parts 5, 14, 18
Wiener, Norbert 21, 23, 334
wisdom 1, 18, 38–9, 45, 47–8,
    50, 71, 101, 126, 163, 164,
    166, 169, 179, 183, 198,
    200, 202, 225, 239, 301,
    316
women, importance of educa-
    tion 247, 267, 268
worlds, future and today's, in
    scenario planning 234,
    235, 238–9